LITTLE GIANT®
ENCYCLOPEDIA
OF

Lucky
Numbers

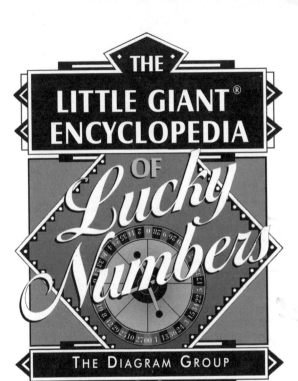

THE
LITTLE GIANT® ENCYCLOPEDIA
OF
Lucky Numbers

THE DIAGRAM GROUP

Sterling Publishing Co., Inc.
New York

Compiled by Quartz Editorial Service

Library of Congress Cataloging-in-Publication Data Available

10 9 8 7 6 5 4 3 2 1

Published by Sterling Publishing Company, Inc.
387 Park Avenue South, New York, N.Y. 10016
A Diagram Book first created by Diagram Visual Information
Limited of 195 Kentish Town Road. London NW5 2JU, England
© 2001 by Diagram Information Visual Limited
Distributed in Canada by Sterling Publishing
c/o Canadian Manda Group, One Atlantic Avenue, Suite 105
Toronto, Ontario, Canada M6K 3E7
Distributed in Great Britain and Europe by Cassell PLC
Wellington House, 125 Strand, London WC2R 0BB, England
Distributed in Australia by Capricorn Link (Australia) Pty. Ltd.
P.O. Box 704, Windsor, NSW 2756 Australia

Manufactured in Canada
All rights reserved

Sterling ISBN 0-8069-2975-8

FOREWORD

Numbers undoubtedly hold a marked fascination for us all. Most people, for instance, would openly admit that they instinctively regard the date of the month in which they were born as somehow of some special significance. They feel it is lucky to them, even if they know nothing about the practice of numerology. The major world religions also hold that certain numbers are not just useful for counting but contain hidden meanings. It is almost as if they are imbued with spirituality. For the ancient Hebrews, for example, the number **4** was very important. This may have been because one of their names for God (*Yahweh*) was spelled with **4** letters. The earth was also believed in ancient times to be flat with **four** distinct corners.

Sacred seven
The number **7** was equally sacred to the Hebrews. It had taken, according to traditional Jewish and later Christian belief, **6** days to create the world, the **7th** being kept as the Sabbath, a day of rest. In every **7th** year, fields were to be left fallow as a means of replenishing the earth. A strict period of mourning lasted **7** days, as did many of the major Hebrew festivals; and the **7**-branch candlestick remains a familiar Jewish symbol. The importance given to the number **10**, meanwhile, clearly relates to the **Ten** Commandments, believed to have been delivered to the Israelites by Moses after a revelation on Mount Sinai.

Such numbers are held as hallow, but others are not favored at all by some religious groups. A prime example must be the number **13**. The fact that the **13th** man at the Last Supper was Judas who was to betray Jesus is deeply engraved in the Christian psyche, so much so that those suffering from even the mildest form of *triskaidekaphobia* (fear of the number **13**) will go out of their way to ensure they do not arrange a dinner party for **13** or will avoid moving into a house with that street number. Some hotels will avoid having a room **13** in case potential guests might be wary of occupying it, and architects of high-rise buildings have been known to miss out a **13th** floor altogether, altering the numbering system so that it jumps straight from the **12th** to the **14th** level.

Lucky for some
Yet not all Christians are ill-disposed towards the number **13**. Some would count it as less ominous, pointing out that **13** is the sum of the Trinity and the **Ten** Commandments; and in Jewish and Central American folklore, **13** is thought to bring good fortune. What is lucky for some of us, it seems, is not so lucky for others. Most of the western world, however, is wary of the number **666**. It is cited biblically as "the number of the beast" or devil; and many people who find they have been given this number as part of a car license plate, for instance, opt to go to considerable expense to change it for fear of bad influences that might result in an accident.

Those who are sceptical about such beliefs, of course, would counter that if you truly believe that something might happen, you may in turn bring it about, even if unconsciously. Nevertheless the majority would probably prefer not to take the risk.

How, though, do numbers come to have such an effect over our lives? Why do we set so much store by them? Scientists have shown what most of us have long known intuitively: that the whole universe is an enormous mathematical structure that operates by strict numerical principles. No wonder, then, that over the centuries mystics have developed the techniques of numerology to help us fathom the nature of the human soul, to enrich our relationships, and to guide us towards a happier future.

Using numerology

If we really can predict, however, where does this leave us when it comes to the question of free will? All-importantly, most practicing numerologists do not claim to reveal an unalterable future. Instead, through certain calculations that relate to your date of birth and given name, for instance, they are able to identify not only personality traits but also marked influences that will help the individual towards greater self-awareness.

You, too, can learn the basics of numerology and many other forms of divination that rely on working with numbers as an essential part of the process, and this is the purpose of this book. Within its many pages you will find, for example, detailed data on predicting with the numbers on dice, dominoes, or cards; information about the numerical equivalents to the letters in names and how they may affect both character and life purpose; lucky numbers for each sign of the zodiac; how to use your birth date in personality assessment; and how to choose the right day for particular activities such as making big decisions, getting married, moving, or for throwing a party.

We feature, too, the Oracle of Napoleon and a female counterpart, the Ladies' Oracle, systems that, through the choice of numbered questions, provide guidance. Sometimes the answers may seem enigmatic, but insight comes with practice on the part of the *querant* (the person seeking a solution to his or her dilemma).

An interest in the significance and symbolism of numbers, as well as an awareness of how they crop up in our daily lives – whether we are selecting numbers for the lottery, deciding on which date to embark on a journey, or considering a name and its numerical equivalent for a newborn child – can bring enormous benefits and will certainly be fun. Like many forms of divination, though, it is best not taken to extremes so that what starts as a fascination turns into an obsession. Far better to continue to use a fresh approach as you work with numbers. Then you will discover all the more clearly how they map our lives and find a route to greater happiness.

CONTENTS

THE ORIGINS OF NUMEROLOGY

THE ORIGINS OF NUMEROLOGY

Many ancient peoples believed in the significance of certain numbers, but it was Pythagoras, the Greek mathematician who, in the 6th century BC, first put forward the theory that numbers pervade our lives and vibrate at distinct levels, providing what he called "the music of the spheres." Everything, he held, is subject to such vibrations. The following is a summary of some of the meanings of numbers **1-10** for certain historical cultures.

1
For medieval alchemists, the number of the Philosopher's Stone, a strange, unidentified catalyst used for turning base metals into gold.
In Judaism, Christianity, and Islam, the **one** God.

2
For the Chinese, the forces of *yin* and *yang*.
For some early Christians, the devil or anti-Christ.
For Zoroastrians, the forces of good and evil.

3
For Christians, the Trinity.
For the Babylonians, creation.

4
For the ancient Hebrews, the four archangels and also the name of God written with **four** letters (YHWH).

5

For the followers of Pythagoras, marriage. (**Five** is the sum of a male and female number).

For the Chinese, the **five** elements

For the Sikhs, the **five** sacred objects that are worn by all adult males of this religion.

6

For Jews, Christians, and Moslems, the number of the day on which Man was created.

For mathematicians since ancient times, the first perfect number.

7

For the early Christians, the **seven** levels of hell.

For the Hebrews, Christians, and Moslems, the Sabbath or **seventh** day.

8

For the ancient Greeks, imperfection.

For the Romans, the mother goddess.

9

For the Chinese, the *lo shi*, a magic square comprising the first **nine** digits

For medieval magicians, Hecate, queen of the witches.

10

For Jews, Christians, and Moslems, the **Ten** Commandments.

NUMBERS AND DEITIES

Different numbers have long been associated with
different planets and therefore also with the spirits
ruling them. In order to invoke a particular spirit, a

Deity	Origin	Associated number
Allah	Islam	1
Amphitrite	Greek	6
Aphrodite (**a**)	Greek	1
Apollo (**b**)	Greek/Roman	1
Athena	Greek	6
Atlas	Greek	10
Bacchus (**c**)	Roman	6
Baldur (**d**)	Norse	12
Boreas	Greek	12
Ceres	Greek	2

magician of old would concentrate on using the corresponding magic number. Provided here are two tables: one lists deities in alphabetical order, their origins, and the numbers with which they are associated; the other, on pages 19–21, shows which deities are associated with the numbers **1–13**.

Deity	Origin	Associated number
Coelus	Roman	10
Con Ticci	Inca	1
Cronos (**e**)	Greek	3
Cybele	Greek/Roman	8
Cythereia	Greek	5
Diana (**f**)	Roman	1
Dionysus	Greek	5
Frey	Norse	1
Freya	Norse	6
Frigga	Norse	2 & 7

d   e   f

Deity	Origin	Associated number
Gaea	Greek	8
God the Father	Christianity	1
Hades	Greek	3 & 9
Hecate	Greek	13
Heimdal	Norse	8
Hella	Norse	9
Hephaestus	Greek	1
Hera	Greek	8
Hermes (**g**)	Greek	6
Holy Trinity	Christianity	3
Iduna	Norse	7
Ishtar	Babylonian	5
Janus (**h**)	Roman	12
Jehova	Judaism	1
Juno	Roman	9
Jupiter	Roman	4
Loki	Norse	2
Lucifer	Christianity	2

Deity	Origin	Associated number
Luna	Roman	9
Magna Mater	Roman	8
Mars	Roman	5
Mercury	Roman	8
Minerva	Roman	7
Mithras	Babylonian	7
Neptune (i)	Roman	11
Neter	Egyptian	1
Niord	Norse	11
Odin (j)	Norse	4 & 9
Pangu	Chinese	1
Pluto (k)	Roman	3 & 13
Poseidon	Greek	11
Proserpine	Greek	9
Ptah (l)	Egyptian	1
Rhea	Greek	2
Satan	Christianity	2
Saturn	Roman	3

j   k   l

Deity	Origin	Associated number
Skuld	Norse	10
Sol	Roman	6
Terpsichore	Greek	9
Thor (**m**)	Norse	5
Tiw	Norse	3
Tyr	Norse	3
Uller	Norse	13
Uranus	Greek	10
Venus (**n**)	Roman	2
Vesta	Roman	1
Zeus (**o**)	Greek	4

NUMBERS AND CORRESPONDING DEITIES

Number	Deities	Origin
1	Allah	Islam
	Aphrodite	Greek
	Apollo	Greek/Roman
	Con Ticci	Inca
	Diana	Roman
	Frey	Norse
	God the Father	Christianity
	Hephaestus	Greek
	Jehova	Judaism
	Neter	Egyptian
	Pangu	Chinese
	Ptah	Egyptian
	Vesta	Roman
2	Ceres	Greek
	Frigga	Norse
	Loki	Norse
	Lucifer	Christianity
	Rhea	Greek
	Satan	Christianity
	Venus	Roman
3	Cronos	Greek
	Hecate	Greek
	Holy Trinity	Christianity
	Pluto	Roman
	Saturn	Roman
	Tiw	Norse
	Tyr	Norse

NUMBERS AND CORRESPONDING DEITIES
(continued)

Number	Deities	Origin
4	Jupiter	Roman
	Odin	Norse
	Zeus	Greek
5	Cythereia	Greek
	Dionysus	Greek
	Ishtar	Babylonian
	Mars	Roman
	Thor	Norse
6	Amphitrite	Greek
	Athena	Greek
	Bacchus	Roman
	Freya	Norse
	Hermes	Greek
	Sol	Roman
7	Frigga	Norse
	Iduna	Norse
	Minerva	Roman
	Mithras	Babylonian
8	Cybele	Greek/Roman
	Gaea	Greek
	Heimdal	Norse
	Hera	Greek
	Magna Mater	Roman
	Mercury	Roman

Number	Deities	Origin
9	Hecate	Greek
	Hella	Norse
	Juno	Roman
	Luna	Roman
	Odin	Norse
	Proserpine	Greek
	Terpsichore	Greek
10	Atlas	Greek
	Coelus	Roman
	Skuld	Norse
	Uranus	Greek
11	Neptune	Roman
	Niord	Norse
	Poseidon	Greek
12	Baldur	Norse
	Boreas	Greek
	Janus	Roman
13	Hades	Greek
	Pluto	Roman
	Uller	Norse

LETTER & NUMBER EQUIVALENTS

The medieval Jewish Kabbalists used a system in which numbers were represented as letters. This system is called *Gemetria* or *Grammatyâ*. Hebrew letters and their number equivalents (*see* chart on pages 23-25) can be used in the construction of magic squares, themselves used as talismans. You will find these magic squares on pages 27-33.

The actual names of Hebrew letters are also words which have meaning. Number equivalents can therefore be used in magic where specific meanings are required. A table of letter and number-meaning correspondences follows.

In addition to the information provided in the chart:

F relates to the number **6**
U relates to the numbers **3** and **21**
V relates to the numbers **3** and **21**
X relates to number **10**
Y relates to the numbers **1** and **10**
O is related to zero and the number **11**

Hebrew letter/number meanings and equivalents

Hebrew name	Numerical value	Meaning	Signifies
Âleph A א	1	Ox	• Independence • Creativity • Innovation
Bêth B ב	2	House	• Family • Inheritance
Gîmel G ג	3	Camel	• Survival • Change • Propagation
Dâleth D ד	4	Door	• Authority • Access • Denial
Hê H ה	5	Window	• Insight • Intuition • Meditation
Vav V ו	6	Peg, nail	• Fertility • Liberty
Zayin Z ז	7	Weapon	• Authority • Defense
Chêth C ח	8	Enclosure	• Intellect • Female

Hebrew name	Numerical value	Meaning	Significance
Têth T ט	9	Snake	● Healing ● Sexual energy
Chai C יח	18	Life	● Survival ● Life
Yôdh Y י	10	Hand	● Destiny
Kâph K כ	20	Palm	● Healing
Lâmedh L ל	30	Ox-goad	● Progress ● Self-sacrifice
Mem M מ	40	Water	● Completion ● Destiny ● Transition
Nûn N נ	50	Fish	● Escape ● Change ● Opportunity
Sâmekh S ס	60	Support	● Communion ● Mutuality ● Charity

Hebrew name	Numerical value	Meaning	Significance
Ayin A ע	**70**	Eye	• Vision • Clairvoyance • Prediction
Pay P פ	**80**	Mouth	• Immortality
Sâdhe S צ	**90**	Fishing hook	Meaning not known
Koph K ק	**100**	Back of head	• Inspiration • Intuition
Rêsh R ר	**200**	Head	• Identity • Individuality • Recognition
Shîn SH שׁ	**300**	Tooth	• Transformation
Tâw T ת	**400**	Sign of cross	• Eternal life
Nûn N ן	**700**	Fish	• Escape • Change • Opportunity

NUMBERS AND COLORS

In magic, all colors have number equivalents, as in this table *below*. When using numbers, it can bring good luck to use an appropriate color – for example, when displaying a house number.

Color	Number	Color	Number
Aquamarine	11	Orange	8
Black	13	Pearl	9
Blue (dark)	2	Purple	7
Blue (light)	10	Red	5
Brown	4	Silver	9
Gold	6	White	1
Green	3	Yellow	12

MAGIC SQUARES

Magic squares were used by medieval and classical numerologists, and by magicians, for the making of talismans. There are seven magic squares. Each one represents a heavenly body and has particular attributes to afford protection.

Traditionally they are made in certain colors and according to elaborate rituals. They are shown on the pages that follow. By the side of some, you will see the Hebrew equivalents.

The Square of Saturn
Added horizontally, vertically, or diagonally, the numbers in this square total **15**. The square totals **45**, the number for Agîêl, the Spirit of Saturn, and Zâzêl, the Demon of the Saturn. For use as a talisman, it is written with black squares and white numbers. Its alchemic metal is lead.

4	9	2
3	5	7
8	1	6

ד	ט	ב
ג	ה	ז
ה	א	ו

The Square of Jupiter

Added horizontally, vertically, or diagonally, the numbers in this square total **34**. The square totals **136**, the number of Yôphîêl, the Spirit of Jupiter, and Hasmâêl, the Demon of Jupiter. Its talismanic colors are blue for the squares, orange for the numbers.

4	14	15	1
9	7	6	12
5	11	10	8
16	2	3	13

ד	יד	יה	א
ט	ו	ז	יב
ה	יא	י	ח
יו	ב	ג	יג

The Square of Mars

Added horizontally, vertically, or diagonally, the
numbers in this square total **65**. The square totals **325**,
the number for Graphîêl, the Spirit of Mars, and
Barsâbêl, the Demon of Mars. For talismans,
individual squares are red and numbers, green.

11	24	7	20	3
4	12	25	8	16
17	5	13	21	9
10	18	1	14	22
23	6	19	2	15

יא	כד	ז	כ	ג
ד	יב	כה	ח	יו
יז	ה	יג	כא	ט
י	יח	א	יד	כב
כג	ו	יט	ב	יה

Square of the Sun

Each line of this square adds up to **111**, the number of the Spirit of the Sun, Nakîêl. The square totals **666**, the number of Sôrath, the Demon of the Sun. Used as a talisman, the squares are yellow and the numbers, purple or magenta.

6	32	3	34	35	1
7	11	27	28	8	30
24	14	16	15	23	19
13	20	22	21	17	18
25	29	10	9	26	12
36	5	33	4	2	31

Square of Venus

There are **49** squares here, the number of the Spirit of Venus, Hagîêl. The sum of each line is **175**, the number of the Demon Kedemèl. The square totals **1225**. Traditional talismanic colors are dark green for the background and yellow for the numbers.

22	47	16	41	10	35	4
5	23	48	17	42	11	29
30	6	24	49	18	36	12
13	21	7	25	42	19	37
38	14	32	1	26	44	30
21	39	8	33	2	27	45
46	15	40	9	34	3	28

Square of Mercury

Lines of this square add up to **260**. The square total is **2080**, the number for Taphthârtharath, the Demon of Mercury. As a talisman, it is orange and decorated with pale blue numbers.

8	58	59	5	4	62	63	1
49	15	14	52	53	11	10	56
41	23	22	44	45	19	18	48
32	34	35	29	28	38	39	25
40	26	27	37	36	30	31	33
17	47	46	20	21	43	42	24
9	55	54	12	13	51	50	16
64	2	3	61	60	6	7	57

Square of the Moon

Lines of this square total **369**, the number for the
Demon of the Moon, Hasmôday. The square totals
3321, the number of Malka Betharshesîm, the Spirit of
the Moon, and Shîedbarshemoth Sharthathan, the
Moon's Demon. As a talismán, it is purple and
decorated with yellow numbers.

37	78	29	70	21	62	13	54	5
6	38	79	30	71	22	63	14	46
47	7	39	80	31	72	23	55	15
16	48	8	40	81	32	64	24	56
57	17	49	9	41	73	33	65	25
26	58	18	50	1	42	14	34	66
67	27	59	10	51	2	43	75	35
36	68	19	60	11	52	3	44	76
77	28	69	20	61	12	53	4	45

A MAGIC CIRCLE

Although talismans commonly contain a magic square, there is no reason why magic numbers should not be used within a circle, as the circle itself is a powerful magic symbol. This is a magic circle said to have been given to Benjamin Franklin. Its magic properties are produced by adding any circle or radial group and including the center number (**12**). This always produces a total of **360**.

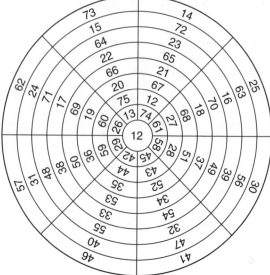

NUMERICAL PROPHECIES

There are several prophecies that involve numbers to be found in the *Old Testament*. Joseph, for example, analyzed the content of the Pharaoh's dreams. In one, **seven** starving cattle ate **seven** fat cattle but remained thin. In another, **seven** withered ears of corn devoured **seven** fine specimens of corn. As a result, Joseph foretold that **seven** years of severe famine would follow **seven** years of plenty in Egypt, and was able to prepare for this eventuality.

Future codes
Recently an Israeli mathematician, Dr Eliyahu Rips, has claimed there is in the *Bible* a secret code that reveals details of events taking place thousands of years after the *Bible* was written. He has discovered this through careful use of a computer. To decode the first five books of the *Bible* (the *Torah* or *Pentateuch*), he eliminated all the spaces between words, turning the text into one long strand.

   Rips was, in fact, continuing the work of a famous Czech rabbi, H.M.D. Weissmandel, who had noticed that, starting at the beginning of *Genesis*, if he skipped **50** letters, then a further **50**, and then **50** more, the letters he came to actually spelled out the word "*Torah*." Then he found the same sequence in each of the other four books of the *Pentateuch* (the first five books of the *Bible*). Most of the prophecies now found to be encoded feature words such as "Man on the

moon" and "Spaceship." But a few also mention
actual numbers that are clearly dates – the stock market
crash in **1929**, for instance (but with the corresponding
Hebrew year of **5690**) and the assassination of Israeli
Prime Minister Yitzhak Rabin in **1995**. The year **1939**
is even encoded with the words "*A. Hitler*,"" and
"*World War*" and "*The Holocaust*" with **1942**. The
code also seems to predict that big earthquakes will hit
Los Angeles in **2010**, and China in either **2000** or
2006.

Other references that have been traced include the
name of Libya's leader *Colonel Kaddafi*; the phrase
"*holocaust of Israel*," and even the words "*asteroid*"
and "*dinosaur*." The *Swift* (-Tuttle) comet is also
encoded with the year **5886**, the equivalent of the
calendar year **2126** when scientists now agree that the
comet is likely to return.

It may be that other books in the *Bible* also feature a
hidden code. Indeed, the discovery of this code is said
by some rabbis to prove the very existence of God.
Perhaps, too, it has been suggested, if the code tells of
events in the future, this is evidence that time does not
flow in the same way that we perceive it to do.

COINCIDENCE AND NUMBERS

Numbers sometimes crop up repeatedly in an individual's life for no apparent reason, unless they are sometimes pointers to the occurrence of significant events. Here are a few examples of such coincidences.

In Ronald Reagan's life, the number **7** has appeared with extraordinary frequency. He first appeared on screen in **1937**, became Governor of California in **1947**, made an acceptance speech for nomination for the presidency on July **17**th (that is, in the **seventh** month); and was **77** at the end of his second term as President of the United States.

The number **7** also dogged the life of another American President, Abraham Lincoln. His names contain **seven** letters each, he was the 16th (1 + 6 = **7**) President of the United States; he was elected **7** times, and died on the **7**th day of the month.

John Lennon found that the number **9** kept appearing in his life, both before and after he became a Beatle. He was born on October **9**, as was his son by Yoko Ono; he was conceived at **9** Newcastle Road; his last home was on 72nd Street (**7** + **2** = **9**), and the number of his apartment there was also **72**.

It does seem that, as the renowned psychologst Carl Jung put it, both numbers and synchronicity have mystery as their common characteristics. You might like to keep a note of how often certain numbers recur in your own life.

FENG SHUI AND NUMBERS

Over recent years a huge interest in the Chinese blend
of fine esthetics and mystical philosophy, known as
Feng Shui (literally "wind and water") has arisen in the
West. Its aim is essentially to ensure harmony in our
surroundings by careful selection of the rooms within a
home or office for specific purposes and the judicious
choice of color schemes, as well as careful positioning
of furniture.

SPECIAL MEASUREMENTS
Feng Shui practitioners hold that certain measurements
and proportions bring good fortune, and to this end
they use a special device known as the *Ting Lan* ruler
which indicates auspicious dimensions. The *Feng Shui*
foot (approximately 17 inches) is
divided into eight sections, each
corresponding to one of the
traditional Eight Trigrams of
Chinese mysticism. In the Far
East, you will even find that
briefcases are made to
precisely this length to
ensure the prosperity of
the business person to
whom it belongs.

The following chart shows the eight divisions of the *Feng Shui* foot and the significance of each.

Division	Measurement	Name	Significance
I	2⅛ ins	*Ts'ai*	Health
II	4¼ ins	*Ping*	Sickness
III	6⁵⁄₁₆ ins	*Li*	Separation
IV	8⁷⁄₁₆ ins	*I*	Righteousness
V	10½ ins	*Kuan*	Promotion
VI	12⅝ ins	*Chieh*	Robbery
VII	14¾ ins	*Hai*	Accidents
VIII	16¹⁵⁄₁₆ ins	*Pen*	Source

A Chinese builder will generally use standard measurements when drawing up plans but may well ensure that these correspond to *Feng Shui* principles. On the *Ting Lan* ruler, fortunate measurements are in red; others will be in black.

FAVORABLE DAYS

Feng Shui principles are also traditionally used in China to find a favorable day for a particular venture, such as moving or going on vacation. The individual's date of birth is used, as is a *Lo P'an*, the Chinese geomancer's Chinese compass. Special Natal Numbers come into play, and procedures can be found in any detailed book on the practice of Chinese geomancy.

THE EIGHT ORIENTATIONS

The drawings shown here are of the eight different orientations of buildings and their portent numbers. Each of the directions, as you can see, provides a different portent for each part of the building.

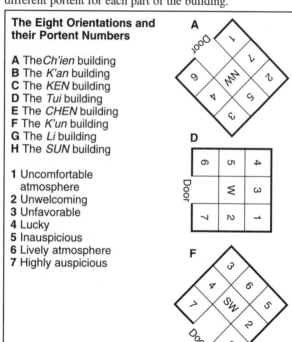

The Eight Orientations and their Portent Numbers

A The *Ch'ien* building
B The *K'an* building
C The *KEN* building
D The *Tui* building
E The *CHEN* building
F The *K'un* building
G The *Li* building
H The *SUN* building

1 Uncomfortable atmosphere
2 Unwelcoming
3 Unfavorable
4 Lucky
5 Inauspicious
6 Lively atmosphere
7 Highly auspicious

The translation of each portent is given opposite. So in
the *Tui* building, in which the door faces West, for
example, the rooms to the right and left of the front
entrance are the most fortunate of all.

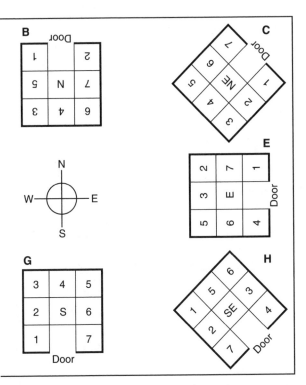

THE CHINESE ALMANAC

The Ancient Chinese Almanac (known as the *T'ung Shu*) is a Chinese classic published annually for over 12,000 years and still issued each year. It features a huge variety of folk wisdom, as still practiced in some Chinese communities, and includes moral precepts as well as astrological information, instructions concerning palmistry and the reading of faces, and much that is related to numerology. Some parts of the book remain the same for each edition; others are changed annually by professional Chinese astrologers and astronomers.

A good deal of the Almanac is very esoteric in tone and deals with concepts that are difficult for the lay person to understand. But there are sections that are more down-to-earth and practical in appeal.

Daily prophecies

One section, for instance, even predicts what will befall you if you wash your hair on particular days of the Chinese month. It is hard to take such prophecies seriously today – if we did, no doubt hairdressers would be closed for much of each month; but it is nevertheless intriguing to consider what was once widely believed. The predictions related to washing one's hair are as follows:

Day 1	You will have a short life
Day 2	You will have good fortune
Day 3	You will have great wealth
Day 4	You will have trouble with your hair color
Day 5	Your hair will fall out
Day 6	You will harm your face
Day 7	You will be in trouble with the law
Day 8	You will have a long life
Day 9	Your marriage will be happy
Day 10	You will be promoted at work
Day 11	Your eyes will sparkle
Day 12	Bad luck awaits you
Day 13	You will have a son
Day 14	You will earn money
Day 15	You will have good fortune
Day 16	Very bad luck in store
Day 17	Your skin will darken
Day 18	You will be robbed
Day 19	Everything will go awry
Day 20	You will be poor
Day 21	You will get ill
Day 22	Good luck awaits you
Day 23	A huge fortune is around the corner
Day 24	You will quarrel
Day 25	You may harm your eyes
Day 26	A huge fortune awaits you
Day 27	You will have a good time
Day 28	An argument in store
Day 29	Good news awaits you
Day 30	You will be visited by ghosts

STROKES IN A NAME

The Chinese have a traditional method of divining by
numerology that involves counting the number of
strokes that there are in the Chinese ideogram spelling
a name. They then interpret the result by checking
against special charts. According to the 14th-century
Secret Book of Chu-Ka's Spirit Calculations, if
someone of Chinese origin wishes to find the answer to
a question such as *Will I find romance this year?* or
Will my business prosper?, the individual's name or the
name of the individual's company should be written in
3 Chinese characters. The number of strokes in each
character is then counted.

   The number of strokes in the first of the three
characters is given the hundreds position in a three-
figure number. So if, for instance, there are **6** strokes in
the first character, the first number achieved will be
600. If the second of the three characters has **12** strokes,
this number will be given the tens position, after being
reduced to a single digit by taking away **10**. The
number will now have become **620**. If the third number
has **13** strokes, **10** is again subtracted, leaving **3** for the
units column. The final secret number is therefore **623**.
There are, however, only **384** secret predictions. It is
therefore necessary in this instance to reduce **623** to **384**
or less. To do this, the fortune-teller subtracts **384** from
623, giving **239**. (If the resulting number after such
subtraction had been more than **384**, the process would
be repeated, using the new number).

In the *Secret Book*, there are many charts, presented three to a page, and totalling 12,700 in all. Taking the figure **239**, the diviner would find the character under the number **239** and write it down. Then he would add **384** to **239** to find a second number, and write down the character corresponding to **623**. The process would be repeated until eventually he would land on **0**, indicating that the prophecy was complete. The diviner could now interpret the prophecy.

English language translations of the *Secret Book* are available but, of course, this form of divination is designed for use with Chinese characters, not the alphabet as used in the West. As might be expected, the more intuitive the fortune-teller is using this method, the more accurate the reading is likely to be.

KIOLOGY

An eastern philosophy akin to numerology, kiology is primarily concerned with the "energies" thought to lie in dates and times. Everyone, it is said, has three *ki* numbers. One relates to the birth year and reveals the inner personality; one relates to the birth month and is a so-called "control" number; and one, called the "tendency" number, relates to attitudes and behavior. A practitioner of kiology will use complex charts and diagrams to advise on the suitability of times and dates for meetings or weddings, when a journey should be undertaken, as well as the suitability of two individuals for a long-term relationship.

Ki, meaning "ether," will not help anyone to change personality but can be used, so exponents claim, to further insight into one's own behavior, the needs of others, and auspicious moments.

One leading practitioner counts Barry Manilow, Yoko Ono, and many other well known show business names, as well as bankers, art dealers, and lawyers, among his clients. Importantly, *ki* calculations need to be done at various stages in an individual's life as circumstances do not remain static. There are few practicing kiologists in the West, and their fees tend to be high. Books on the subject do exist but the methodology requires considerable concentration if any degree of expertise is to be achieved.

SPIRITUAL WEIGHTS

According to another system of Chinese fortune-telling, we all have a spiritual weight to our bones that will provide divination about the future. This does not involve weighing the physical body, however, but calculations relating to hours, days, and months which, on detailed charts, provide specific figures in the form of weights. These lead the diviner to a predictive verse about the individual's whole life. The weights are in the form of *liang* and *chin*, which we might regard as pounds and ounces.

HOUSE NUMBERS

The Chinese regard the house number **88** as particulary auspicious as it closely resembles the ideogram for "Double Happiness." **Eight** is also the number of the immortals of Chinese mythology; **eight** times **eight** (64) is the number of the hexagrams in the **I Ching**; and **eight** is the number of characters in the Chinese date of birth.

If a Chinese family bought a house with the number **9**, however, they might well use the western numeral as it resembles the character for "Long life," if written in script. **Nine** is also the number of lights in Heaven, according to ancient Chinese belief.

The number **4**, meanwhile, is considered very inauspicious by the Chinese.

TABLETS OF FATE

Use of the Tablets of Fate combines the occult
significance of numbers with the random element of
casting lots.

History The precise origins of Tablets of Fate cannot
be traced, although they are known to have been
popular in the 17th century, when they were on sale in
the form of cheap pamphlets sold in the street. These
were called *chap books*. In the 19th century, they were
used more as parlor games than as a serious means of
divination.

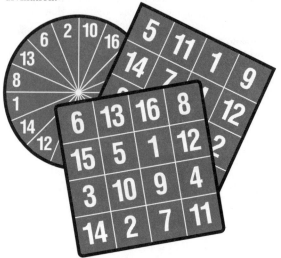

Modern methods Tablets of Fate are popular among some diviners because they can be devised so that answers have particular relevance to a person's lifestyle. Although experts may differ as to the frequency with which you may ask questions, and the exact rituals employed, all the tablets shown here are used in essentially the same way. Popular tablets include the *Sphinx*, and tablets for love, home and family, time, justice, work and finance, and travel.

Equipment Modern tablets can be simply made using numbers written onto shapes of paper. It is quite permissible for you to devise your own number sequence and list of answers. You will also need a pencil or pointer.

Using Tablets of Fate

Consult the Tablet of the *Sphinx* first. It is on page 51. This will tell you whether the present moment is suitable for using this method of divination. You may only put your questions to an appropriate tablet if the *Sphinx* gives a positive answer. It is helpful to have someone else present when you use the tablets.

1 Shut your eyes.
2 Concentrate on the question you wish to ask.
3 If someone else is present, ask him or her to turn the tablet round *three* times.
4 Using the thumb and forefinger of your left hand, take the pencil by the blunt end and dangle it over the table.
5 The other person present should move the Tablet of Fate so that it is just under the pencil.

6 Some diviners trace a circle or square in the air **three** times, using the pencil.

7 Bring the point of the pencil down on to the tablet, and open your eyes.

8 See which number the pencil has come down on and consult the key to find your answer.

- If the pencil misses the tablet completely **three** times, do not try again for at least 24 hours.

- If, when you open your eyes, the page is upside down, take the answer that is given after the word "reversed" in the key.

Tablet of the Sphinx

This tablet should be consulted first as it tells you whether the other tablets will give you true answers at the present time.

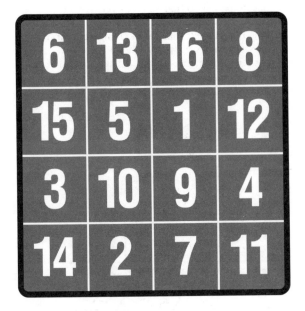

See *the next page* for meanings.

Tablet of the Sphinx: meanings

Number and position of paper		Meaning
1	Upright	Now is the time to test your fate.
	Reversed	*Today is not the time.*
2	Upright	Tomorrow will be preferable.
	Reversed	*Yes, straight away.*
3	Upright	Thursday is the best day.
	Reversed	*Try any day but Thursday.*
4	Upright	You are too impatient.
	Reversed	*Leave it as it is.*
5	Upright	Try on Sunday.
	Reversed	*Not on Sunday.*
6	Upright	Lose no time.
	Reversed	*Wait one week exactly.*
7	Upright	The answers are waiting.
	Reversed	*Do not even try.*
8	Upright	Try on Tuesday.
	Reversed	*Not until next week.*

Number and position of paper		Meaning
9	Upright	Try again on the day on which you were born.
	Reversed	*Soon, if you do not lose your temper.*
10	Upright	Saturday is preferable.
	Reversed	*No Saturday is suitable.*
11	Upright	There is nothing to say.
	Reversed	*Secrets wait.*
12	Upright	Monday will be auspicious.
	Reversed	*Monday is inauspicious.*
13	Upright	Lose no time.
	Reversed	*First be sure of your own mind.*
14	Upright	Try on Friday.
	Reversed	*Good fortune awaits you.*
15	Upright	Try on Wednesday.
	Reversed	*Certainly not.*
16	Upright	Straight away.
	Reversed	*Do not try at all.*

Tablet of Venus

This tablet will answer questions connected with *love*.

5	11	1	9
14	7	4	12
8	3	16	2
6	15	10	13

See *opposite* for meanings.

Tablet of Venus: meanings

Number and position of paper		Meaning
1	Upright	This love is true.
	Reversed	*Think hard—this person disagrees with you.*
2	Upright	Expect some delay.
	Reversed	*Not the kind who is easily deceived.*
3	Upright	Follow your heart.
	Reversed	*Flatterers are dangerous.*
4	Upright	Yes, if you are really sure of your own mind.
	Reversed	*If you knew the truth you'd forgive.*
5	Upright	All's well.
	Reversed	*Yours was a hasty judgment.*
6	Upright	You will be to blame if you lose this love.
	Reversed	*True love can weather misfortune.*
7	Upright	You are causing unhappiness.
	Reversed	*Look beyond appearances.*
8	Upright	Do not let jealousy come between you and your loved-one.
	Reversed	*A friend who loves you truly.*

Tablet of Venus: meanings (continued)

Number and position of paper		Meaning
9	Upright	You are the only one who is loved.
	Reversed	*You are too fond of amusements.*
10	Upright	You are in someone's thoughts.
	Reversed	*Beware of a flirt.*
11	Upright	A passing cloud.
	Reversed	*A misunderstanding on both sides.*
12	Upright	Someone has defintely had a change of mind.
	Reversed	*Evil tongues, evil minds.*
13	Upright	Yes, but not the one you are thinking of.
	Reversed	*You should not act hastily.*
14	Upright	What reason is there for doubt?
	Reversed	*It was an infatuation—forget it.*
15	Upright	Try to remember what was said as you parted.
	Reversed	*There is no reason to be jealous.*
16	Upright	It is true love.
	Reversed	*Be sensible before it is too late.*

Tablet of the Moon

This tablet will answer questions concerning your
home, *relatives*, and *friends*.

See *the next page* for meanings.

Tablet of the Moon: meanings

Number and position of paper		Meaning
1	Upright	All is well, so be patient.
	Reversed	*You are your own worst enemy.*
2	Upright	The fault is yours.
	Reversed	*Less than ever.*
3	Upright	Do not let them worry you.
	Reversed	*If you can do so with a clear conscience.*
4	Upright	Love will find a way.
	Reversed	*There'll be none.*
5	Upright	It is a question of jealousy.
	Reversed	*It may possibly come about.*
6	Upright	You are indulging in fantasy.
	Reversed	*None, if you are discreet.*
7	Upright	A fair woman.
	Reversed	*Sometimes, but rarely.*
8	Upright	It is most unlikely.
	Reversed	*Matters will improve.*

Number and position of paper		Meaning
9	Upright	You will be disappointed in this matter.
	Reversed	*You will do more harm than good.*
10	Upright	Hasty works will be regretted.
	Reversed	*Do not take any of them into your confidence.*
11	Upright	Groundless suspicions.
	Reversed	*Current gossip maligns you.*
12	Upright	There is a marvelous friend to help.
	Reversed	*The secret is at risk.*
13	Upright	Be content.
	Reversed	*Trust a woman speaking her mind.*
14	Upright	Your neighbor is a true friend.
	Reversed	*It will soon be over.*
15	Upright	You will have your wish.
	Reversed	*There is no reason for doubt.*
16	Upright	A removal.
	Reversed	*Everything is for the best.*

Tablet of the Sun

This tablet answers questions concerning *time*.

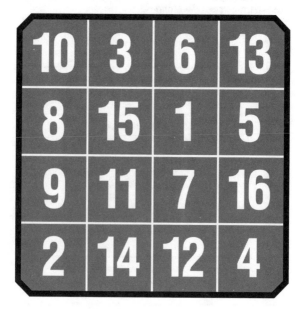

10	3	6	13
8	15	1	5
9	11	7	16
2	14	12	4

See *opposite* for meanings.

Tablet of the Sun: meanings

Number and position of paper		Meaning
1	Upright	In six month's time.
	Reversed	*Wait exactly one week.*
2	Upright	Never.
	Reversed	*In two weeks.*
3	Upright	It will soon come out.
	Reversed	*Time will tell.*
4	Upright	Soon.
	Reversed	*Not for a long time.*
5	Upright	Continue and you will flourish.
	Reversed	*Not yet.*
6	Upright	In less time than you think.
	Reversed	*Very gradual change.*
7	Upright	This year.
	Reversed	*The hundredth day of the year.*
8	Upright	Yes.
	Reversed	*The fifteenth day of the month.*

Tablet of the Sun: meanings (continued)

Number and position of paper		Meaning
9	Upright	There is some cause of delay.
	Reversed	*In two years' time.*
10	Upright	You are wrong to be impatient.
	Reversed	*Never.*
11	Upright	Right away.
	Reversed	*In months rather than days.*
12	Upright	Very soon.
	Reversed	*Three times.*
13	Upright	Find your lucky day.
	Reversed	*Sooner than you imagine.*
14	Upright	There is not much longer to wait.
	Reversed	*Leave well alone for as long as you can.*
15	Upright	It seems to have no chance of happening.
	Reversed	*Highly improbable.*
16	Upright	In one year's time.
	Reversed	*In a while.*

Tablet of Jupiter

This tablet will answer questions concerned with *doubts*, *worries*, *legal problems*, and *justice*.

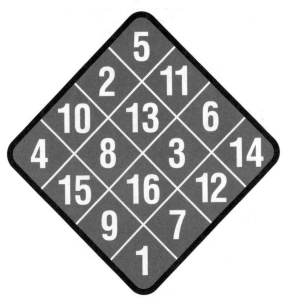

See *the next page* for meanings.

Tablet of Jupiter: meanings

Number and position of paper		Meaning
1	Upright *Reversed*	You have been misjudged. *Your judgment was hasty.*
2	Upright *Reversed*	The truth will out. *You will not play a major part.*
3	Upright *Reversed*	Your judgment was much too hasty. *You could not escape this trouble.*
4	Upright *Reversed*	This cloud will pass. *Things will soon improve.*
5	Upright *Reversed*	You are in the wrong. *Be brave, you have done no wrong.*
6	Upright *Reversed*	You are most certainly right. *This is an injustice.*
7	Upright *Reversed*	Learn from your own experience. *Take care.*
8	Upright *Reversed*	You already know the truth. *There is no danger.*

Number and position of paper		Meaning
9	Upright	No one can answer the question.
	Reversed	*Justice will triumph in the end.*
10	Upright	There will be little delay.
	Reversed	*Do not be afraid without reason.*
11	Upright	Try once more.
	Reversed	*Speak out boldly.*
12	Upright	Do not be afraid.
	Reversed	*No, which is a good thing.*
13	Upright	Yes, and right will prevail.
	Reversed	*You are not in error.*
14	Upright	Things are not as black as you think.
	Reversed	*Make your plans slowly and carefully.*
15	Upright	It is a foolish scandal.
	Reversed	*Do not be anxious.*
16	Upright	You were in the worng.
	Reversed	*Everything will come right in the end.*

Tablet of Mars

This tablet will answer questions to do with *work*, *business*, or *money*.

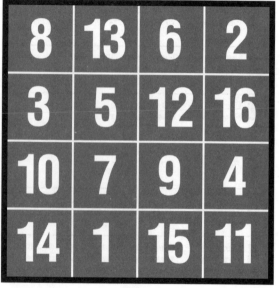

See *opposite* for meanings.

Tablet of Mars: meanings

Number and position of paper	Meaning
1 Upright *Reversed*	Money changes. *Friends are more valuable than money.*
2 Upright *Reversed*	New work. *It will be very expensive.*
3 Upright *Reversed*	It's up to you. *There is a high risk.*
4 Upright *Reversed*	Happiness is preferable to wealth. *Do not rely on it.*
5 Upright *Reversed*	The bad times will soon be over. *There is the prospect of wealth.*
6 Upright *Reversed*	A big surprise. *Be ready to take some blame.*
7 Upright *Reversed*	Think hard before giving your consent. *Look at it from a different angle.*
8 Upright *Reversed*	Hard work is what is needed. *Be less selfish and more considerate of others.*

Tablet of Mars: meanings (continued)

Number and position of paper		Meaning
9	Upright	Prove that you can be trusted.
	Reversed	*If you persevere no one can rob you of success.*
10	Upright	Be very careful.
	Reversed	*Turn back.*
11	Upright	Expect problems ahead.
	Reversed	*Take counsel of your second thoughts.*
12	Upright	Your worries will soon be over.
	Reversed	*Exactly what you deserve.*
13	Upright	Expect good luck.
	Reversed	*Money.*
14	Upright	Be bold.
	Reversed	*It will be an improvement.*
15	Upright	All's well.
	Reversed	*You will gain by an accident.*
16	Upright	Have patience.
	Reversed	*Be brave.*

Tablet of Mercury

This tablet will answer questions about *journeys*.

See *the next page* for meanings.

Tablet of Mercury: meanings

Number and position of paper		Meaning
1	Upright	In a while.
	Reversed	*Wants to be with you.*
2	Upright	Yes, it's all for the best.
	Reversed	*It's inadvisable.*
3	Upright	Better to stay where you are.
	Reversed	*You will decline.*
4	Upright	The prospect of a long journey.
	Reversed	*When you least expect it.*
5	Upright	Distant thoughts are turned to you.
	Reversed	*Some loss and some gain.*
6	Upright	A disappointment.
	Reversed	*It should not be long now.*
7	Upright	Not far.
	Reversed	*An enjoyable time.*
8	Upright	Yes, though it's not so very important.
	Reversed	*After careful thought.*

Number and position of paper		Meaning
9	Upright	Modern transport has made the world shrink.
	Reversed	*Very doubtful indeed.*
10	Upright	It will happen very suddenly.
	Reversed	*An unexpected route to happiness.*
11	Upright	Definitely for the better.
	Reversed	*Westward.*
12	Upright	Expect many changes.
	Reversed	*All will not be happiness.*
13	Upright	Your hopes will be fulfilled.
	Reversed	*The distance is great.*
14	Upright	Wait awhile.
	Reversed	*Soon.*
15	Upright	All's for the best.
	Reversed	*The East beckons.*
16	Upright	Don't go.
	Reversed	*Not yet.*

NUMEROLOGY TODAY

Throughout this book, you will find information about the way in which you can use numbers to best advantage by producing your own meaningful calculations. You do not need to be a skilled mathematician to do this, however. You will not even need a calculator. The figure work is very basic and you should be able to work everything out in your head or on paper. Nevertheless you may sometimes consider consulting a professional numerologist – if you have specific health, emotional, or career problems, for example. At such times their insight can be extremely valuable.

You should be able to find the address of a numerologist by using the Internet, in your local press, on the bulletin board of an alternative lifestyle bookshop, or by calling a psychic studies center. Personal recommendation may also lead you to one who is highly regarded. Some numerologists require you to visit personally; others do readings by post or will perhaps be prepared to speak with you by telephone.

A consultation

A visit to a numerologist is unlikely to last more than an hour, and you should ask about the charge in advance. You will need to provide your full name, as on your birth certificate, the current name by which you are known, and your age. Don't be tempted to be reticent about giving your true date of birth. This is essential for the numerologist to forecast the potential for change and the outcome of any current difficulty. You might like to ask in advance if you can bring along a cassette recorder, as it can be useful to play back the numerologist's reading later. One visit to a numerologist may be sufficient for current needs, but you may choose to seek a further reading another time. If a problem concerns compatibility, it may be very helpful to attend with the other party so that the relationship can be reviewed by both of you and better mutual understanding encouraged.

Business matters

Individuals sometimes seek a reading on behalf of their business. In this case, they need to give the full company name, the date of incorporation or commencement of trading, and the registration number. The numerologist may suggest a change of name, or use of a new trading name if profits have not been up to expectations. They may also be able to advise on suitable staff, as well as auspicious dates for the launch of new products or advertising campaigns. The viability of a new product name can also be calculated using the principles of numerology.

All modern numerologists work according to the findings of a team of highly talented women from southern California who, in the early part of the 20th century, began a thorough investigation of the theories of Pythagoras. The group was led by Dr Juno Jordan, who formed the California Institute of Numerological

Research. Just as Pythagoras had somehow intuitively known, the team reached the conclusion that numbers are a vital source of form and energy.

Now, at the beginning of the 21st century, scientific research has led us to accept that everything in this universe vibrates with set energy patterns. This is true not only of objects but of human beings. Indeed, numerologists believe that each of us vibrates according to our own set of personal numbers. It has even been said that these numbers represent our very essence. Could it therefore be that, when we meet someone with whom we instantly feel a rapport, it is because we share a rate of vibration? Once we become aware of these personal numbers and their significance, a whole new level of understanding will emerge.

Living by numbers

But numerology does not only help to provide greater self-awareness. Some use the system for analyzing dreams, when gambling, or even when family planning. Others use it for financial transactions, for naming a child, to improve relationships, or as a guide to general health or midlife problems. The sections that follow in this book explain the calculations you will need to use when seeking a guide to these and many other areas of modern life.

TAKE
A DATE!

FIGURING IT OUT

Numerologists hold that the figures in your date of
birth provide a clue to your nature – good points and
failings. The numbers making up the year in which we
are living at any one time, moreover, are also said to
have an effect on us all. These readings can be used as
guidelines only to greater self-awareness and
predictively.

The day of birth
According to one simple form of calculation, the so-
called Personality Number is based on the day of the
month in which you were born. It does not matter
whether you were born on September **9**, July **9**, or May
9, your Personality Number will still be **9**. If, however,
you were born on a date with double figures, you need
to use a reading for each of the figures, and then
temper these with one for the total of the two figures.
Say you were born on **23** August; you need first to use
readings for the figures **2** and **3**, and then a reading for
their total, **5**. If, however, were born on **10**, **20**, or **30** of
any month, according to this method you will only
need use a reading for one Personality Number as there
are no readings for zero. If you were born on **11** or **22**
of any month, you can proceed with an additional
reading for the totals which are **2** and **4** respectively;
but you should also note that characteristics for
Personality Numbers **1** and **2** may be more pronounced
since they are repeated.

PERSONALITY NUMBER 1

Those with this Personality Number are frequently highly individualistic and tend to stand out in a crowd. They are often extremely extrovert and tend to dress stylishly. Sometimes outrageous in the way that they behave, yet never without some degree of feeling for others who are more retiring, they are very ambitious. Stand in their way and you will soon find that they voice a strong and loud complaint.

Example: Marilyn Monroe, actress
Born June 1, 1926

PERSONALITY NUMBER 2

Quick to take umbridge and often very sensitive, those with the Personality Number **2** can be highly strung and need to be treated with kid gloves. They are never speedy at making decisions and will dither until their minds are made up for them by someone else. Stubborn by nature, too, they are wary of advice, regarding it as an intrusion in their lives. On the positive side, however, they are very caring and will always provide a shoulder to cry on.

Example: Maria Callas, opera singer
Born December 2, 1923

PERSONALITY NUMBER 3

Those with this Personality Number may have two completely different sides to their nature. On occasions they may seem very withdrawn, separating themselves from the crowd. At other times, however, they will be far more extrovert. Even their friends may not know what to expect due to their mood swings. With a deep concern for humanity at large, and a strict code of conduct from which they rarely depart, they would rather suffer personally than let anyone down.

Example: Marlon Brando, actor
Born April 3, 1924

PERSONALITY NUMBER 4

Strike up a relationship with someone who has the Personality Number **4** and the chances are you will still be in touch in old age, even if only exchanging Christmas cards, because they make the very best of friends. They may not be the most organized of people, however, and often need someone else's assistance to ensure that everything is kept in order. The frequent need to both give and receive expressions of affection is particularly marked.

Example: Gina Lollobrigida, actress
Born July 4, 1927

PERSONALITY NUMBER 5

No other Personality Number provides such a degree of sparkle. Extremely outward-going, vivacious, and full of curiosity about all sorts of subjects, these people are intelligent (even if not highly educated), quick-witted, full of fun, and highly adventurous. They are often admired by others but will not always respect anyone else's opinion. They tend to change careers midstream, possibly because they have such lively minds and so many interests.

Example: Neil Armstrong, astronaut
Born August 5, 1930

PERSONALITY NUMBER 6

Extremely generous by nature and usually fun-seeking, those with this Personality Number tend to be relied on to find something amusing that will cheer even the gloomiest of moments. They enjoy the good life and do not worry about tomorrow. If, by chance, someone annoys them, however, they are likely to remain resentful for a long period rather than expressing their anger in the first place in order to clear the air.

Example: Ronald Reagan, actor/politician
Born Feburary 6, 1911

PERSONALITY NUMBER 7
The most likely person to be able to influence
public opinion and make people change their
minds is someone with the Personality
Number **7**. Impatience, sarcasm, and overt
criticism of behavior seen as inappropriate are
compensated for by a tremendous creativity
and originality. Those with this Personality
Number are also very generous of spirit and
not at all possessive, except when it comes to
personal relationships.

Example: Anthony Quayle, actor
Born September 7, 1913

PERSONALITY NUMBER 8
Very self-possessed, confident, and assertive,
those with the Personality Number **8** are
frequently born leaders and will be at their best
when at the helm. They may need to avoid a
tendency to be overpowering at times, however, if
others are not to resent what are basically
excellent qualities. Highly organized and
practical, as well as hard-working, they have the
ability to sum up a situation at speed and are
quick decision-makers.

Example: Jesse Jackson, politician
Born October 8, 1941

PERSONALITY NUMBER 9

A tendency to be over-critical of others is a common fault among those with this Personality Number. They set very high standards for themselves in all areas of life. Some would even go so far as to label them stuffy, old-fashioned, or prudish. But such qualities can be put to good use because there will always be others who need to be reminded of life's ground rules. They frequently have a good sense of humor. Respect for others is shown at all times.

Example: Alan Bennett, author
Born May 9, 1934

Assessing others

After you have read through the Personality Number tables on pages 77-81, it can be an interesting exercise to try and assess the Personality Number of people you are familiar with but whose birth dates you do not know. Famous examples given within the table on these pages may not always seem to correspond to the outer persona but will relate to the true inner nature of the individual and his or her psychological make-up.

LIFE NUMBERS

The full date of birth can be used to reveal much about
the direction that an individual's life is likely to take.
The calculation is a simple one. Say you were born on
March 1, 1972 (3.1.1972). Add the digits together as
follows: $3 + 1 + 1 + 9 + 7 + 2 = 23$ Now reduce this to
$2 + 3 = 5$. Your Life Number would therefore be **5**. If
you were born on December 14, 1980 (12.14.1980) you
would calculate as follows: $1 + 2 + 1 + 4 + 1 + 9 + 8 +
0 = 26$. Now reduce this again to $2 + 6 = 8$. Your Life
Number would therefore be **8**. According to one school
of numerology, however, Life Numbers **11** and **22** are
never reduced.

LIFE NUMBER 1
Highly ambitious, those with the Life Number **1**
are likely to succeed in most things they do and
will always seem to forge ahead with great drive.
But they should be wary of taking on too much.
Example: Truman Capote, author
Born September 30, 1924.

LIFE NUMBER 2
Since those with this Life Number are generally
creative, unselfish, and cheerful by nature. They
make excellent diplomats, negotiators, social
workers, counsellors, and entertainers.
Example: Stephen Sondheim, composer
Born March 22, 1930.

LIFE NUMBER 3

You will find that inventors, explorers, and scientists
will often have the Life Number **3**. They face up to
both intellectual and practical challenges without any
sign of fear but this may cause resentment at times in
others who are not so talented. They usually have
considerable staying power and a natural intelligence.
Example: Sir Alec Guinness, actor
Born April 2, 1914

LIFE NUMBER 4

Diligent, charitable, and loyal by nature, those
with the Life Number **4** may often enter one of the
caring professions. But whatever they do, they
will always be very well organized and rarely let
others down. Everything will be undertaken with
great enthusiasm and vigor.
Example: Arnold Palmer, golfer
Born September 10, 1929.

LIFE NUMBER 5

When difficult situations arise, those with the Life
Number **5** often find they can fall back on a sense of
humor to keep them on track. They frequently need
to watch their stress levels, however, as a tendency
to push themselves too much may sometimes cause
physical problems.
Example: Moshe Dayan, general/politician
Born May 20, 1915

LIFE NUMBER 6
Few people succeed in balancing the demands of
work and family responsibilities as well as those
with the Life Number **6**. They are frequently very
successful in business in spite of this, and will
usually be able to count their colleagues, who
respect them greatly, as true friends.
Example: Dame Alicia Markova, ballerina
Born December 1, 1910.

LIFE NUMBER 7
Intuitive, spiritual, introspective, and in many ways
too idealistic, those with the Life Number **7** often
dismiss the material things in life, opting instead for
a far simpler way of living than most of their
generation enjoy. It will serve them in good stead
not to worry unduly about the world's problems.
Example: Arthur Miller, playwright
Born October 17, 1915.

LIFE NUMBER 8
Very concerned with their careers, those who have
the Life Number **8** spend a good part of their lives
trying to climb the ladder in whatever field of work
they have chosen. They tend to perform best within
large organizations, and will be highly regarded as
reliable colleagues in all respects.
Example: Jesse Owens, athlete
Born September 12, 1913.

LIFE NUMBER 9

Compassionate, charitable, creative, and full of original ideas, those with the Life Number **9** are excellent initiators. They often have a competitive streak, however, and do not take kindly to criticism. They will readily go out on a limb, and like to be thought of as different and somehow apart from the crowd.
Example: Allen Ginsburg, poet
Born June 3, 1926.

LIFE NUMBER 11

Very determined and self-possessed, those with the Life Number **11** are good communicators and often reach high office, though not without taking a number of calculated risks on the way. They seem to thrive on thorny problems and, through sheer endeavor, usually win through.
Example: Shirley Temple Black, actress/politician
Born April 23, 1928.

LIFE NUMBER 22

Unmaterialistic and happy-go-lucky by nature, those with the Life Number **22** will take things as they come and are rarely upset by the sort of problems that would totally confuse others. They have a tendency, however, to be taken advantage of since they are often a poor judge of character.
Example: Thor Heyerdahl, explorer
Born October 6, 1914.

UNIVERSAL NUMBERS

In addition to being influenced by your date of birth
which provides both a Personality and a Life Number,
you will also need to take into account a Universal
Year Number which is calculated from the figures of a
current year and is therefore the same for everyone
during that year.

Method
If, for example, the current year is 2002, you will need
to do the sum $2 + 0 + 0 + 2 = 4$. This means that in the
course of 2002, everyone will be influenced by
energies corresponding to the number **4**.

If this Universal Year Number happens to
correspond to your Personal Year Number (calculate
this by adding together the digits in the year of your
birth), then this will be a particularly auspicious year
for you.

If, for example, you were born in 1975, do the
calculation $1 + 9 + 7 + 5 = 22$. Then reduce this to $2
+ 2 = 4$. Your Personal Year Number would therefore
be the same as the number for the Universal Year
2002, **4**, showing that this is likely to be a very lucky
time for you.

UNIVERSAL YEAR TRENDS

During each Universal Year, we are all likely to experience particular trends, and the Universal Year cycle renews itself every **9** years. The following chart outlines the sort of things we might expect during each Universal Year according to the number of our Personal Year, calculated as on page 86.

If a **Universal Year 1** coincides with:

A Personal Year 1
This is a highly auspicious year for you.

A Personal Year 2 or 3
You will find that energies are renewed.

A Personal Year 4 or 5
Many new opportunities will present themselves.

A Personal Year 6 or 7
You will start to feel more positive about life.

A Personal Year 8 or 9
There will be more challenges than ever.

If a **Universal Year 2** coincides with:
A Personal Year 1
This will be a particularly creative period.
A Personal Year 2
This is a highly auspicious year for you.
A Personal Year 3 or 4
Delay making any big decisions this year.
A Personal Year 5 or 6
You may meet and need to overcome certain obstacles.
A Personal Year 7 or 8
Work at developing a new relationship.
A Personal Year 9
It is time to learn to be more tolerant of others.

If a **Universal Year 3** coincides with:
A Personal Year 1 or 2
It will be a particularly busy year.
A Personal Year 3
This is a highly auspicious year for you.
A Personal Year 4 or 5
Romance may well be in the offing.
A Personal Year 6 or 7
Grasp every opportunity that presents itself.
A Personal Year 8 or 9
All your efforts are rewarded.

If a **Universal Year 4** coincides with:
A Personal Year 1 or 2
This will be an expensive time for you.
A Personal Year 3
Bide your time by making careful plans.
A Personal Year 4
This is a highly auspicious year for you.
A Personal Year 5 or 6
Devote time to providing for future needs.
A Personal Year 7 or 8
Do not take on too many responsibilities this year.
A Personal Year 9
Do not be unduly influenced this year.

If a **Universal Year 5** coincides with:
A Personal Year 1 or 2
Changes are highlighted this year.
A Personal Year 3 or 4
There are lots of decisions to be made this year.
A Personal Year 5
This is a highly auspicious year for you.
A Personal Year 6 or 7
Be prepared for the entirely unexpected.
A Personal Year 8 or 9
Do not allow others to impede your progress this year.

If a **Universal Year 6** coincides with:
A Personal Year 1 or 2
Be sure to give sufficient attention to all sorts of
family matters.
A Personal Year 3 or 4
Try to resolve any longstanding disputes this year.
A Personal Year 5
A more realistic approach to life will undoubtedly
serve you best.
A Personal Year 6
This is a highly auspicious year for you.
A Personal Year 7 or 8
You will want to put down roots.
A Personal Year 9
This year augurs well for your love life.

If a **Universal Year 7** coincides with:
A Personal Year 1 or 2
It is time to reassess your lifestyle.
A Personal Year 3 or 4
You will benefit from taking more time out.
A Personal Year 5 or 6
Spending more time on your own will prove to
be beneficial.
A Personal Year 7
This is a highly auspicious year for you.
A Personal Year 8 or 9
You will start to climb the ladder of success.

If a **Universal Year 8** coincides with:
A **Personal Year 1 or 2**
You will reap all the rewards for past efforts.
A **Personal Year 3 or 4**
Take care this year not to weaken under pressure.
A **Personal Year 5 or 6 or 7**
This will be an exciting time.
A **Personal Year 8**
This is a highly auspicious year for you.
A **Personal Year 9**
Prospects for financial gain are well augured.

If a **Universal Year 9** coincides with:
A **Personal Year 1 or 2**
You will do best to mark time this year.
A **Personal Year 3 or 4**
This is not the time to gamble on a large scale.
A **Personal Year 5 or 6**
Look after your health and conserve your energies.
A **Personal Year 7 or 8**
A year for taking stock of achievements.
A **Personal Year 9**
This is a highly auspicious year for you.

UNIVERSAL MONTH NUMBERS

The Universal Month Number is calculated by using the number of the current month (the number for July, for example, would be **7**, and the number for October would be **10**) and adding this to the appropriate Universal Year Number.

The Universal Month Number for May 2003 would involve the calculation $5 + 2 + 0 + 0 + 3 = 10$. This is then reduced to $1 + 0 = 1$. The Universal Month Number for May 2003 is therefore **1**.

In a similar way, you can find your Personal Month Number by adding the number of the month in which you were born to the digits of the year in which you were born. Someone born in April 1962, for example, would do the calculation $4 + 1 + 9 + 6 + 2 = 22$. This is then reduced to $2 + 2 = 4$. The Personal Month Number for this person is therefore **4**.

When both the Universal Month Number and the Personal Month Number are the same, this may be taken as a sign that influences, as listed on page 93, will be doubly strong.

UNIVERSAL DAY NUMBERS

The Universal Day Number is calculated by adding the calendar day of the date in question to the Universal Year and Month Number. The Universal Day Number for July 28th, 2004, is therefore calculated as $7 + 2 + 8 + 2 + 0 + 0 + 4 = 23$. This is then reduced to $2 + 3 = 5$. The Universal Day Number for July 28th 2004 is therefore **5**.

Influences

Universal Year, Month, and Day Numbers bring with them very distinct vibrations or influences which can be summarized as follows:

1 Opportunities, new beginnings
2 Thoughtfulness, peacefulness
3 Self-expression, enjoyment
4 Making plans, looking ahead
5 Changes, excitement
6 Creativity, increased responsibility
7 Inner quests, reassessing values
8 Achievements, ambitions
9 Concern for humanity, tying up loose ends

TURNING POINTS

According to one school of numerology, we all
experience four distinct turning points at various
stages in our lives. Not everyone has them at the same
time – it all depends on your date of birth; and when
they occur, you will find your inner strength is
somehow revitalized and that very significant events
take place.

You can identify when the first turning point in your
life either took or is about to take place by subtracting
your Life Number (calculated by adding together all
the digits in your full date of birth) from **36**.

Say, for example, you were born on **5 September
1945**. You would subtract your Life Number, **6**, from
36 to give **30**. The age at which you would experience
a turning point would therefore be **30**. The next three
turning points would occur at **9**-year intervals – in this
instance, therefore, at the ages **39**, **48**, and **57**.

THE NAME'S THE THING

SOUL NUMBERS AND NAMES

The soul is thought to be that part of you which makes you a human being and which, according to certain beliefs, lives on after your physical body dies. It is unique to you, and numerologists believe it is possible to tap its depths by means of a Soul Number that will reveal aspects of your character that are not obvious on the surface.

You can find your Soul Number by combining all your names as on your birth certificate and then adding the numerical value of all the vowels. This may seem strange at first, but our names are very much part of us and have a strong influence on our lives. The value of the vowels is calculated as follows:

$$
\begin{array}{ll}
\textbf{A} & \textbf{1} \\
\textbf{E} & \textbf{5} \\
\textbf{I} & \textbf{9} \\
\textbf{O} & \textbf{6} \\
\textbf{U} & \textbf{3}
\end{array}
$$

Some numerologists count the letter Y as a vowel, particularly if there is no other vowel in the name, or no other vowel in the same syllable. In the names Yvonne, Cy, Myra, or Gary, for example, the letter Y is counted as a vowel, but not in the names Audrey, May, Rodney, or Gaynor. It has the value **7**.

Calculating a Soul Number
If **Amelia Joyce Muirhead** (the name on her birth
certificate and not her married name) wishes to find
her Soul Number, she will find the value of the vowels
in the full name she was given and then add them
together. The resulting sum is as follows:
1 + 5 + 9 + 1 + 6 + 5 + 3 + 9 + 5 + 1 = 45.

These two digits are then reduced to **4 + 5 = 9**.
Her Soul Number is therefore **9**, and she can obtain a
reading from page 101. Even though she now calls
herself **Amy Johnson**, if she wishes to find out
something concerning the spirit with which she was
born, she needs to use her given name in full. (You can
discover what difference changing your name can
make on page 112).

SOUL NUMBER 1
People who have the Soul Number **1** are deemed
to be the pioneers among us. They have the
confidence to tread new paths, to try new
approaches rather than accepting existing methods
as the only way, and delight in experimentation.
When used to its full extent, such a spirit of
enterprise can bring enormous benefits both to the
individual with the Soul Number **1** and to
humanity at large. Original and even flamboyant
at times, they are true individualists.

SOUL NUMBER 2

Those with this Soul Number have a valuable
lesson to learn in their journey through life. They
will come to realize that life is never a simple
case of black and white. They need to develop the
wisdom to view difficult situations impartially,
while never losing a degree of compassion for the
feelings of people beleaguered by problems.
These qualities tend to come to those with the
Soul Number 2 over the years via first-hand
experience. Everything that happens to them in
life should therefore be regarded as contributing
to their spiritual education.

SOUL NUMBER 3

Ambitious, talkative, sometimes vain, highly
creative, and easily bored, those with the Soul
Number 3 often need to take onboard the fact that
everyone has to accept to a certain degree the
hand that destiny has dealt. They may try to better
themselves by all means, and will usually
succeed, but they should not forget their origins.
Altering one's image may not always be for the
best, and will not ensure happiness. People with
this Soul Number are often more attractive and
successful if they do not try too hard.

SOUL NUMBER 4

Orderly, conventional, and thriving within a stable environment, those with the Soul Number **4** frequently find they have to strive to provide a degree of harmony in the lives of others as well as in their own family circle. Fortunately they are innately realistic and will be able to find practical solutions for situations in which others would flounder. A rock in times of trouble, someone with this Soul Number will usually be able to find a sensible solution when difficulties arise. They make reliable friends and will always provide a shoulder for someone to cry on if the need arises.

SOUL NUMBER 5

This Soul Number reveals a driving force that will influence a latent talent for communication. Progressive in attitudes, versatile, and eloquent, those with the Soul Number **5** readily convey ideas and are acknowledged as being adept at stimulating enthusiasm in others about unfamiliar concepts. They are not slow in coming forward and may sometimes appear egoistic, yet they are sensitive to the feelings of others and may even be telepathic in this respect. They often make excellent teachers and can hold the attention of a whole class without difficulty.

SOUL NUMBER 6

With a very clear sense of what is right and wrong, and an inner need to see justice done, those with this Soul Number generally expect others to have similar standards. They also expect the best of themselves continually and feel dreadful if they fail for any reason. They strive for perfection on every level and will complain if this is not achieved by others. Those with the Soul Number 6 need to learn as a lesson in this life that it is possible to accept and love others, warts and all. In the end, we are all human and fallible.

SOUL NUMBER 7

Those with the Soul Number 7 are independent by nature and strong-willed. They have a need to try out everything for themselves and will not readily rely on the experience of others. They will do well, however, to develop a heightened sensitivity to the spiritual needs of those with whom they live and work. In turn, everyone will benefit from the realization that sensitivity is not necessarily a weakness but often a strength. Only if they become over-emotional are problems likely to arise.

SOUL NUMBER 8

Single-minded and with a burning ambition to succeed, those with the Soul Number **8** are frequently described as stubborn and may be ruthless in their attempts to reach the top. But it is not necessary an entirely selfish spirit that drives them. The individual with this Soul Number frequently strives for the best for his or her family, the community, or even humanity as a whole. There is often a need to get things into perspective, however, if all this effort is to bear fruit for everyone. There may be simpler routes to happiness.

SOUL NUMBER 9

Compassionate, romantic, creative, and with a strong love of life, those with the Soul Number **9** often display a wonderful sense of humor. Always kindly towards others, they nevertheless often seem to fail to appreciate their own spiritual needs. A sense of humility is also frequently lacking and this may need to be worked at. It is often necessary for them to stand back and view themselves as others see them. There are times, too, when it will be sensible to accept a helping hand.

KARMIC NUMBERS

In addition to Personality, Life, and Soul Numbers, we
all have a Karmic Number. According to cosmic
principles that make up the Law of Karma – a belief
originating in the East but now increasingly recognized
in the West – we always get back in life what we put
into it. By extension, some people also believe this
may apply to future lives, and that behavior in a past
life may have influenced our destiny in this life.

Calculating a Karmic Number

You can calculate your Karmic Number by adding
together the numerical equivalents of all the letters in
your full name, both vowels and consonants, as given
at birth. The following table should be consulted when
making this calculation.

A	J	S	1
B	K	T	2
C	L	U	3
D	M	V	4
E	N	W	5
F	O	X	6
G	P	Y	7
H	Q	Z	8
I	R		9

Example:
The calculation for **Bruce George Robbe** would
involve adding the following digits:
$2 + 9 + 3 + 3 + 5 + 7 + 5 + 6 + 9 + 7 + 5 + 9 + 6 + 2 + 5$
which gives the total **85**.
Now reduce this to $8 + 5 = 13$, and further to
$1 + 3 = 4$. In this instance, the Karmic Number is
therefore **4**.

The following summary shows the significance of
Karmic Numbers **1-9**.

KARMIC NUMBER 1
Show others the way and *you* will be guided to success
and happiness, too, as you are a natural leader.

KARMIC NUMBER 2
Just as you help others to solve their problems and to
make sensible decisions, so you will benefit from
living your life on an even keel.

KARMIC NUMBER 3
Use your natural creative talents to benefit the lives of
others and their enjoyment will spur you on to far
greater things.

KARMIC NUMBER 4
Just as you bring a sense of calm to those who are
troubled, so such steadfastness will help you cope with
any difficulties that arise in your own life.

KARMIC NUMBER 5
Use your natural intelligence wisely and, slowly but
surely, you will achieve your ambitions.

KARMIC NUMBER 6
It is your nature to put others before yourself. When
you need a helping hand in life, it will therefore surely
come to you.

KARMIC NUMBER 7
Intuitive and spiritual, you will readily recognize those
with whom you can form a lifelong bond, and they
will appreciate your excellent qualities.

KARMIC NUMBER 8
A strong sense of responsibility encourages you to
work diligently, and this in turn brings great rewards
by way of satisfaction at what is achieved, and often
great financial gain.

KARMIC NUMBER 9
Providing you do not become too opinionated, your
views on what you regard as matters of importance
will bring you huge respect.

DOUBLING UP

During any sort of numerological calculation, if a
number that contains the same two digits together is
achieved, this is said to have great influence. Indeed, it
is thought to *double* the effect of the single digit.
Finding a double digit (also known as a *Master
Number*) may well help an individual to highlight a
certain aspect of his/her talents or character. This can
be particularly helpful when it comes to choosing a
career, for instance.

Double digits may occur when you calculate your
Soul, Karma, Life, Personality or other numbers
before reducing them to a single figure. A guide to
each of the Master Numbers and the effects that they
exert as an aid to greater self-awareness follows.

---

11 indicates a tendency to be highly strung and
intuitive, and with a very caring attitude towards
others. Prepared to go out on a limb on someone
else's behalf, those with this Master Number often
make good therapists or may choose a career in
the performing arts. They frequently take control
of situations and do not suffer fools gladly.
(This Master Number reduces to the digit **2**).

22 indicates a painstaking individual who does not get distracted when trying to climb the ladder to success. They may appear self-centered but the motive is not always entirely a selfish one. Those with this Master Number often play a very supportive role and will go to the ends of the earth to protect the interests of a loved one.
(This Master Number reduces to the digit **4**.)

33 indicates a highly generous personality who is perhaps excessively liberal with the time that he/she devotes to others or with donations to charitable causes. Those with this Master Number make very good listeners and will often appreciate the true nature of a situation rather than accepting what merely seems to be the case.
(This Master Number reduces to the digit **6**.)

44 indicates someone who has tremendous panache and who is a born leader. Those with this Master Number can usually be trusted with a lot of responsibilities and may be relied upon to give others a helping hand up the ladder without feeling at all resentful if those whom they assist finally achieve far more recognition than they ever do.
(This Master Number reduces to the digit **8**.)

55 indicates a superb communicator with a real gift of the gab, who would make a powerful politician or barrister. Those with this Master Number, however, are not entirely self-centered and will frequently speak up for the shy and retiring. They also have very agile minds, and can readily switch from one topic to another.
(This Master Number reduces to the digit **1**.)

66 indicates someone who enjoys both giving and receiving affection, and who deems love above all else in life. Frequently at the hub of a family circle or social group, those with this Master Number are always compassionate to friends going through trying times – so much so that they risk becoming over-emotionally involved in such set-backs.
(This Master Number reduces to the digit **3**.)

77 indicates someone adept at putting things in order and who thinks clearly. Because of this, those with this Master Number risk being put upon by others and, as a result, may become overburdened. Provided such pressure is avoided, there may be enormous personal achievements in the course of a lifetime.
(This Master Number reduces to the digit **5**.)

88 indicates an individual who enjoys being in a position of power. Authoritarian at times, and with a strong sense of what is right and wrong, those with this Master Number are usually looked up to by others, but it is more usually out of fear than out of admiration, respect, or love. Once a friend, however, they remain loyal for life.
(This Master Number reduces to the digit **7**.)

99 indicates the sort of personality who will always appreciate that there is another point of view. Those with this Master Number usually show a willingness to nurture the talents of friends and casual acquaintances alike, even if this is to their own detriment. With lots of creative gifts, many with this Master Number will be admired by the public.
(This Master Number reduces to the digit **9**.)

REPEATED NUMBERS

When calculating a name number, one digit may appear many more times than any of the others. The significance of such repeated numbers is as follows.

1 The desire to be innovative and to have an interesting lifestyle.

2 Wanting to be accepted as one of the crowd.

3 A need to be sociable and to look on the bright side at all times.

4 Marked staying power and determination.

5 Adaptability and a dislike of routine.

6 An innate sense of justice and social responsibility.

7 Self-sufficiency and a tendency not to take the advice of others.

8 Efficient and well organized.

9 Sympathetic to the problems of others.

Examples:

Take the following names:

S U S A N   J A M E S
1 3 1 1 5   1 1 4 5 1

The number **1** appears most frequently and points to an extremely extravert personality.

L U K E   F O X
3 3 2 5   6 6 6

The number **6** appears most frequently in this name, indicating a caring nature and awareness of the needs of the community. Such repeated numbers are sometimes called *Numbers of Intensity*.

MISSING NUMBERS

When working out your Soul or Karmic number, you will be sure to notice that certain numbers are missing. If any of these missing numbers are also missing from a birth number calculation, this is taken to be a sign of a quality that needs to be developed.

The significance of missing numbers 1-9

1 A need to become more assertive and self-confident.

2 Empathy with the situation in which others may find themselves may be lacking.

3 Imagination needs to be stimulated.

4 More self-discipline and patience are required.

5 There may be a reluctance to try anything new.

6 A need to be more reliable and to be prepared to take on additional responsibilities.

7 Greater understanding of what makes himself or herself tick is required by this individual.

8 Practicality may be lacking.

9 This individual may be too tolerant.

Example

Take the following names:

H A R R Y   B U S H
8 1 9 9 7   2 3 1 8

The numbers missing for this name are **4, 5, 6**. If **4, 5,** and **6** are missing from Harry Bush's birth number calculation, too, then this is a sign that he may well need to concentrate on developing greater tenacity when it comes to work and a more structured routine.

L U C Y   A N N E   B O Y S
3 3 3 7   1 5 5 5   2 6 7 1

The numbers missing for this name are **4, 8, 9**. If **4, 8,** and **9** are also missing from the birth number calculation for Lucy Anne Boys, then she might do well to take herself in hand and set realistic targets for herself and daydream less.

C A R O L   S A R A   C U R T I S
3 1 9 6 3   1 1 9 1   3 3 9 2 9 1

The missing numbers for this name are **4, 5, 7** and **8**. This seems to indicate that, if these numbers are also missing from her birth number calculation, Carol Sara Curtis may require more self-discipline, and should be prepared to consider new options. She would do well to become more self-aware and take a more practical attitude to life.

CONFLICTING NUMBERS

Those who find that their Personality, Life, and Soul
Numbers are the same will be extremely fortunate.
Opportunities that arise are likely to match innermost
needs and desires, and they may rarely encounter
difficulties in making decisions. When these numbers all
differ, however – and particularly if two are odd and one
is even, or one is odd and two are even – the individual
may feel pulled in different directions at various stages
in life. Taking careful account of the motivation revealed
by the Soul Number often helps with an acceptance of
what is revealed by the Life Number.

CHANGING YOUR NAME

Names exert such influence over our lives that at times
– usually when things are not running smoothly – some
people think of taking on a different identity. This
happens anyway if a woman opts to adopt her
husband's surname on marriage. Others may want to
use a pseudonym professionally. If such a situation
arises, it may be a good idea to take into account the
new numerological calculation. Interestingly, some
people report finding that they choose a name with an
identical numerical value completely subconsciously. If
you select a name with a different value, you may well
change the energies emitted by the original name,
thereby altering your wheel of fate.

CHOOSING A NAME

Theoretically, if we accept the that a name can provide us with a Soul Number (see pages 96-97), then we must regard the choice of a name for a baby as an important one. When considered together with a middle name or names, and the surname, it will also provide a Karmic Number. Some practitioners of numerology go so far as to state that while we think that we might consider picking any name, it does not happen by chance.

Calculations
To assist you with calculating a baby's Soul Number when selecting a name, and by extension his or her Karmic Number, the table that you will find on pages 114-119 lists currently popular names and their vowel and vowel/consonant numerical equivalents.

Note that the different spelling of what is basically the same name may have a profound effect upon the Soul or Karmic Number achieved. For example, the name Stewart has the Soul Number **6** and the Karmic contribution Number **7**; but if it is written as Stuart, this gives the Soul Number **4** and the Karmic contribution Number **9**. Remember that you will need the whole given name to calculate a Karmic Number. This does not, of course, mean that two people with exactly the same name will be exactly alike. Their temperaments will be affected by their Personality and Life Numbers, too.

BOYS' NAMES	Soul Number	Karmic Contribution
Adam	2	1
Adrian	2	2
Ali	1	4
Alvin	1	4
Andrew	6	2
Anthony	7	7
Barnaby	2	9
Bart	1	5
Boris	6	9
Bradley	6	4
Brian	1	8
Christian	1	2
Christopher	3	4
Claude	4	1
Clive	9	6
Colin	6	8
Crispin	9	7
Daniel	6	9
Darren	6	6
Daryl	1	6
David	1	4
Derek	1	6
Earl	6	9
Edward	6	1
Eliot	2	7
Eric	5	8
Errol	2	5
Frank	1	5
Frederick	6	7

BOYS' NAMES	Soul Number	Karmic Contribution
Gareth	6	5
Gavin	1	8
George	7	3
Gideon	2	9
Gordon	3	1
Grant	1	6
Guy	3	8
Harry	1	7
Harold	7	4
Ian	1	6
Jack	1	7
James	6	3
Jason	7	5
John	6	2
Jonathan	8	2
Jordan	7	8
Justin	3	3
Julian	4	4
Keith	6	8
Kevin	6	7
Laurence	5	7
Lee	1	4
Luke	8	4
Magnus	4	3
Mark	1	7
Matthew	6	9
Melvyn	5	1
Michael	6	6
Miles	5	4

BOYS' NAMES	Soul Number	Karmic Contribution
Mitchell	6	6
Nicholas	7	9
Oliver	2	9
Patrick	1	6
Paul	4	5
Peter	1	1
Randy	1	8
Raymond	7	9
Robert	2	6
Robin	6	4
Roger	2	9
Roland	7	1
Sam	1	6
Samuel	9	8
Saul	4	8
Stephen	1	6
Steven	1	6
Stewart	6	7
Stuart	4	9
Simon	6	7
Thomas	7	4
Tim	9	4
Timothy	6	2
Tom	6	3
Victor	6	6
Warren	6	7
Will	9	2
William	1	7
Zak	1	2

GIRLS' NAMES	Soul Number	Karmic Contribution
Abigail	2	5
Alison	7	7
Amber	6	3
Amy	1	3
Angela	7	4
Annabel	7	4
Annabelle	3	3
Barbara	3	7
Belinda	6	2
Bethany	6	3
Camilla	2	6
Candida	2	9
Carol	7	4
Caroline	3	7
Carolyn	7	7
Catherine	2	1
Christina	1	2
Christine	5	6
Corinna	7	2
Daisy	1	2
Danielle	2	8
Davina	2	6
Dee	1	5
Elizabeth	2	5
Emily	5	1
Emma	6	5
Erica	5	9
Estelle	6	6
Eve	1	5

GIRLS' NAMES	Soul Number	Karmic Contribution
Faith	1	8
Felicity	5	8
Fiona	2	9
Frances	6	3
Francesca	7	7
Gabrielle	2	8
Gail	1	2
Geraldine	2	3
Gloria	7	8
Hannah	2	1
Helen	1	8
Helena	2	9
Irma	1	5
Isolde	2	1
Jacqueline	2	7
Jasmin	1	3
Jemima	6	6
Jessica	6	3
Joy	6	8
Judith	3	9
Kate	6	1
Kathryn	1	7
Kerry	5	5
Kirsty	9	3
Laura	5	8
Lorna	7	6
Louise	9	9
Madeleine	7	5
Melanie	2	5

GIRLS' NAMES	Soul Number	Karmic Contribution
Melissa	6	6
Milly	6	8
Moira	6	2
Molly	6	5
Nina	1	2
Olivia	7	5
Pamela	7	3
Patricia	7	5
Polly	6	8
Rachael	7	3
Rebeccah	2	9
Rhiannon	7	3
Rosalind	7	2
Rosie	2	3
Ruth	3	4
Sadie	6	2
Sandra	2	3
Sarah	2	2
Sharon	7	3
Sophie	2	9
Stephanie	2	7
Susan	4	2
Susannah	5	7
Tamara	3	9
Tanya	2	7
Tracey	6	9
Valerie	2	9
Victoria	7	5
Yvonne	9	5

COLORS AND NUMBERS

According to numerological theory, numbers from **1-9**
all have color associations. One method used to find
your lucky color, according to a particular school of
numerology, involves adding your name and birth date
numbers. If, for example, this gives the answer **3**, your
lucky color will be yellow, as shown on the chart
opposite. You are likely to find that it suits you best,
that others respond well to you when you wear this
shade, and that you feel particularly at ease in a room
setting that is predominantly that color.

Example:

Alice Joy Grant was born on August **14**th 1963.
Her Karmic number is calculated as follows:
$$1 + 3 + 9 + 3 + 5 + 1 + 6 + 7 + 7 + 9 + 1 + 5 + 2 = 59$$
This reduces to **5 + 9 = 14**.
14 further reduces to **1 + 4 = 5**.
Her Life Number is calculated as follows (*see* page
82):
$$8 + 1 + 4 + 1 + 9 + 6 + 3 = 32.$$
This further reduces to **3 + 2 = 5**.
Now add the Karmic Number to the Life Number.
5 + 5 = 10. This further reduces to **1 + 0 = 1**.
Alice Joy Grant's lucky color is therefore likely to be
a shade of red, as revealed on the chart *opposite*.

Color chart

Having worked out the sum of a name and a birth
number, consult the chart shown here to discover the
color most likely to bring an individual contentment
and good fortune.

1	Red, crimson, scarlet, cherry
2	Orange, gold, tangerine, peach
3	Yellow, lemon, primrose, deep cream
4	Green, eau-de-nil, emerald
5	Mid-blue, turquoise
6	Deep blue, navy, royal blue
7	Violet, purple, plum
8	Pink, rose, blush
9	White, off-white, pale cream

Note that brown and black are not generally regarded
by numerologists as particularly lucky colors.

NUMBERS AND GEMSTONES

Many numerologists believe that gemstones have numerical associations according to their color. You can find out which precious or semi-precious stone or metal is likely to bring you most luck by using the same method as that outlined on page 120 for discovering your most fortunate color. Then consult the chart *below*.

1	Ruby, garnet
2	Gold, coral
3	Topaz
4	Jade, emerald
5	Turquoise, aquamarine
6	Sapphire, lapis lazuli
7	Amethyst
8	Rose quartz, opal
9	Silver, platinum, diamond, pearl

NUMBERS AND FLOWERS

By extension from a color and numbers calculation as outlined on page 120, it is possible to identify which flowers may bring good fortune, particularly when part of a bridal bouquet or corsage. Consult the following chart.

1	Red roses, red carnations
2	Freesias, orange roses, orange lilies
3	Yellow roses, orchid
4	Ornamental foliage
5	Pale anemones
6	Dyed blue carnation or any natural blue flower
7	Irises, deep purple roses
8	Pink roses, pink carnations, pinks
9	White carnations, white roses, gypsophila, lily of the valley

ODD AND EVEN NUMBERS

The odd numbers between **1** and **9** (that is, **1**, **3**, **5**, **7**, and **9**) are all traditionally regarded as *masculine* numbers. As such, they symbolize outward-going energies and activity. The even numbers between **1** and **9**, meanwhile (that is **2**, **4**, **6**, and **8**), are regarded as *feminine*. They symbolize more inward-looking energy and passive qualities.

Numbers have no true sexual connotations, however; so it is perfectly possible for a woman to have only or predominantly masculine numbers in her name or birth date calculations. In the same way, a man may have all or predominantly feminine numbers in such calculations.

When masculine numbers predominate, the individual is likely to be particularly assertive and full of drive. When feminine numbers predominate, the individual is likely to be more introspective and perhaps more intuitive than average.

The significance of such so-called masculine and feminine numbers applies to all forms of numerological calculations.

Masculine numbers	**1, 3, 5, 7, 9, etc**
Feminine numbers	**2, 4, 6, 8, etc**

Example:
Pauline Elizabeth Miller
Born July 14th, 1973

We can assess her Personality and Life Numbers from
her date of birth, and her Soul and Karmic Numbers
from her full name.

Personality Number **14** (from the date of birth),
which reduces to **4 + 1 = 5**.

Life Number **5** (from the whole date of birth)
1 + 4 + 7 + 1 + 9 + 7 + 3 = 32
which reduces to **3 + 2 = 5**

Soul Number **7** (calculated from the vowels in
her name)
1 + 3 + 9 + 5 + 5 + 9 + 1 + 5 + 9 + 5 = 52
This reduces to **5 + 2 = 7**

Karmic Number **1** (from her full name)
7 + 1 + 3 + 3 + 9 + 5 + 5 + 5 + 3 + 9 + 8 + 1 + 2 + 5 +
2 + 8 + 4 + 9 + 3 + 3 + 5 + 9 = 109
This reduces to **1 + 0 + 9 = 10** which further reduces to
1 + 0 = 1.

Masculine numbers predominate, and so this subject is
likely to be essentially extrovert, with fewer of the
softer qualities traditionally thought of as feminine.

EXPRESSION NUMBERS

These are also sometimes known as Childhood
Numbers and are calculated using only the consonants
in the full name as given at birth. Use the chart on
page 102 to make the calculation.

Example
The Expression Number for Frances Rachael
Freedman is calculated as follows:
6 + 9 + 5 + 3 + 1 + 9 + 3 + 8 + 3 + 6 + 9 + 4 + 4 + 5 = 75
This is then reduced to **7 + 5 = 12**, and further to **1 + 2
= 3.** The Expression Number for Frances Rachael
Freedman, relating to characteristics that are inborn
and perhaps carried through from a past live, is
therefore **3.** The following chart provides a summary
of characteristics for the Expression Numbers **1-9.**

Expression Number 1
Those with this Expression Number seem very self-
assured. They have an independent streak and at
times may even seem arrogant. But this is often an
illusion. Underneath they are as soft as butter.

Expression Number 2
Very caring and modest by nature, those with the
Expression Number **2** do not seek the limelight and
are quite content to take a back seat in any situation
or relationship, providing lots of support to others
in trying times.

Expression Number 3

Playful even as an adult, and with a quirky sense of
humor, someone with the Expression Number **3** is
usually very extrovert in behavior and dress. But in
many respects they are like the sabra fruit: tough on
the outside, but far softer inside.

Expression Number 4

Conscientious as a child and student, the individual
with the Expression Number **4** continues to be
reliable and hard-working in adult life. He or she
will present a rather conservative personality to the
world and may worry unnecessarily at times.

Expression Number 5

Popular but rather moody and restless at times,
those with the Expression Number **5** nevertheless
make good friends and colleagues. They thrive on
change and enjoy travel. This may also mean that
they flit from one job to another.

Expression Number 6

Sociable by nature and with an intense dislike of
disagreement, those with the Expression Number **6**
will do anything they can to keep the peace. In
childhood, they may have been a little spoiled.

Expression Number 7

Those with this Expression Number sometimes
have a very spiritual or religious side to them and
tend to be deep thinkers. They can be very
withdrawn at times, too. As children (or in a
previous incarnation) they may have shown
promise at an early age.

Expression Number 8

As a child (or, again, in a previous incarnation)
those with the Expression Number 8 may well have
been precocious, enjoying showing off to the
crowd. As adults, too, they tend to like to prove
they are smart. Providing others do not resent this
too greatly, they make excellent colleagues and
very good friends.

Expression Number 9

Good students, energetic, and very polite, those
with the Expression Number 9 are often very
critical of others, even if they do not actually voice
that criticism. They have very high standards and
will never follow the crowd for the sake of
conformity.

RELATIONSHIPS
BY NUMBERS

COUNTING ON LOVE

Just as astrologers base the likelihood of compatibility on the birth charts of two individuals, so numerologists use birth dates to assess the chances of a couple having a lasting and rewarding relationship. The aim is not so much to help anyone choose a life partner but to assist both parties towards greater awareness of each other's character and needs.

Method
Add up all the figures in the birth date of each individual. Say, for example, one partner was born on March 18, 1972. His or her calculation would be as follows:
$3 + 1 + 8 + 1 + 9 + 7 + 2 = 31$. This should now be reduced to $3 + 1 = 4$. If the other partner was born on April 5, 1970, his or her calculation would run:
$4 + 5 + 1 + 9 + 7 + 0 = 26$. This is then further reduced to $2 + 6 = 8$. They can now consult the table on pages 131-141 for a numerological reading for numbers **4** and **8**. This will reveal how someone who is a Number **4** is likely to get on with a partner with the Number **8**. Each might also consult the charts on pages 82-85 for further insight into these Life Numbers.

It can be an interesting exercise to compare the reading for each birth date of one's parents in order to understand more about the nature of their relationship.

Readings

1/1
The love of life that both share is likely to sustain the relationship by continually refreshing it. Each needs to be aware, however, that the inevitable element of competition in this partnership could, if taken to extremes, sever the bond.

1/2
Both of these personalities will need to learn to open up more readily and express their feelings. The Number **2**, meanwhile, must resist a tendency to become over-emotional.

1/3
This combination of personalities is one in which each will enrich the life of the other, providing all the support and encouragement necessary for them both to develop to their full potential.

1/4
Number **4** will help to keep Number **1**'s feet on the ground so that the partnership should prove a very stable one.

1/5

Both personalities are outward-going and very independent. The Number **1** personality in particular will need his or her own space at home to which to retreat at times.

1/6

Opposites often attract, and this is likely to be what will help to keep the relationship alive once a Number **1** and a Number **6** get together. But Number **1** might need some coaxing towards putting the partnership on to a permanent level.

1/7

Number **7** personalities tend to spend a lot of time in their own fantasy worlds; but a relationship with a Number **1** should help them develop a more realistic approach to life.

1/8

Each may lead a fairly independent life within this relationship, but this will only make the time they do spend together all the more precious and exciting.

1/9

This relationship will always be buoyant due
principally to the shared ability to see a problem as
a challenge and not a set-back. Together, it
sometimes seems, they could conquer the world.

2/2

Both parties may be very sensitive and will
therefore need to take teasing or the occasional
lack of consideration on the chin if the bond is to
last.

2/3

The Number **3** personality will help the Number **2**
not to take life so seriously, while the Number **2**'s
contribution to the relationship will be that of a rock
in troubled times.

2/4

Both parties tend to be romantics at heart, and it
will be the constant attempt to keep the original
courtship alive that helps the relationship go from
strength to strength.

2/5

The sensitivity of a Number **2** personality will be highly valued by the Number **5**. In return, the Number **5** will help the Number **2** to become more spontaneous.

2/6

This relationship will blossom if both parties, who hate to argue, come to realize that the occasional overt disagreement does no harm and will help clear the air.

2/7

Both parties tend to be highly sensitive; but if this quality is directed towards appreciation of the other partner's needs, the future should certainly be rosy.

2/8

The rational approach to life of the Number **8** will almost certainly help the Number **2** to be more confident both within and outside the relationship.

2/9

The Number **9** and Number **2** are both loyal and sensitive. However each should remember that constantly and obviously striving to please may become boring in its own right in the end.

3/3

Taking care not to squabble over who takes center stage, as these parties are both very outward-going, will pay dividends. One must learn to give way to the other every now and then.

3/4

These two personalities like to have fun and will enjoy life all the more together provided that the Number **4** can tolerate the Number **3**'s tendency to be disorganized.

3/5

If the Number **5** tries to be more open than his or her character normally allows, then they will both benefit from complete honesty within the relationship and a solid mutual trust will develop.

3/6

Number **6** is generally quite financially astute and this should help to keep the couple solvent – an important aspect of the relationship as someone with the Life Number **3** can be a spendthrift at times.

3/7

These two personalities complement each other very well, since Number **7** will soften Number **3**'s more extravert approach to life.

3/8

The Number **3** personality usually has a good sense of the ridiculous – a useful quality when it comes to coping with Number **8**'s often exaggerated sense of self-importance.

3/9

The Number **9** can be highly demanding of others and the Number **3** may find this oppressive at times due to extreme sensitivity. Nevertheless, this relationship should greatly improve the quality of life of both parties.

4/4
Both parties are utterly reliable by nature and thus quickly come to know what they can expect of one another. Variety, each needs to learn, however, is the spice of life.

4/5
The Number **5** is often quick to make decisions and may need to take into account a Number **4**'s reluctance to express emotions before feeling completely confident and at ease within a long-standing relationship.

4/6
It will take time for a Number **4** to develop trust, while the Number **6** may not readily display affection either. Each will have to be very patient with the other.

4/7
Both will need to allow time for a bond to form. Patience is its own reward, however, because the relationship will ultimately become a very stable one.

4/8

There could be considerable competition within this relationship. Each must learn to allow the other to score a point every now and then if controversy is to be kept to a minimum.

4/9

This relationship will never be boring since both are strong personalities. They need to take care not to blame each other when no blame is due, however, and to accept the rough with the smooth. Their love runs deep in spite of this.

5/5

Both partners thrive on an element of surprise. So if the relationship is to last, both will need to introduce the unexpected into their shared lives. Nothing must be allowed to become too routine.

5/6

Number **5** will find that learning to open up, as Number **6** does very readily, rather than hiding true feelings, will benefit the relationship enormously.

5/7
Neither partner excels at facing up to reality.
However, if each gives support to the other, what
started off as weaknesses may turn into strengths
before too long.

5/8
Number **8** is more reserved in most aspects of life.
But with a Number **5**'s encouragement, he or she
will develop more confidence and a more sensual
side to his or her personality.

5/9
Number **9** has a very spiritual side that Number **5**
finds attractive. They may not always agree about
things but can learn to have respect for each
other's point of view.

6/6
Romance thrives in this relationship but should not
be allowed to cloud the more practical things in life
if the partnership is to be an enduring one.

6/7
Number **6** knows how to keep a sense of proportion
and to look on the bright side of life, which should
help to assuage any anxieties felt by Number **7**.

6/8

Each has a lesson to learn from the other. Number **6** probably needs to be more practical, while Number **8** needs to be wary of taking things too seriously.

6/9

Number **9** may not find it easy to open up and can set excessively high standards. It takes all the warmth that is readily provided by Number **6** to help the relationship to flourish.

7/7

Both partners will continue to find the relationship a very rewarding one if they regularly step back and reassess the partnership, cherishing its very best aspects and making a mutual promise to improve those areas that either party finds irritating.

7/8

Number **7** is a worrier by nature but the determination of a Number **8** will see this couple through the darkest hours. These individuals would be lost without one another.

7/9
These two personalities are well suited.
The Number **7** is very sensitive and will make
allowances for Number **9**'s idealism. Number **9**'s
spirituality, meanwhile, will help him or her to accept
Number **7**'s quiet nature.

8/8
These partners will need to decide fairly early on
who is to take the lead in particular areas of life.
There will be times when one needs to step back.

8/9
The Number **8** will have tread warily in this
relationship because the Number **9** is very exacting
in his or her priorities in life.

9/9
Both partners have very high principles and should
not be too disappointed if they occasionally realize
that the other does not quite come up to
expectations. However, neither would wittingly let
the other down. Their relationship should prove as
solid as a rock.

THE GEOGRAPHY OF NUMBERS

Some numerologists believe that a person's Soul
Number, and the Soul Number of both the country and
city or town where he or she lives, should all be
compatible if this individual is to have a particularly
happy life there and enjoy a good rapport with the
character of the place. You can check this out for
yourself by calculating the appropriate Soul Numbers
as described on pages 96-97.

Example
If Susanna Clark lives in Brisbane, Australia, the
relevant Soul Numbers will be calculated as follows:

Susanna Clark $3 + 1 + 1 + 1 = 6$

Brisbane $9 + 1 + 5 = 15$
            This then reduces to $1 + 5 = 6$

Australia $1 + 3 + 1 + 9 + 1 = 15$
             This then reduces to $1 + 5 = 6$

The Soul Number for her name, town, and country are
all therefore **6**, which is said to promise a contented
life in this part of the world.

THE ORACLE OF NAPOLEON

The following method of divination is based upon an oracle said to have been found among Napoleon's papers in Leipzig, Germany, after his army had been routed there. The original is thought to have been found in an Egyptian tomb at the beginning of the 19th century, and was first translated into French and then into German.

This is an abbreviated version but still fascinating to use. It can be consulted to find an answer to any of this list of questions on page 145:

PROCEDURE

1 First find pencil and paper, and make *five* rows of dots on the sheet. Be sure not to think about how many you will make in each row. There have to be at least *eleven*, but there can be as many as your mind tells you to make. Try not to think about it as you make the dots. They should be put down instinctively. You might, for instance, put *eighteen* dots in the first row, *thirteen* dots in the second row, *fifteen* dots in the third row, *twelve* dots in the fourth row, and *nineteen* dots in the fifth row, as shown here.

Row **1**   • • • • • • • • • • • • • • • • • •
Row **2**   • • • • • • • • • • • • •
Row **3**   • • • • • • • • • • • • • • •
Row **4**   • • • • • • • • • • • •
Row **5**   • • • • • • • • • • • • • • • • • • •

2 The next step is to look at each row in turn and see whether your random choice for each is odd or even. Then construct a small table, using one dot for an odd number and two dots for an even number. Using the above example, the numbers of dots run as follows: even, odd, odd, even, odd. Your table will therefore look like this:

$$\begin{array}{cc} \bullet & \bullet \\ \bullet & \\ \bullet & \\ \bullet & \bullet \\ \bullet & \end{array}$$

3 Now consider the question you would like to ask the Oracle of Napoleon, choosing from those listed on page 145. You might, for example, choose question **17** – *Will I achieve happiness?*

4 On pages 146-184, you will find a key to all possible sequences of dots. Look for the page featuring Q17. Run across the column until you find where it meets your sequence of dates at **15**.

5 Look up or down column **15** until you find where it meets row **17** running across. In this box you will find the letter "*e.*"

6 You now need to look for answer **15** in list "*e*" on page 184. The answer reads: "*Laughter and tears.*"

No one has proven whether the Oracle of Napoleon always provides an accurate answer to a question, of course. But at the very least it provides some intriguing entertainment.

1 Will I succeed?
2 Will I gain financially?
3 Will I come up against any problems?
4 Will I lose out?
5 Will I make a profit in the near future?
6 Will I get promoted at work?
7 Is it worth taking a gamble?
8 Will I marry (named person)?
9 Will this friendship prove lasting?
10 Will I have a family?
11 Should I go on this trip?
12 Is he/she faithful to me?
13 Will we have financial security?
14 Will things work out all right?
15 Shall I change things?
16 Is it a wise move?
17 Will I achieve happiness?
18 Will I gain by making changes?
19 If I do this, will it be advantageous?
20 Shall I benefit?
21 How will girlfriends affect the outcome?
22 Shall I go ahead and spoil myself?
23 Shall I send this letter/fax/Email?
24 Will I come first/win?
25 Shall I ask about possible promotion?
26 Would marriage bring contentment?
27 Is it safe to do what I intend doing?
28 Is someone against what I propose doing?
29 Will this be a successful partnership?
30 Shall I remain financially secure?
31 Will my status improve?
32 Is there a chance I will succeed?

The Key

	1	2	3	4	5	6	7	8	9	10	11	12	13	14	15	16
Q	(dots)	(dots)	(dots)	(dots)	(dots)	(dots)	(dots)	(dots)	(dots)	(dots)	(dots)	(dots)	(dots)	(dots)	(dots)	(dots)
1	A	B	C	D	E	F	G	H	I	J	K	L	M	N	O	P
2	B	C	D	E	F	G	H	I	J	K	L	M	N	O	P	Q
3	C	D	E	F	G	H	I	J	K	L	M	N	O	P	Q	R
4	D	E	F	G	H	I	J	K	L	M	N	O	P	Q	R	S
5	E	F	G	H	I	J	K	L	M	N	O	P	Q	R	S	T
6	F	G	H	I	J	K	L	M	N	O	P	Q	R	S	T	U
7	G	H	I	J	K	L	M	N	O	P	Q	R	S	T	U	V
8	H	I	J	K	L	M	N	O	P	Q	R	S	T	U	V	W
	(dots)	(dots)	(dots)	(dots)	(dots)	(dots)	(dots)	(dots)	(dots)	(dots)	(dots)	(dots)	(dots)	(dots)	(dots)	(dots)
	1	2	3	4	5	6	7	8	9	10	11	12	13	14	15	16

	17	18	19	20	21	22	23	24	25	26	27	28	29	30	31	32
Q	(dice)	(dice)	(dice)	(dice)	(dice)	(dice)	(dice)	(dice)	(dice)	(dice)	(dice)	(dice)	(dice)	(dice)	(dice)	(dice)
1	Q	R	S	T	U	V	W	X	Y	Z	a	b	c	d	e	f
2	R	S	T	U	V	W	X	Y	Z	a	b	c	d	e	f	A
3	S	T	U	V	W	X	Y	Z	a	b	c	d	e	f	A	B
4	T	U	V	W	X	Y	Z	a	b	c	d	e	f	A	B	C
5	U	V	W	X	Y	Z	a	b	c	d	e	f	A	B	C	D
6	V	W	X	Y	Z	a	b	c	d	e	f	A	B	C	D	E
7	W	X	Y	Z	a	b	c	d	e	f	A	B	C	D	E	F
8	X	Y	Z	a	b	c	d	e	f	A	B	C	D	E	F	G
	(dice)	(dice)	(dice)	(dice)	(dice)	(dice)	(dice)	(dice)	(dice)	(dice)	(dice)	(dice)	(dice)	(dice)	(dice)	(dice)
	17	18	19	20	21	22	23	24	25	26	27	28	29	30	31	32

	1	2	3	4	5	6	7	8	9	10	11	12	13	14	15	16
Q	(dots)	(dots)	(dots)	(dots)	(dots)	(dots)	(dots)	(dots)	(dots)	(dots)	(dots)	(dots)	(dots)	(dots)	(dots)	(dots)
9	I	J	K	L	M	N	O	P	Q	R	S	T	U	V	W	X
10	J	K	L	M	N	O	P	Q	R	S	T	U	V	W	X	Y
11	K	L	M	N	O	P	Q	R	S	T	U	V	W	X	Y	Z
12	L	M	N	O	P	Q	R	S	T	U	V	W	X	Y	Z	a
13	M	N	O	P	Q	R	S	T	U	V	W	X	Y	Z	a	b
14	N	O	P	Q	R	S	T	U	V	W	X	Y	Z	a	b	c
15	O	P	Q	R	S	T	U	V	W	X	Y	Z	a	b	c	d
16	P	Q	R	S	T	U	V	W	X	Y	Z	a	b	c	d	e
	(dots)	(dots)	(dots)	(dots)	(dots)	(dots)	(dots)	(dots)	(dots)	(dots)	(dots)	(dots)	(dots)	(dots)	(dots)	(dots)
	1	2	3	4	5	6	7	8	9	10	11	12	13	14	15	16

	17	18	19	20	21	22	23	24	25	26	27	28	29	30	31	32
Q	⁙	⁙	⁙	⁙	⁙	⁙	⁙	⁙	⁙	⁙	⁙	⁙	⁙	⁙	⁙	⁙
9	Y	Z	a	b	c	d	e	f	A	B	C	D	E	F	G	H
10	Z	a	b	c	d	e	f	A	B	C	D	E	F	G	H	I
11	a	b	c	d	e	f	A	B	C	D	E	F	G	H	I	J
12	b	c	d	e	f	A	B	C	D	E	F	G	H	I	J	K
13	c	d	e	f	A	B	C	D	E	F	G	H	I	J	K	L
14	d	e	f	A	B	C	D	E	F	G	H	I	J	K	L	M
15	e	f	A	B	C	D	E	F	G	H	I	J	K	L	M	N
16	f	A	B	C	D	E	F	G	H	I	J	K	L	M	N	O
	⁙	⁙	⁙	⁙	⁙	⁙	⁙	⁙	⁙	⁙	⁙	⁙	⁙	⁙	⁙	⁙
	17	18	19	20	21	22	23	24	25	26	27	28	29	30	31	32

	1	2	3	4	5	6	7	8	9	10	11	12	13	14	15	16
Q																
17	Q	R	S	T	U	V	W	X	Y	Z	a	b	c	d	e	f
18	R	S	T	U	V	W	X	Y	Z	a	b	c	d	e	f	A
19	S	T	U	V	W	X	Y	Z	a	b	c	d	e	f	A	B
20	T	U	V	W	X	Y	Z	a	b	c	d	e	f	A	B	C
21	U	V	W	X	Y	Z	a	b	c	d	e	f	A	B	C	D
22	V	W	X	Y	Z	a	b	c	d	e	f	A	B	C	D	E
23	W	X	Y	Z	a	b	c	d	e	f	A	B	C	D	E	F
24	X	Y	Z	a	b	c	d	e	f	A	B	C	D	E	F	G
	1	2	3	4	5	6	7	8	9	10	11	12	13	14	15	16

	17	18	19	20	21	22	23	24	25	26	27	28	29	30	31	32
Q																
17	A	B	C	D	E	F	G	H	I	J	K	L	M	N	O	P
18	B	C	D	E	F	G	H	I	J	K	L	M	N	O	P	Q
19	C	D	E	F	G	H	I	J	K	L	M	N	O	P	Q	R
20	D	E	F	G	H	I	J	K	L	M	N	O	P	Q	R	S
21	E	F	G	H	I	J	K	L	M	N	O	P	Q	R	S	T
22	F	G	H	I	J	K	L	M	N	O	P	Q	R	S	T	U
23	G	H	I	J	K	L	M	N	O	P	Q	R	S	T	U	V
24	H	I	J	K	L	M	N	O	P	Q	R	S	T	U	V	W
	17	18	19	20	21	22	23	24	25	26	27	28	29	30	31	32

	1	2	3	4	5	6	7	8	9	10	11	12	13	14	15	16
Q																
25	Y	Z	a	b	c	d	e	f	A	B	C	D	E	F	G	H
26	Z	a	b	c	d	e	f	A	B	C	D	E	F	G	H	I
27	a	b	c	d	e	f	A	B	C	D	E	F	G	H	I	J
28	b	c	d	e	f	A	B	C	D	E	F	G	H	I	J	K
29	c	d	e	f	A	B	C	D	E	F	G	H	I	J	K	L
30	d	e	f	A	B	C	D	E	F	G	H	I	J	K	L	M
31	e	f	A	B	C	D	E	F	G	H	I	J	K	L	M	N
32	f	A	B	C	D	E	F	G	H	I	J	K	L	M	N	O
	1	2	3	4	5	6	7	8	9	10	11	12	13	14	15	16

	17	18	19	20	21	22	23	24	25	26	27	28	29	30	31	32
Q																
25	I	J	K	L	M	N	O	P	Q	R	S	T	U	V	W	X
26	J	K	L	M	N	O	P	Q	R	S	T	U	V	W	X	Y
27	K	L	M	N	O	P	Q	R	S	T	U	V	W	X	Y	Z
28	L	M	N	O	P	Q	R	S	T	U	V	W	X	Y	Z	a
29	M	N	O	P	Q	R	S	T	U	V	W	X	Y	Z	a	b
30	N	O	P	Q	R	S	T	U	V	W	X	Y	Z	a	b	c
31	O	P	Q	R	S	T	U	V	W	X	Y	Z	a	b	c	d
32	P	Q	R	S	T	U	V	W	X	Y	Z	a	b	c	d	e
	17	18	19	20	21	22	23	24	25	26	27	28	29	30	31	32

A

Figure			Figure		
1	⋮	Very likely	17	⠿	Extremely happy
2	⋮	Good chances	18	⠿	Good possibilities
3	⋮	If you use your talents	19	⋮	Do so
4	⋮	They remain yours	20	⋰	Yes
5	⋮	It opens up opportunities	21	⋮	Every chance
6	⋮	No	22	⋮	He is reliable
7	⠿	Safe	23	⋮	It will be successful
8	⋮	More than now	24	⋮	Children maybe
9	⋮	Promotion ahead	25	⋮	Friends bring you luck
10	⋰	Very likely	26	⋮	Happiness likely
11	⋮	Write at once	27	⠿	A good chance
12	⋮	Yes	28	⋮	Very likely
13	⋮	Quite well	29	⋮	Probable
14	⋮	You cannot fail	30	⋮	Nothing
15	⋮	Possible good results	31	⋮	Unlikely
16	⋮	Probably	32	⠿	For sure

B

Figure			Figure		
1		A little, maybe	17		Unlikely
2		Success unlikely	18		Not very happy
3		Not much yet	19		Few opportunities
4		To a degree	20		Uncertainty
5		Mostly, yes	21		Possibly
6		Status quo	22		If you try hard
7		A little	23		Uncertainty
8		Only if you take care	24		There is no point
9		Some, maybe	25		Not much chance
10		Not worthwhile	26		Friendship does not help
11		Not much chance	27		Chances are poor
12		Write, if you want to	28		Uncertainty
13		Does not matter	29		Little chance
14		Fairly well	30		Few possibilities
15		You are wrong	31		Little profit
16		Difficulties	32		Few, if any

C

Figure			Figure		
1		Yes	17		Success
2		Yes	18		Benefits ahead
3		Yes	19		Rejoicing
4		Good chances	20		A good idea
5		Fame and regard	21		Do it!
6		For sure	22		Yes
7		Excellent	23		Yes
8		Very much so	24		A reliable friend
9		Few risks	25		Yes
10		Much more than you imagine	26		A few
11		Promotion ahead	27		Benefits
12		Success	28		Yes
13		Go ahead	29		Yes
14		You should	30		Yes
15		Very well	31		Yes
16		Expect good opportunities	32		You are unlikely to lose

D

Figure			Figure		
1		Some loss and some gain	17		Good chances
2		Evens	18		A rocky boat
3		Good chances	19		You could gain
4		Evens	20		Both laughter and tears ahead
5		Evens	21		Good possibilities
6		Yes	22		Status quo
7		Yes, if you are careful	23		Only if you keep trying
8		If you are creative	24		The chances are good
9		Strong opposition	25		Occasionally
10		You will overcome difficulties	26		Even chances
11		Some joy, some sorrow	27		Yes, perhaps
12		You have a rival	28		Gains *and* losses from a friend
13		No profit	29		It is likely
14		Why not?	30		Possibilities
15		Uncertain	31		Good chances
16		Good influences	32		Some

E

Figure			Figure		
1		Good fortune	17		Success
2		A sure profit	18		A large gain
3		Good luck	19		Happiness
4		Good fortune will be yours	20		Profits to be made
5		A good outcome	21		Happiness
6		Opportunities will appear	22		Success
7		Fame lies ahead	23		Great success lies ahead
8		Definitely	24		Excellent outcome
9		Profit lies ahead	25		Good fortune lies ahead
10		You will win	26		Your friend is reliable
11		It is safe	27		Good fortune after the journey
12		Great happiness	28		Much luck
13		Take a big step	29		You are lucky to have such a friend
14		You will overcome	30		Good fortune
15		A good outcome	31		Success
16		Do	32		A good chance

F

Figure			Figure		
1		Chances are good	17		A little
2		A wonderful opportunity ahead	18		Only a little, but it is fine
3		Good odds	19		Gain
4		Likely success	20		A good outcome
5		Good chances	21		You will be treated kindly
6		The prospects are good	22		Contentment
7		All bodes well	23		Excellent outcome
8		You will be one of the lucky few	24		All will be fine if you are sensible
9		Why not?	25		Excellent possibilities
10		A fine pairing	26		They are well disposed to do so
11		Yes, but not much	27		You are lucky to know this person
12		For sure	28		It is a good idea
13		A good chance	29		Your dreams will come true
14		Now is the hour	30		This person is kind
15		Good chances	31		A good opportunity awaits
16		The right moment	32		Opportunities ahead

G

Figure			Figure		
1		No	17		Do not write
2		No	18		Abandon it
3		No	19		Badly
4		A great loss	20		Not now
5		No	21		A bad outcome
6		No	22		No profit
7		No	23		Unhappiness
8		None	24		Unwise
9		Very unlikely	25		Not sensible
10		May be lost	26		Leave alone
11		Not a good idea	27		Hope unrealized
12		Not sensible	28		Deceit
13		Do not be tempted	29		Do not go
14		Unhappiness	30		No
15		No success	31		It will bring bad luck
16		Failure	32		No

H

Figure			Figure		
1		A change of mind	17		Your luck changes
2		Changes ahead	18		Uncertain outcome
3		Changes occur	19		Yes, but no satisfaction
4		The outcome is uncertain	20		Changeable influence
5		Circumstances alter a lot	21		Variable results
6		More good luck than bad	22		Only for a while
7		Swings and roundabouts	23		Make the change
8		Prospects may change	24		An unhappy feeling
9		A lot if you are determined	25		Too many extremes
10		Gradually	26		Not successful
11		A friend changes	27		They need to change
12		The outcome is not certain	28		Possibly
13		Sometimes	29		Do not trust him
14		Plans change	30		Reconsider
15		Marriage is for the best	31		Your present attitude will alter
16		Only if you are determined	32		This friend is unreliable

I

Figure			Figure		
1		Do not be too trusting	17		The future is in your own hands
2		Marriage unlikely	18		Success
3		Yes	19		Think carefully first
4		Some chances	20		Status quo
5		Gamble	21		Uncertainty
6		Losses unlikely	22		Gamble
7		Uncertainty	23		Perhaps, but only for a while
8		Unlikely but some chances	24		There are risks
9		Results uncertain	25		Unlikely
10		Quite good	26		Only if you like risks
11		Uncertainty	27		The results are uncertain
12		Success	28		Give this more thought
13		Success	29		Uncertainty
14		A friend will help	30		There is deceit
15		Great risks	31		Unlikely
16		Special happiness ahead	32		Few, if at all

J

Figure			Figure		
1		Children may be born	17		More than now
2		Friends bring luck	18		Promotion ahead
3		Happiness likely	19		Very likely
4		Chances are good	20		Write now
5		Unlikely	21		Do so
6		Likely	22		Quite well
7		None	23		Success
8		Not much chance	24		Possible gain
9		For sure	25		Probably
10		Yes	26		Happiness
11		The chances are good	27		A good chance
12		If you use your talents	28		Do so
13		They remain yours	29		Yes
14		Good chances	30		Every chance
15		No	31		He is reliable
16		It is safe	32		Success

K

Figure			Figure		
1		Not worthwhile	17		Only if you take care
2		Not much chance	18		Maybe some
3		This friendship is of little value	19		Not worthwhile
4		Not much chance	20		Not much hope
5		Unlikely	21		Write if you feel like it
6		Little chance	22		It does not matter
7		Unlikely	23		Fairly well
8		Little gain	24		You are wrong
9		Only a few, if any	25		Bad feeling
10		A little, maybe	26		Unlikely
11		Success unlikely	27		Not very happy
12		Not much yet	28		Few opportunities
13		To a degree	29		Unknown
14		Mostly	30		Possibly
15		Uncertain	31		If you try hard
16		A little	32		A slight chance

L

Figure			Figure		
1		A reliable friend	17		Greatly
2		Yes	18		Few dangers
3		Several	19		A lot more than you imagine
4		Great benefit	20		Promotion ahead
5		Yes	21		Good prospects
6		Yes	22		Go ahead
7		Yes	23		Do so
8		Yes	24		Excellently
9		Losses are unlikely	25		Good opportunities
10		Yes	26		Success
11		Yes	27		Benefits
12		Yes	28		Joyous outcome
13		A good chance	29		Sensible
14		Famous and well regarded	30		Go ahead
15		For sure	31		Yes
16		Positive	32		For sure

M

Figure			Figure		
1		A good chance	17		If you are creative
2		Sometimes	18		There is opposition
3		Even chances	19		You will overcome difficulties
4		Yes, maybe	20		Some joy, some sorrow
5		Some profit, some loss from a friend	21		There is a rival
6		Marriage may take place	22		No profit
7		Possibilities	23		It is fine
8		A good chance	24		Doubtful
9		A few	25		Good influences
10		Some loss, some gain	26		There are good chances
11		Evens	27		Instability
12		The chances are quite good	28		Profits are likely
13		Evens	29		Laughter and tears
14		Evens	30		A good likelihood
15		By all means	31		A fairly good outcome
16		If you are careful	32		Only if you try hard

N

Figure			Figure		
1		A good outcome	17		For sure
2		Good fortune will come your way	18		Profits ahead
3		Your friend is reliable	19		You win all along the line
4		A lucky journey	20		Of course – it is quite safe
5		Yes, and it will bring good fortune	21		Great happiness
6		You are fortunate in your friend	22		A big, surprising leap is before you
7		Good fortune attends the matter	23		Victory
8		First-rate chances of much success	24		Amazingly good results if you do so
9		Excellent possibilities	25		Do – you will not regret it
10		Good luck in yours	26		They will help it to success
11		Success	27		Great profit
12		Fortune will dispel them	28		The whole affair brings happiness
13		Good luck	29		Much gain will be made
14		Much good fortune is promised	30		Happy, because it is fortunate
15		Great opportunities	31		You will be successful
16		Fame lies ahead	32		Great success lies ahead

O

Figure			Figure		
1		All will go well if you take care	17		You will be one of the fortunate
2		Excellent possibilities	18		Why not?
3		They should like to do so	19		A good partnership
4		Try to appreciate this person	20		A little
5		You should go	21		Definitely
6		Your dreams will come true	22		Good possibilities
7		This person is kindly	23		The time is right
8		A good opportunity ahead	24		Excellent chances
9		Great opportunities	25		Now is the hour
10		Circumstances are right	26		Only slightly
11		Good opportunities arise	27		A little
12		Good chance	28		Gain
13		Success	29		A good outcome
14		A good outcome	30		You will be well treated
15		Good prospects	31		Fairly happy
16		A good outcome	32		A good outcome

P

Figure			Figure		
1	⋮	Unwise	17	⁞⁞	None
2	⋮	Unhappy outcome	18	⁞⁞	Unlikely
3	⋮	Leave them	19	⁞⁞	May be lost
4	⋮	Your dream may not be realized	20	⁞⁞	Not a good idea
5	⋮	Deceit	21	⁞⁞	Unwise
6	⋮	Do not go	22	⁞⁞	Do not be tempted
7	⋮	No	23	⁞⁞	Unhappiness
8	⋮	Bad luck	24	⁞⁞	No success
9	⋮	No	25	⁞⁞	Failure
10	⋮	No	26	⁞⁞	Do not write
11	⋮	No	27	⁞⁞	Leave it alone
12	⋮	No	28	⁞⁞	Badly
13	⋮	Big losses	29	⁞⁞	Not now
14	⋮	No	30	⁞⁞	An unhappy outcome
15	⋮	No	31	⁞⁞	No profit
16	⋮	No	32	⁞⁞	Unhappiness

Q

Figure			Figure		
1	⁞	Bad feeling	17	⁞⁞	Prospects vary
2	⁞	Unsettled	18	⁞	Plenty, if you are determined
3	⁞	Lack of success	19	⁞	Gradually
4	⁞	They need to change	20	⁞	A friend brings changes
5	⁞	More stability needed	21	⁞	Instability
6	⁞	He is unreliable	22	⁞	Only sometimes
7	⁞⁞	Rethink	23	⁞	Plans change
8	⁞	Your attitude now will change	24	⁞	Marriage is a good idea
9	⁞	The friend is unreliable	25	⁞⁞	Only if you are determined
10	⁞	You will change your mind	26	⁞	Conditions change for the best
11	⁞	There will be change	27	⁞⁞	Uncertainty
12	⁞	Changes ahead	28	⁞⁞	Yes, but unsatisfactory
13	⁞	Prospects vary	29	⁞⁞	Changes in influence
14	⁞	Circumstances are changeable	30	⁞⁞	A variable outcome
15	⁞	More good luck than bad	31	⁞	Only for a while
16	⁞	Many twists and turns	32	⁞⁞	Go ahead

R

Figure			Figure		
1		It is risky	17		Good opportunities
2		Uncertain	18		Uncertainty
3		Only if you like taking risks	19		Quite good
4		Uncertainty	20		Doubtful
5		More thought needed	21		Gains
6		Uncertain	22		You win
7		Deceit	23		It will be a friend, probably
8		Unlikely	24		Too many risks
9		Few, if any at all	25		Rare happiness
10		Do not be too trusting	26		Your fortune is in your own hands
11		Think carefully about marriage	27		Go ahead
12		Yes	28		Think it over carefully
13		An opportunity may be lost	29		No profit
14		Speculate	30		Uncertainty
15		Losses can be avoided, mostly	31		Gamble
16		Uncertainty	32		If so, not for long

S

Figure			Figure		
1		Possibly	17		Not likely
2		Every likelihood	18		Yes
3		Content	19		Strong possibilities
4		A good chance	20		Every chance
5		Do so	21		If you use your talents
6		Yes	22		They remain yours
7		Possibilities	23		Good chances ahead
8		Reliable	24		No
9		Success	25		It is safe
10		Children born	26		More than now
11		Friends bring benefits	27		You will be promoted
12		Happiness likely	28		Probably
13		A good chance	29		Write now!
14		Likely	30		Yes
15		Strong probabilities	31		Quite well
16		None	32		You will!

T

Figure			Figure		
1	⋮	You are wrong	17	⁚⁚	Little profit
2	⋮	Uncertainty	18	⋮	Few, if at all
3	⋮	Unlikely	19	⋮	A little, maybe
4	⋮	Not very happy	20	⋮	Little likelihood of success
5	⋮	Not many opportunities	21	⋮	Not a lot for now
6	⋮	Uncertainty	22	⋮	A little
7	⁚⁚	Possibly	23	⋮	A lot
8	⋮	If you try hard	24	⁚⁚	Status quo
9	⋮	Possibly	25	⁚⁚	A little
10	⋮	No point	26	⋮	Only if you take care
11	⋮	Not much chance	27	⁝⁝	Some, maybe
12	⋮	Friendship does not help	28	⁝⁝	Hardly worth the bother
13	⋮	Your chances are few	29	⋮	Not much hope
14	⋮	Unlikely	30	⁝⁝	Write, if you want to do so
15	⋮	Not much chance	31	⁝⁝	It does not matter
16	⋮	Unlikely	32	⁝⁝	Fairly well

U

Figure			Figure		
1		Positive	17		Yes
2		Excellent opportunities	18		Gains likely
3		All goes well	19		Yes
4		Benefits	20		Yes
5		Great joy	21		Yes
6		Sensible	22		A good chance
7		Forge ahead	23		Yes
8		Yes	24		For sure
9		Yes	25		Sound
10		Reliable	26		Very much so
11		Do so	27		Few risks
12		A few	28		More than you imagine
13		Benefits	29		Promotion lies ahead
14		Yes	30		Very well
15		Yes	31		Yes
16		Yes	32		Yes

V

Figure			Figure		
1		Doubts	17		A fair chance
2		Good influence	18		A few
3		It could be	19		Swings and roundabouts
4		Uncertainties	20		Evens
5		Possible	21		Possibly
6		Both laughter and tears	22		Maybe
7		Good possibilities	23		An even chance
8		Not good, not bad	24		Likely
9		Carry on trying	25		If you take care
10		Good chances	26		If you are creative
11		Sometimes	27		Strong opposition
12		Evens	28		You will overcome difficulties
13		Yes, perhaps	29		Joy and sadness
14		Some benefits, some drawbacks	30		You have a rival
15		A good chance	31		Nothing gained
16		Good possibilities	32		Do not worry

W

Figure			Figure		
1		Fabulous results if you do	17		Much success
2		No regrets	18		Excellent outcome
3		Success	19		Good fortune
4		Profits	20		No losses
5		Happiness	21		Luck lies ahead
6		Gains	22		Success
7		Lucky	23		Good fortune
8		Success	24		Great opportunities
9		Fortune	25		Fame
10		A great outcome	26		For sure
11		Good fortune ahead	27		Gain
12		Your friend is reliable	28		You will win
13		A promising journey	29		It is safe
14		Yes	30		Happiness
15		You are lucky to have this friend	31		Changes ahead
16		Good fortune ahead	32		You will overcome

X

Figure			Figure		
1		You may win	17		Good opportunity on the horizon
2		Now is the right time	18		Excellent opportunities soon
3		Only a little	19		A good moment
4		Only a little but that is fine	20		Good prospects in the offing
5		Gains	21		Loss unlikely
6		Good results	22		Good chances of success
7		You will be treated well	23		Favorable prospects
8		Happiness	24		Favorable outcome
9		A good outcome	25		All bodes well
10		Take care and all will be well	26		You will be favored
11		Every chance	27		By all means
12		They are used to it	28		A good combination
13		You are lucky to know this person	29		Yes, reasonably
14		You ought to go	30		For sure
15		You will have your heart's desires	31		Good possibilities
16		You are well thought of	32		Now is the right time

Y

Figure			Figure		
1		Failure, alas	17		A bad outcome
2		Unsuccessful	18		No
3		Do not write it	19		No
4		Leave it alone	20		No
5		Badly	21		No
6		Not now	22		Losses
7		Uncertainty	23		No
8		No profit to be had	24		No
9		Sadness	25		No
10		Unwise	26		None
11		Not advisable	27		Unlikely
12		Forget it/them	28		May be lost
13		Few chances	29		Not prudent
14		Deceit	30		Not wise
15		Do not go	31		Resist the temptation
16		No	32		Sadness

Z

Figure			Figure		
1		Marriage is for the best	17		Your attitude will change
2		Only if you are determined	18		Your friend is not constant
3		Conditions alter for the better	19		You will change your opinion
4		Uncertain	20		Changes
5		Yes, but you will be dissatisfied	21		Changes ahead
6		Influences vary	22		Uncertainty
7		Uncertain	23		Circumstances vary
8		Only for a while	24		Some luck, a little misfortune
9		Try it	25		Good and bad
10		Bad feeling	26		Nothing is certain
11		Instability	27		A lot, if you are determined
12		Unlikely	28		Bit by bit
13		Changes to be made	29		A friend helps make changes
14		Maybe	30		Instability
15		Too unreliable	31		Only once in a while
16		Give it more thought	32		Plans change

a

Figure			Figure		
1		Uncertainties	17		Unlikely
2		You will enjoy it	18		Precious few
3		You are your own master	19		Do not be too trusting
4		Be confident	20		Doubts about marriage
5		Plan and then go ahead	21		Yes
6		Status quo	22		Possibly lost opportunities
7		Uncertainty	23		Speculate
8		Gamble	24		You may not lose
9		If so, only for a while	25		Unknown
10		It is risky	26		Unlikely
11		Unlikely	27		Unknown
12		Only if you like taking risks	28		Fairly good
13		Unlikely	29		Unlikely
14		More thought needed	30		Fruitfulness
15		No one knows	31		You will win
16		Deceit	32		A friend is involved

b

Figure			Figure		
1		No	17		Cannot be trusted
2		No risks	18		A good outcome
3		Better things ahead	19		Children may be born
4		Rewards ahead	20		Your friends bring you luck
5		Possibly	21		Happiness
6		Write now	22		Fairly likely
7		Yes	23		Very likely
8		Quite well	24		A good probability
9		You will succeed	25		None
10		A good outcome is possible	26		Not likely
11		Probably	27		Yes
12		Very happy	28		Yes, it is likely
13		Strong possibilities	29		Could be
14		Go ahead	30		If you try hard
15		Yes	31		They will be yours still
16		Likely	32		Opportunities arise

c

Figure			Figure		
1		Neutral	17		With a lot of effort
2		Slightly	18		It is possible
3		Only if you take care	19		There is no point
4		Some, maybe	20		Little chance
5		Not worth the effort	21		Friendship does not help
6		Not much hope	22		The chances are not good
7		Write, if you want to do so	23		Uncertain
8		It does not matter	24		Not much chance
9		Only fairly well	25		Hardly likely
10		You are wrong	26		Not much profit
11		A bad feeling	27		Not many, if any at all
12		Possible, but unlikely	28		A little, maybe
13		Not very happy	29		Little chance of success
14		Few opportunities	30		Not a lot yet
15		The outcome is uncertain	31		To some degree
16		Maybe	32		Largely so

d

Figure			Figure		
1	⠇	Definitely	17	⠿	Yes
2		Reliable	18		Definitely
3		Very much so	19		This person is a faithful friend
4		Few difficulties	20		Go ahead
5		More than you imagine	21		Several
6		Promotion ahead	22		You will gain
7		You will do well	23		Yes
8		Do so!	24		Yes
9		Go ahead	25		Yes
10		Their influence is good	26		Yes
11		Good opportunities	27		You are unlikely to lose out
12		All will go well	28		Yes
13		Good results	29		Yes
14		Celebrations!	30		Yes
15		A good idea	31		Good chances
16		Do so!	32		More famous and admired

e

Figure			Figure		
1		Why not?	17		Status quo
2		Yes, if you are sensible	18		Only if you carry on trying
3		If you are creative	19		A good chance
4		There is opposition	20		Occasionally
5		You will conquer difficulties	21		Evens
6		Some joy, some sorrow	22		Maybe
7		You have a rival	23		Some profit and loss from a friend
8		No profit	24		Marriage perhaps
9		It is safe	25		Fairly likely
10		Uncertainty	26		Quite good chances
11		Their influence is good	27		Some
12		Good chances	28		Some loss, some profit
13		Lack of stability	29		Evens
14		Likely	30		Reasonable
15		Laughter and tears	31		Evens
16		A good chance	32		Evens

f

Figure			Figure		
1	⋮	Great opportunities	17	⠇⠇	Success
2		Fame lies ahead	18		Great success
3		Definitely	19		A good outcome
4		Profit	20		Good fortune
5		You will win	21		Your friend is reliable
6	⋮	It is safe	22		Good fortune follows a journey
7		Great happiness	23		Good fortune
8		A big, surprising leap before you	24		You are fortunate to have this friend
9		Victory	25		Good fortune
10		Good results are promised	26		Success is likely
11		Do so!	27		Excellent possibilities
12		Success	28		Good fortune
13		You will gain	29		You will not lose
14		Happiness ahead	30		Good fortune
15		Profit	31		Luck
16		Good luck	32		A great outcome

THE LADIES' ORACLE

This method of fortune-telling dates back to the 19th century and was designed as a guide for young women in doubt about relationships. There are 96 questions that can be asked of the oracle. These, presented on pages 188-191, have been updated slightly in content for this book, as have the answers.

1. The first step is to choose a question from those that are listed on pages 188-191 and to keep it silently in your head. Each question is numbered.

2. Look at page opposite where you will find a layout of numbers. Close your eyes and try to place an index finger on one of these boxed numbers.

3. Identify the number on which or nearest to which you have landed and now turn to the tables you will find on pages 192-197.

4. Locate the number of your question down the lefthand column and run along the row until you find the column headed by the number that you have already picked at stage **2**. You will find another number in this position.

5. Next, turn to the chart with that number and on pages 198-245 read the answer corresponding to your chosen number at stage **2**.

THE LAYOUT

1	7	10	14
12	13	4	11
6	16	5	2
9	3	8	15

Questions for the Ladies' Oracle
Read through the following 96 questions and decide
which one you would like to ask the Ladies' Oracle.
Do not ask too many questions in quick succession,
however, as this may prove confusing rather than
revealing.

1 Will I soon have a boyfriend?
2 What does he think of me?
3 Does everyone still think I'm a child?
4 Is he as warm-hearted as I am?
5 How can I make him happy?
6 Shall I answer his Email/letter/fax?
7 What will happen if I keep our date?
8 Shall I agree to what he wants?
9 Will my husband be young?
10 How many husbands will I have?
11 How many lovers will I have?
12 What does he really think of me?
13 Should I believe him when he says he loves me?
14 Does this person love me?
15 Does this person think I love him?
16 What should I do to make him love me?
17 Will I marry young?
18 Will I have lots of affairs?
19 Will my husband make me happy?
20 Is the man I love faithful to me?

21 Will my husband suspect me?

22 Ought I to break it off or give in?

23 Shall I have any children?

24 Will I come into a fortune?

25 Will my secret be discovered?

26 Do people think I'm pretty?

27 What is generally thought of my intelligence?

28 If my mistake is discovered, will it be forgiven?

29 Shall I lose my virginity before I marry?

30 Shall I marry the man I am now thinking about?

31 Shall I always enjoy good health?

32 Ought I to go ahead with my plans?

33 Am I paid properly?

34 Shall I be happy in love?

35 Shall I be happy long?

36 Shall I marry a rich man?

37 What sort of character will my husband have?

38 Will my husband be handsome or ugly?

39 Will my husband be intelligent?

40 Have I any rivals?

41 Is all the praise he gives me sincere?

42 Shall I be happy in what I do?

43 How can I prevent them finding out?

44 Will I marry a man I already know?

45 How long will our quarrel last?

46 Will the reconciliation be for the best?

47 Does my husband love me as much now?

48 Am I the first woman my husband has loved?

49 Has my husband loved another woman as much?

50 Will the person I am thinking about return?

51 Does my husband always tell me the truth?

52 Will my unhappiness last long?

53 Shall I soon be pregnant?

54 Will this affair last long?

55 Which of the two people I am thinking about should I prefer?

56 Shall I receive the presents I am expecting?

57 Will I go on many long voyages?

58 Will this friendship last?

59 Will there be changes?

60 Will my weakness bring what I dread?

61 Will they keep all the promises they made me?

62 Ought I to forgive?

63 Is the repentance sincere?

64 Shall I confess?

65 Ought I to try to make-up?

66 Does my husband trust me?

67 Ought I to oppose my husband's ideas?

68 Am I in trouble?

69 Should I expect any loss of money?

70 What is the person about whom I am thinking doing right now?

71 Is anyone envious of me?
72 Will I receive any unexpected property?
73 Ought I to fear a tête-à-tête?
74 Will my reputation always be good?
75 Ought I to follow the advice given to me?
76 What will be the result?
77 Shall I be loved forever?
78 Will my life be a peaceful one?
79 Ought I to prefer the countryside or town life?
80 Has my fear any foundation?
81 Ought I to accept the proposals?
82 What will happen if I do what they ask?
83 Shall I die an old maid, wife, or widow?
84 What profession will my husband follow?
85 Will my wish be granted?
86 Are they thinking of me?
87 What does the world think of me?
88 Will my heart be without love for long?
89 Will my old age be happy?
90 When shall I stop loving?
91 Have I any enemies?
92 Will what I want to happen come to pass?
93 Will what I dread come to pass?
94 Ought I to stop having fun?
95 Will they miss me?
96 Shall I have more sorrow than joy?

Numbers relating to answers from the Ladies' Oracle

Question	1	2	3	4	5	6	7	8	9	10	11	12	13	14	15	16
1	20	26	32	38	44	50	56	62	68	74	80	86	92	98	8	14
2	21	27	33	39	45	51	57	63	69	75	81	87	93	99	9	15
3	22	28	34	40	46	52	58	64	70	76	82	88	94	100	10	16
4	23	29	35	41	47	53	59	65	71	77	83	89	95	5	11	17
5	24	30	36	42	48	54	60	66	72	78	84	90	96	6	12	18
6	25	31	37	43	49	55	61	67	73	79	85	91	97	7	13	19
7	26	32	38	44	50	56	62	68	74	80	86	92	98	8	14	20
8	27	33	39	45	51	57	63	69	75	81	87	93	99	9	15	21
9	28	34	40	46	52	58	64	70	76	82	88	94	100	10	16	22
10	29	35	41	47	53	59	65	71	77	83	89	95	5	11	17	23
11	30	36	42	48	54	60	66	72	78	84	90	96	6	12	18	24
12	31	37	43	49	55	61	67	73	79	85	91	97	7	13	19	25
13	32	38	44	50	56	62	68	74	80	86	92	98	8	14	20	26
14	33	39	45	51	57	63	69	75	81	87	93	99	9	15	21	27
15	34	40	46	52	58	64	70	76	82	88	94	100	10	16	22	28
16	35	41	47	53	59	65	71	77	83	89	95	5	11	17	23	29

Numbers relating to answers from the Ladies' Oracle

Question	1	2	3	4	5	6	7	8	9	10	11	12	13	14	15	16
17	36	42	48	54	60	66	72	78	84	90	96	6	12	18	24	30
18	37	43	49	55	61	67	73	79	85	91	97	7	13	19	25	31
19	38	44	50	56	62	68	74	80	86	92	98	8	14	20	26	32
20	39	45	51	57	63	69	75	81	87	93	99	9	15	21	27	33
21	40	46	52	58	64	70	76	82	88	94	100	10	16	22	28	34
22	41	47	53	59	65	71	77	83	89	95	5	11	17	23	29	35
23	42	48	54	60	66	72	78	84	90	96	6	12	18	24	30	36
24	43	49	55	61	67	73	79	85	91	97	7	13	19	25	31	37
25	44	50	56	62	68	74	80	86	92	98	8	14	20	26	32	38
26	45	51	57	63	69	75	81	87	93	99	9	15	21	27	33	39
27	46	52	58	64	70	76	82	88	94	100	10	16	22	28	34	40
28	47	53	59	65	71	77	83	89	95	5	11	17	23	29	35	41
29	48	54	60	66	72	78	84	90	96	6	12	18	24	30	36	42
30	49	55	61	67	73	79	85	91	97	7	13	19	25	31	37	43
31	50	56	62	68	74	80	86	92	98	8	14	20	26	32	38	44
32	51	57	63	69	75	81	87	93	99	9	15	21	27	33	39	45

Numbers relating to answers from the Ladies' Oracle

Question	1	2	3	4	5	6	7	8	9	10	11	12	13	14	15	16
33	52	58	64	70	76	82	88	94	100	10	16	22	28	34	40	46
34	53	59	65	71	77	83	89	95	5	11	17	23	29	3,5	41	47
35	54	60	66	72	78	84	90	96	6	12	18	24	30	36	42	48
36	55	61	67	73	79	85	91	97	7	13	19	25	31	37	43	49
37	56	62	68	74	80	86	92	98	8	14	20	26	32	38	44	50
38	57	63	69	75	81	87	93	199	19	15	21	27	33	39	45	51
39	58	64	70	76	82	88	94	00	0	16	22	28	34	40	4.6	52
40	59	65	71	77	83	89	95	5	11	17	23	29	35	41	47	53
41	60	66	72	78	84	90	96	6	12	18	24	30	36	42	48	54
42	61	67	73	79	85	91	97	7	13	19	25	31	37	43	49	55
43	62	68	74	80	86	92	98	8	14	20	26	32	38	44	50	56
44	63	69	75	81	87	93	99	9	15	21	27	33	39	45	51	57
45	64	70	76	82	88	94	100	10	16	22	28	34	40	46	52	58
46	65	71	77	83	89	95	5	11	17	23	29	35	41	47	53	59
47	66	72	78	84	90	96	6	12	18	24	30	36	42	48	54	60
48	67	73	79	85	91	97	7	13	19	25	31	37	43	49	55	61

Numbers relating to answers from the Ladies' Oracle

Question	1	2	3	4	5	6	7	8	9	10	11	12	13	14	15	16
49	68	74	80	86	92	98	8	14	20	26	32	38	44	50	56	62
50	69	75	81	87	93	99	9	15	21	27	33	39	45	51	57	63
51	70	76	82	88	94	100	10	16	22	28	34	40	46	52	58	64
52	71	77	83	89	95	5	11	17	23	29	35	41	47	53	59	65
53	72	78	84	90	96	6	12	18	24	30	36	42	48	54	60	66
54	73	79	85	91	97	7	13	19	25	31	37	43	49	55	61	67
55	74	80	86	92	98	8	14	20	26	32	38		50	56	62	68
56	75	81	87	93	99	9	15	21	27	33	39	45	51	57	63	69
57	76	82	88	94	100	10	16	22	28	34	40	46	52	58	64	70
58	77	83	89	95	5	11	17	23	29	35	41	47	53	59	65	71
59	78	84	90	96	6	12	18	24	30	36	42	48	54	60	66	72
60	79	85	91	97	7	13	19	25	31	37	43	49	55	61	67	73
61	80	86	92	98	8	14	20	26	32	38	44	50	56	62	68	74
62	81	87	93	99	9	15	21	27	33	39	45	51	57	63	69	75
63	82	88	94	100	10	16	22	28	34	40	46	52	58	64	70	76
64	83	89	95	5	11	17	23	29	35	41	47	53	59	65	71	77

Numbers relating to answers from the Ladies' Oracle

Question	1	2	3	4	5	6	7	8	9	10	11	12	13	14	15	16
65	84	90	96	6	12	18	24	30	36	42	48	54	60	66	72	78
66	85	91	97	7	13	19	25	31	37	43	49	55	61	67	73	79
67	86	92	98	8	14	20	26	32	38	44	50	56	62	68	74	80
68	87	93	99	9	15	21	27	33	39	45	51	57	63	69	75	81
69	88	94	100	10	16	22	28	34	40	46	52	58	64	70	76	82
70	89	95	5	11	17	23	29	35	41	47	53	59	65	'71	77	83
71	90	96	6	12	18	24	30	36	42	48	54	60	66	72	78	84
72	91	97	7	13	19	25	31	37	43	49	55	61	67	73	79	85
73	92	98	8	14	20	26	32	38	44	50	56	62	68	74	80	86
74	93	99	9	15	21	27	33	39	45	51	57	63	69	75	81	87
75	94	100	10	16	22	28	34	40	4.6	52	58	64	70	76	82	88
76	95	5	11	17	23	29	35	41	47	53	59	65	71	77	83	89
77	96	6	12	18	24	30	36	42	48	54	60	66	72	78	84	90
78	97	7	13	19	25	31	37	43	49	55	61	67	73	79	85	91
79	98	8	14	20	26	32	38	44	50	56	62	68	74	80	86	92
80	99	9	15	21	27	33	39	45	51	57	63	69	75	81	87	93

Numbers relating to answers from the Ladies' Oracle

Question	1	2	3	4	5	6	7	8	9	10	11	12	13	14	15	16
81	100	10	16	22	28	34	40	46	52	58	64	70	76	82	88	94
82	5	11	17	23	29	35	41	47	53	59	65	71	77	83	89	95
83	6	12	18	24	30	36	42	48	54	60	66	72	78	84	90	96
84	7	13	19	25	31	37	43	49	55	61	67	73	79	85	91	97
85	8	14	20	26	32	38	44	50	56	62	68	74	80	86	92	98
86	9	15	21	27	33	39	45	51	57	63	69	75	81	87	93	99
87	10	16	22	28	34	40	46	52	58	64	70	76	82	88	94	100
88	11	17	23	29	35	41	47	53	59	65	71	77	83	89	95	5
89	12	18	24	30	36	42	48	54	60	66	72	78	84	90	96	6
90	13	19	25	31	37	43	49	55	61	67	73	79	85	91	97	7
91	14	20	26	32	38	44	50	56	62	68	74	80	86	92	98	8
92	15	21	27	33	39	45	51	57	63	69	75	81	87	93	99	9
93	16	22	28	34	40	46	52	58	64	70	76	82	88	94	100	10
94	17	23	29	35	41	47	53	59	65	71	77	83	89	95	5	11
95	18	24	30	36	42	48	54	60	66	72	78	84	90	96	6	12
96	19	25	31	37	43	49	55	61	67	73	79	85	91	97	7	13

Answers from the Ladies' Oracle

Chart 1

1 A pleasant outcome
2 Very good, if you are careful
3 He wants to return but cannot
4 Forgiveness follows
5 It ought to last forever
6 As long as it has already lasted
7 Swings and roundabouts
8 Two pretty ones, one plain
9 Happiness prevails
10 Foolish to hope for it
11 Yield and romance is lost
12 Weep less, laugh more
13 As many as your faults
14 He is more affectionate
15 Time to repent
16 Wait one or two days

Chart 2

1 Widow, for the second time
2 Nothing is lasting
3 No, but your fortune brings envy
4 If you do so, you must continue
5 Yes, if you behave well
6 If it arrives, it will be there in three days
7 He loves you more than he shows
8 Not a word was meant
9 If you know how to please
10 You cannot wait
11 As much as before
12 Young but not young enough for you
13 At the least thirty
14 Let him see you love him
15 With a pretence of regret
16 Your old age will be enjoyable

Chart 3

1 Not a lucrative one
2 Peaceful, if you are wise
3 Not rewarding
4 Yes, definitely
5 More happy than wise
6 Do not expect it for now
7 You make the twenty-fifth
8 Yes, with patience
9 No gold for you
10 Yes, as soon as you like
11 Yes, but will you enjoy it
12 The first stops you seeking others
13 That you are a pearl
14 First letters can cause tears
15 Nothing more to fear
16 When folly turns to wisdom

Chart 4

1 Impossible
2 Stay where you are comfortable
3 To be feared
4 With all your power
5 Only half – it is enough
6 To the one you think most about
7 He has done so, and will again
8 Be confident and assertive
9 As bad as yours is good
10 Yes, even against wind and tide
11 It has never been a secret
12 Yes, if you can cope with little
13 It is safer to doubt them
14 Many more to come
15 That should never arrive
16 A waste of time

Chart 5

1 They are not interested in you
2 No danger but in your own fears
3 For a long time, but not forever
4 It will not arrive for a while
5 Take the advice of real friends
6 Presents to entrap come quickly
7 No thought of returning
8 Choose from a known and unknown
9 He gives a good impression
10 It is ruinous
11 Beautiful as a wingless angel
12 You made him unfaithful
13 Tomorrow is uncertain
14 He is not impatient
15 He never acts rashly
16 After dinner

Chart 6

1 What you deserve
2 Refuse them
3 Follow them
4 There is not always gain
5 More sincere than you deserve
6 Some good things come in small parcels
7 Sometimes, when he fears you will guess
8 Take the first step
9 Less than you
10 You do not deserve it
11 Out of sight, out of mind
12 Never, unless you make him
13 He thinks you love someone else
14 Middle-aged, but not wise
15 A child with nothing more to learn
16 At midday, in the shade

Chart 7

1 It is already lost
2 Inability to refuse ensues
3 Do not take any notice
4 He wishes he could be with you
5 Frankness never hurt anyone
6 It will depend on your conduct
7 It ought to last longer than it will
8 A great calamity
9 Yes, someone you regard as a friend
10 Sometimes, in the night
11 You will be despised
12 It is better to bend than break
13 Try to be less perfect
14 As many as your first loved-one married
15 He is confused
16 Within a year

Chart 8

1 More than you deserve
2 Widow, if you do not marry by 20
3 As many as you can deceive
4 Yes, but they are not powerful
5 Be wary and let them come to you
6 Only if you change it
7 Good news comes quickly
8 No, because you are not friendly
9 The person praising you is truthful
10 The more your joy, the sooner it ends
11 You will marry sooner than you think
12 Several who will make you very happy
13 You will have the chance but refuse
14 Carry on counting
15 You must be less light-headed
16 They will never regret you enough

Chart 9

1 When you die
2 A financially rewarding profession
3 Much more peaceful than it was
4 You will inherit nothing
5 He only believes the truth
6 There is no more danger
7 It is better for you if it continues
8 Six blondes and nine brunettes
9 Do not build on their successes
10 His fortune is as shallow as his love
11 But you are already engaged
12 Enough for your happiness
13 Too many or too few
14 There are good and bad sides to you
15 Answer it later
16 A lucky time will soon come

Chart 10

1 Many
2 When you least expect it
3 You are too sophisticated
4 It is not safe
5 Yes, when he wants to be assertive
6 Yes, if you keep promises
7 To someone who takes things slowly
8 If he said "no," he would be lying
9 Follow your heart
10 Things may get worse
11 The Oracle says "yes"
12 Do not worry
13 He will not bother after the 40th year
14 No
15 Swings and roundabouts
16 When you gain more wisdom

Chart 11

1 You are sensible at night
2 A little sometimes
3 It is silly to be frightened
4 You do not know how to keep it
5 If so, of your own making
6 Do not rush things
7 Bide your time
8 He is on his way
9 He knows you, but you don't know him
10 Neither one nor the other
11 It is too late
12 Too much so, sometimes
13 Men are not faithful if they no longer love
14 He loves you, but in a different way
15 He may take it if you do not give it
16 Give him some encouragement

Chart 12

1 You ought never to be
2 They think you better than you are
3 There is nothing to risk
4 Think it over
5 You have lost more than ever again
6 Hypocrisy
7 A rolling stone gathers no moss
8 Believe it
9 Forever
10 Much more than you will ever have
11 They give you more than you return
12 They cannot excuse your pretensions
13 Perhaps, but he will say nothing
14 He believes in your love
15 Middle-aged
16 They only need to see you

Chart 13

1 Sometime, after today
2 But a very short time
3 A bad outcome
4 Folly cannot produce good effects
5 He is chatting up to a very pretty woman
6 Promise, if you have the courage
7 You cannot break it off too soon
8 By the next new moon it will be over
9 Very favorable, if you act well
10 That should not trouble you
11 Yes
12 They have already forgiven too much
13 If you do not yield today, tomorrow
14 Get rich and be loved
15 Four
16 Not at first

Chart 14

1 They'll forget you too soon
2 Yes, if a little is sufficient
3 Maid, if you wait another year
4 Until you are well known
5 Do not be curious and fear nothing
6 Be content with being the second
7 You have not long to wait for changes
8 He'll arrive when you least expect him
9 It depends on the time and his mood
10 They are not to be depended on
11 Happiness brings long visits
12 Two things happen on the same day
13 Three
14 You will be married young
15 You feel like adding four more
16 Nothing, for he loves you

Chart 15

1 As much of one as the other
2 After your 60th birthday
3 A very lucrative and honorable one
4 Peace will follow
5 Never depend upon yourself
6 Your virtue is prized
7 It cannot have any
8 Wait patiently
9 You are equal
10 Rarely, perhaps once in ten times
11 Small fortune and little intellect
12 If you marry him, you may regret it
13 Yes
14 A wise woman always has too many
15 That you have little love
16 Reply and say farewell

Chart 16

1 Much too soon for happiness
2 Those you have are to be feared
3 You will sigh a long time for it
4 Town-life suits you
5 It promises you nothing but pleasure
6 You are already too opposed to them
7 You must be mad to believe it
8 To the one who knows your secret
9 Yes, but it has not been so long
10 Defy all those around you
11 He will drink like a fish
12 Doctors will not ruin you
13 No, but talk less at night
14 Everywhere and at all times
15 Promises are good, security is better
16 Nothing that will surprise you

Chart 17

1. He thinks more about you by night
2. By day and by night
3. Yes, but it will be badly arranged
4. Stay calm and all will go well
5. It is absolutely impossible
6. Frequent but not lasting sorrow
7. Make them wait for it
8. It depends what you do to merit them
9. He will soon return
10. You will marry a former lover
11. He will be handsome enough for you
12. Whenever you do it, it will be too soon
13. You are generally thought pretty
14. He says "yes," the Oracle says "no"
15. You are his first true love
16. It will make him ungrateful

Chart 18

1. All know you are no longer one
2. You should want what you fear
3. Neither good nor bad
4. You can, without danger
5. Yes, but not blindfolded
6. Lose money, rather than friends
7. Has sincerity anything to do with it?
8. Only one and that will cost you a lot
9. He has never told lies
10. Until the first fine day in May
11. Enough to consume his wealth
12. They don't know enough about you
13. Take care of what you have
14. Suspicions soon pass away
15. He thinks you are a flirt
16. He will be younger than you

Chart 19

1 He is more generous than you
2 Yes, if you wish them to regret you
3 Why throw yourself away
4 Neither good nor bad will result
5 No success
6 He wants to deceive you
7 Do as you will
8 It will last half as long again
9 You could have ended it
10 You will not profit much
11 Keep calm and you will
12 Yes, until you are wrinkled
13 They forgive you, but you begin again
14 Some say that women should obey
15 Don't tell him off, even if he's wrong
16 Three if you are married in three weeks

Chart 20

1 Give him all that he asks
2 Never
3 With great wealth
4 Widow, if you are one now
5 It will not last long, but begins again
6 Many, among people you think friends
7 That would be wrong
8 It will become brighter, but not better
9 Sooner than you ought for happiness
10 Sometimes more, sometimes less
11 Sincere and merited
12 Happiness is too fragile to last
13 How could you doubt it?
14 Only one, as amiable as yourself
15 Young girls like you marry
16 A great many

Chart 21

1 It is nearly over
2 Little pleasure, little grief
3 Never
4 Not any
5 Agitate the ocean, expect a storm
6 Do not count upon it
7 He loves only you
8 Others are more to be feared
9 Obstacles delay the outcome
10 He has not done better than you, nor worse
11 Always in spite of reason
12 Too much for his honor and yours, too
13 If he leaves you, goodbye to happiness
14 Yes
15 They are preparing for you
16 You will soon deceive him

Chart 22

1 You have nothing to lose
2 You are in too great a hurry
3 You have none at present
4 Never completely
5 You have false values
6 If you are married, yes; if not, no
7 Give advice, but don't tease him
8 With difficulty, but they will keep them
9 To the youngest, if he is 30
10 No, and that will never happen
11 Trust no one but God and yourself
12 Honest, upright, and trusting
13 Good health and a long life
14 Tomorrow if not today
15 Morning, noon, and night
16 Do not believe them

Chart 23

1 Today or tomorrow, since you must do it
2 More important things on his mind
3 At night
4 They sing your praises
5 It has not the slightest foundation
6 It will not last as long as it has
7 The worst is over
8 Yes, but make them give guarantees
9 The longer you wait, the more valuable they are
10 Sooner than you wish
11 You will marry your first or last lover
12 Much more handsome than those before him
13 The results are uncertain
14 It was thought you would be prettier
15 Ask him this, and believe what he says
16 Slightly

Chart 24

1 He is not yet born
2 Yes, but an influential one
3 In the middle of the night
4 A bad opinion
5 They have set a trap
6 Take care
7 Swings and roundabouts
8 You can believe it
9 Several by land and sea
10 He is a great boaster
11 If it ends tonight, it begins again tomorrow
12 He will not have much
13 Sincere and constant
14 That it is a flame that will soon go out
15 Suspicions seldom enter a noble heart
16 Yes, but he will not believe it long

Chart 25

1 Only one, and one too many
2 His heart is empty
3 In ten or twelve years
4 Yes, if you are wise
5 When peas are sown, beans do not grow
6 It will end happily
7 He is thinking seriously
8 Better today than tomorrow
9 It will last long but not happily
10 A sharp pain does not last long
11 If you are too easy, you will regret it
12 Rivalry will not last
13 More pain than pleasure
14 Yes, they cannot do otherwise
15 Break it off if possible
16 Take trouble over him

Chart 26

1 Can the stars be counted?
2 You must try to improve
3 They will weep for a long time
4 It ought not to be but will
5 The same as you are now
6 Always, if you do not change
7 They will disappear
8 It will not take place unless you do
9 Yes, and you will not be happier for it
10 You need much patience
11 Are flies preserved in vinegar?
12 Such words are light as air
13 Nothing is lasting
14 Who do you think would want to know you?
15 Yes, when you have found out what you need
16 Be patient

Chart 27

1 He finds you charming... Love is blind
2 Words fly away but writing remains
3 Joy follows grief
4 When your hair goes gray
5 Several, and not one good one
6 The worry will not last
7 Industry is the best fortune
8 He begins to suspect the truth
9 Yes, but they will forgive you
10 There are many obstacles to overcome
11 You had enough experience to notice
12 One step forward, two back
13 You will only marry him for money
14 Marry, if you can
15 No, if your taste does not change
16 You will have too many

Chart 28

1 Promises are not always kept
2 You have one more fault only
3 A change of character is needed for this
4 You had some, but none now
5 Not without difficulty
6 The country is good for health, but you like the town
7 Your happiest moments will be spent there
8 It would disturb your home life
9 They will be only too happy to do so
10 To the one that seems the most patient
11 A man loves only once
12 There is a plot
13 Passionate
14 Yes, if you keep your head
15 Sooner or later it must arrive
16 You will be happy with him

Chart 29

1 He is not fool enough for that
2 You do not know how to say "no"
3 He never has, and never will
4 By day or by night, the results will be the same
5 They think a great deal about you
6 You have nothing to fear
7 It is already lost
8 Many trials ahead, but resign yourself
9 Forgive them, and in 8 days they begin again
10 It is wrong to think about them
11 Soon enough to anger you
12 Your future husband is an old family friend
13 Morally handsome but physically ugly
14 It ought to have been done
15 Yes, but they do not love you more
16 Not now but he may become so

Chart 30

1 Only fools believe in impossibilities
2 He will have neither teeth nor hair
3 All know you do not wish to be thought one
4 In sunshine
5 They think you are envious
6 Yes, if they please you
7 Follow them – they are good
8 Sacrifice a little to prevent great loss
9 Much less than he seems to have
10 Uncertainty
11 Yes
12 Say one word and it will instantly stop
13 Just enough to be able to manage himself
14 You love less than you are loved
15 That is not much good to yourself nor to others
16 He will always have too much self-esteem

Chart 31

1 Nothing, as he already adores you
2 As many as you have had lovers
3 As affectionate, but more faithful
4 Why give up happiness?
5 It will not be so tomorrow
6 That you will soon regret it
7 Do not count on its success
8 He is making mistakes
9 Wait until the storm dies down
10 It will have more charm than duration
11 You have not to suffer much more
12 It will be your greatest misfortune
13 They fear you too much for that
14 Love will be its own reward
15 It is prudent not to count on it
16 Break it off

Chart 32

1 It will always arrive too soon
2 As many as you find to deceive
3 You must be wise, devoted, and amiable
4 Very much
5 Very happy
6 You cannot die a maid
7 As much as you love yourself
8 You will soon have many
9 Admit you are wrong
10 It will change sooner or later
11 Hope and wait patiently
12 He would love you if you were friendly
13 Sincere, but little merited
14 You are too inconstant
15 A pretty woman can be anything she likes
16 You will have some sooner or later

Chart 33

1 A little by day and very much by night
2 He thinks positively
3 Yes, if you want to refuse nothing
4 More grief than joy
5 Within ten years
6 He will be good for nothing
7 Very agitated, but it will be your fault
8 Yes, but it is very distant
9 He did believe it, but no longer
10 Yes, and it will be profitable
11 It will be better if it does not end soon
12 Forgive him as he loves you
13 Two steps forward, one step back
14 You think he is rich, but he is poor
15 Alas, a little too late
16 Fortune through pleasure

Chart 34

1 Yes, every other day
2 Seeing is believing
3 Do not accept it, you will be laughed at
4 What a waste of time!
5 Not among gentlemen
6 Yes, in a short time
7 The country would be very dull for you
8 Those not wishing to do wrong, should not fear
9 Slowly and imperceptibly
10 If they do not keep them, it will be your fault
11 Today to one, tomorrow to the other
12 He has loved them all in the same way
13 Do not trouble yourself about the first word
14 False, quarrelsome, dissipated
15 Always without a doctor, never with one
16 Yes, but more good than bad will result

Chart 35

1 Some times for two whole days
2 A little, as he has loved a thousand others
3 You will not make him a very beautiful present
4 Sometimes, when he has nothing better to do
5 During the day, if in summer
6 They think more of themselves than you
7 You should desire what you now fear
8 It will soon be reduced to its real value
9 You will have more than you had
10 Yes, as the repentance is sincere
11 They have changed their minds
12 Too late for him, too soon for you
13 The one destined for you is not yet born
14 Physically handsome, morally ugly
15 You must walk upright
16 Ugly and foolish

Chart 36

1 He will never know all the truth
2 He knows you want his love
3 Young and handsome
4 They take you for what you are
5 Once by night, twice by day
6 You are thought very silly
7 No, if you have not made up your mind
8 You will not know how to find better
9 You are lucky if you only lose money
10 Sincerity is lacking
11 A very short sentimental voyage
12 He would sooner tear out his tongue
13 Until you change your behavior
14 A good mind
15 You have no sincerity yourself
16 That you can make better use of it

Chart 37

1. To break is difficult, but to yield is easy
2. Be discreet
3. You will have twelve before marrying
4. He will try to find out first if you are affectionate
5. Wait until you are older
6. It will be the same in three months as today
7. One concession always calls for others
8. You will succeed, but with difficulty
9. He is thinking of a separation
10. It is always best to tell all
11. More duration than charm
12. Time alone can calm it
13. It will not cost you much, nor bring much
14. A prettier and cleverer one than you
15. Yes, if you are content with little
16. Yes, but after much punishment

Chart 38

1. A boy and a girl
2. The later the better
3. As many as you wish
4. Be loving and show it
5. They only regret those they really love
6. Enough to make you regret life
7. You will die before your first husband
8. Until you are wrinkled
9. One is always envied by inferiors
10. Neither the first nor the last
11. It will change during the year
12. In one more day
13. He adores you
14. They wished to blind you with praise
15. It will depend on you
16. Virgin or not, you'll be adored

Chart 39

1 Poor and impatient
2 Yes, but they will end badly
3 He thinks only of loving you
4 Speak a little and write less
5 Joy and no sorrow
6 Very soon
7 Your love hinders his work
8 More peaceful than most thought
9 You do not want what you receive
10 He knows you very well
11 No
12 Before the end of the next moon
13 Yes, as he never loved before he loved you
14 Yes, if you change your behavior
15 Good fortune will soon pass away
16 Yes, but it will be a shotgun wedding

Chart 40

1 It was known for a long time
2 Not as much as you deserve
3 Similar promises are generally forgotten
4 First pleasure, then grief
5 You will be wrinkled before then
6 Defy the women around you
7 If it is not soon, it will never be
8 Only town life suits you
9 You should fear the consequences
10 His projects are wise
11 They want to get rid of them, but cannot
12 Keep them both
13 He will never love you as he loved others
14 Always hold you tongue
15 He will be a misanthrope
16 Your health is in your own hands

Chart 41

1 You would have to change your appearance
2 He gives you value for money
3 Yes, like you love him
4 Grant it, as you will get it back
5 He thinks too much
6 The night, if in winter
7 They are only making fun of you
8 Do what is right, fear nothing
9 You may deceive but not forever
10 Childish sorrow that will soon disappear
11 He is incorrigible
12 They are preparing them for you
13 Too soon for him, too late for you
14 You'll marry the man courting you now
15 As handsome as you can wish
16 Without hesitating an instant

Chart 42

1 That it is more brilliant than solid
2 You can make him believe all you like
3 He did believe, but does not now
4 He was grown up before you were born
5 They wish you really were one
6 In the night, happily for you
7 They all agree you are not very friendly
8 No harm can result from it
9 Your heart is your best guide
10 What you lose is not worth having
11 No, it is only a pretence
12 You are too changeable to remain stable
13 He respects truth but never speaks it
14 Until you deserve forgiveness
15 You will never have met such an intellectual man
16 Yes, they cheat you as you cheat them

Chart 43

1 It may be forgiven but not forgotten
2 You will not break it off
3 Be tolerant, and know how to forgive
4 An old one and a young one
5 Very sensitive but not constant
6 You ought to have given it up already
7 It has been more than it will ever be
8 You cannot go back along which it is impossible to stop
9 You will be poorer than before
10 He is not thinking about you
11 To sin and to confess is to be half-forgiven
12 You are not constant enough
13 You are not a woman to die of grief
14 I should not like what lies ahead
15 You will soon be surrounded by them
16 Never – it is your destiny

Chart 44

1 More than ten years before
2 Yes, that is for sure
3 Yes, it is urgent
4 A dozen, and a very little one make thirteen
5 Follow their advice
6 They will appear to do so
7 As much as to youthfulness
8 All these before your death
9 Yes, until you go white
10 The envious only suffer
11 If you do it, you will regret it
12 Yes, very often like your temper
13 An unforeseen event prevents it
14 Much less, but he will love you more
15 A bait thrown out to your vanity
16 Yes, but not always in the same way

Chart 45

1 Yes. and several others
2 Hopefully
3 You look for more than you find
4 Oysters live but do not think
5 Yes, as it is dangerous
6 Enough suffering – now rejoice
7 Today... or tomorrow
8 A dangerous profession
9 Calm always follows a storm
10 Neither hope nor fear
11 He does not know about them
12 You deserve them but you do not get them
13 If not in three days, in three months
14 He has had several
15 You only succeed in minor things
16 Great fortune, little heart, very little brain

Chart 46

1 No good health without wisdom
2 Everybody knows it
3 Much more than you deserve
4 Not to examine would be foolish
5 It will not make much difference
6 Yes, but only to make fun of you
7 You ought to fear just one
8 Yes, and it is the worse for you
9 Live in the country if you want good health
10 Yes, and many other things
11 Oppose him and regret it
12 They would retract if they could
13 The youngest for pleasure, not fortune
14 A deep love
15 You are watched
16 Brave, liberal, and gallant

Chart 47

1 As soon as possible
2 Very pretty, but not likeable
3 Yes, he cannot do otherwise
4 His love is a caprice
5 Take care to retain his heart
6 How can he avoid it? He adores you
7 Perhaps it will never arrive
8 They are too busy to worry about you
9 Never was fear more ridiculous
10 It will be what you deserve
11 Give way to what you cannot prevent
12 Forgive them today, and they laugh at you tomorrow
13 They have not had time to think
14 He will always play tricks
15 You will marry one who often annoys you
16 Too handsome

Chart 48

1 They are making fun of you
2 That it is the Devil's intelligence
3 Yes
4 He jokes about it
5 Hoary-headed and white-bearded
6 You are not innocent enough
7 It often arrives at all hours
8 They think you do lots of silly things
9 Yes, they make no difference
10 Lots of advisers, little wisdom
11 You should not lose anything
12 You regret it most
13 You will do so, though you do not have to
14 You'd be surprised if he did not fib sometimes
15 Another month or so
16 Enough not to ask about the last

Chart 49

1 Those happy in love do not always deserve it
2 Forgive but never forget
3 Break it off if you are wise
4 Do as he wishes
5 As many as your children
6 He's like a cock that struts about
7 Yes – there is no good in it
8 The longer the better
9 That a second step follows the first
10 It will be prompt and fruitful
11 He is building castles in the air
12 There are many ways
13 You tried to break it off too soon
14 Yes, but we do not die to learn suffering
15 It will give you pleasure
16 You will have them again

Chart 50

1 A few hours, in a few years
2 When you marry, your first children have teeth
3 Three, and they will be very handsome
4 Yes, without rector or parson
5 Yes, as many as your bad thoughts last night
6 Show yourself wiser than you are
7 They will show you justice
8 Your position will not change
9 You will die a maid, if you do not marry before 30
10 A long time, but not strongly
11 Yes, but they seldom have any power
12 It will be profitable for you
13 No change in a month, and it will never change
14 They are trying to send it to you
15 Love before and after marriage is not comparable
16 No, the one making them was blind

Chart 51

1 Neither rich nor poor
2 He will not marry you
3 Fortune and you will never meet
4 Enough to make you regret it
5 You have more sense than love
6 It does not matter
7 The future is rosy
8 At the next snowstorm
9 A good profession
10 A little agitation, but much peace
11 Never, nor a title
12 He will always believe it
13 It ought to make you feel it, but will not
14 It is nearer to the end than you think
15 One only, and she deceived him
16 Always, thanks to your boldness

Chart 52

1 Foolish, wicked, and jealous
2 You will suffer, but not badly
3 A secret confided to two is no secret
4 It depends on your future conduct
5 Credulity is dangerous
6 Nothing that will frighten you
7 Nobody thinks of it – they know you wish it
8 Your greatest enemy is yourself
9 You will do better not to desire it
10 Live in town if you like pleasure
11 Yes, above all after dinner
12 Leave him alone and be silent
13 Their promises are soon forgotten
14 To the youngest, if you prefer wealth
15 No, he has loved someone else
16 Be wise by night and by day

Chart 53

1 Ugly
2 Do not be too hasty
3 Much prettier than good
4 He has always been so
5 He has loved you more
6 You could if you had it
7 Much more than you think of him
8 Neither by night nor day
9 They do not think it worth their while
10 Your fear is without foundation
11 It remains as it is, if you don't change
12 You are smiled upon
13 Forgive once, and forgive a thousand times
14 If you receive with one hand, give with the other
15 It is likely he will never return
16 The one you marry appears in a dream within 3 days

Chart 54

1 He has enough for himself and you
2 They are deceiving you – and it is your own fault
3 That it is in accordance with your face
4 Do not let him suspect anything
5 Yes, and he loves you
6 He was born before your father and mother
7 They have reason to think so
8 At night, after supper
9 They do not think you very cruel
10 Send them packing
11 All who advise should be suspected
12 You will lose a lot, but gain more
13 Not more so than your vows
14 They will be more productive than long
15 No, and it is as well
16 Until tomorrow morning

Chart 55

1 You had them, but they are gone
2 You will be happy and unhappy
3 Yes, if you know how to deserve it
4 It may be too late to break it off
5 Be faithful to him, and do not complain
6 Two, and they will not be worth much
7 An iron head, icy hand, and leaden brain
8 That is more than you can cope with
9 Only a few hours more
10 Much less evil than may otherwise occur
11 Begin again
12 He regrets not being with you
13 Moderation in all things
14 Everything is there
15 It has already half diminished
16 It will cause you more pain than pleasure

Chart 56

1 You are foolish to believe them
2 You ought to do so always
3 To cease to be so, you should be one now
4 A charming one, and several awful ones
5 You already seem married
6 Three at a time to begin with
7 Act in disguise
8 Very little
9 Sorrow generally follows too much pleasure
10 You will die a wife, not a widow
11 Always, and very fondly
12 You envy others more than you are envied
13 Obey your conscience
14 Yes, for your happiness
15 A lame messenger walks slowly
16 His love is like yours

Chart 57

1 That depends on how wise you are
2 Rich in love, poor in money
3 There is an insurmountable obstacle
4 A moderate fortune, but honestly acquired
5 They will cause you grief
6 You could not be nicer, but could be wiser
7 To reply would be wrong
8 Fortune smiles from now on
9 When time shall have made you wiser
10 His work will often keep him away
11 Frequent storms
12 A rich relative often thinks of you
13 He does not trust women
14 Less disastrous than you think
15 Not soon, but it ends to your advantage
16 He has been wiser than you

Chart 58

1 Be more prudent
2 Sweet-tempered, modest, easily persuaded
3 Someone will cure your illness
4 It will not be discovered for a long time
5 You may not meet with an accident, but be careful
6 Promises are often forgotten
7 The first man to propose is still a child
8 He will try to do so but without success
9 You ought never to have any
10 No, you are insatiable
11 They both suit you
12 If you allow it, you will be lost
13 You will do better to attend to matters at home
14 They could only keep the first
15 Two are not too many for you
16 You are his first love, and his last

Chart 59

1 Yes, one you know very well
2 As ugly as you are pretty
3 Everything comes to those with patience
4 Your flatterers will say "yes," but the Oracle says "no"
5 He has been more than he will ever be again
6 He does not know himself
7 How can you give what you have not?
8 He is madly in love with you
9 Between the two
10 Yes, but do not say anything good
11 The evil is done
12 You do not take care enough of it for that
13 You are surrounded by pleasure
14 Forgiveness will have no good results
15 That will depend on a whim
16 He is preparing to start a journey

Chart 60

1 Long enough for a great reconciliation
2 Just as much as you have
3 You will be wrong if you doubt it
4 It would be better if less lively
5 He will have suspicions
6 Did you not make mistakes to win him?
7 As young as you, and not wiser
8 Yes, a spoilt child
9 At every time, and in every place
10 That you are too lively
11 You may accept them, but not yet
12 Advisers are generally worthless
13 You have lost all you had to lose
14 Sincerity is not for you
15 Yes, and you will soon begin them
16 He is not simple enough for that

Chart 61

1 It will be pleasant, not advantageous
2 You will soon be troubled by them
3 Love and happiness are not the same
4 You have no hope of forgiveness
5 With care you may prevent both
6 To suffer and be silent is a great virtue
7 Several in jest, and one who causes pain
8 It is the most honest and loving heart
9 Do not be in too much of a hurry
10 For an entire year
11 That which has already happened
12 Very bad, if you are not cautious
13 He is pining away
14 Everybody knows anyway
15 Yes, if you are indulgent
16 It has lasted too long

Chart 62

1 He would do so, but...
2 you know they cannot be
3 The first day only
4 That is laughable
5 Yes, before and after
6 In twelve years that will be talked about
7 One for the day, afternoon, and night respectively
8 To be loved, you must be kind
9 You ought to be eternally regretted
10 It will be troubled by repentance
11 You will be a widow, but will marry again
12 The love you inspire will not last
13 That ought not to prevent you sleeping
14 You ought to, but you will not
15 If it should have changed, it would
16 Yes, if he does not get lost

Chart 63

1 You are the first of the third series
2 You will sail against the wind
3 Rich in money, poor in wisdom
4 Yes, if you wish to die of grief
5 Much more than you deserve
6 Enough to make you know the world
7 It is very difficult for the learned to be kind
8 Yes, do it, or you will die
9 No more sorrow
10 When you cease to feel for others
11 He will have two professions
12 Very violently, but not for long
13 Yes, a fine one but lawyers take much
14 As good as most women
15 You are at fault and must be punished
16 It is nearly at an end

Chart 64

1 He has loved many in different ways
2 You would have a great deal to do
3 Careless but kind-hearted
4 You will be a charming imaginary invalid
5 No, if you keep calm
6 Your home will be a paradise
7 That would be foolish
8 Nothing if you are strong, much if weak
9 There is time enough yet
10 Yes, but you will soar above them
11 It will be perfectly satisfied
12 In the town, if you want to be rich
13 You will become rich through him
14 Do not meddle with what is not understood
15 Not without difficulty
16 To the first that causes you to weep

Chart 65

1 He does not think of returning but thinks of marrying
2 A man who did not know you would not marry you
3 He will be charming, but know too much
4 The later the better
5 Yes, at night
6 Uncertainty
7 He is fortunate
8 Not much risk
9 Do not let him suffer for long
10 Nothing of the sort should happen
11 They are relating your adventures
12 There are remedies for all evils
13 You have already tried to lose it
14 No, if you are prudent
15 Wait until they deserve forgiveness
16 Do not wait for them

Chart 66

1 He has told more stories than he ever will again
2 Until you take the first step
3 The results alone will prove that
4 That you wish it to appear more than it is
5 Husbands are always the last to suspect
6 He knows it well but is not affected
7 He will be an old man
8 They have often showed you the contrary
9 In the middle of the day
10 They think you are not modest enough
11 Yes, but without conditions
12 The advice is not worth taking
13 Know how to lose to learn how to gain
14 Another piece of foolishness
15 One only
16

Chart 67

 1 It will soon disappear
 2 It will cost you tears
 3 One only which is not dangerous
 4 Love is not the road to happiness
 5 They will not forgive you
 6 Your heart should be your guide
 7 Hide the past, do better in the future
 8 Too many if you only have one
 9 His heart is affectionate, but you will deceive him
10 If you give it up too soon, you will return to it
11 Much longer than you want
12 You know it by experience
13 It will not be brilliant enough
14 He is dreaming of a sweet future
15 Do not deny the truth
16 Yes, if you become reasonable

Chart 68

 1 You will have to wait as long again
 2 Very much so, and it is right
 3 As sincere as it is possible to be
 4 As happy as you were before
 5 You will do as your mother did before you
 6 It would be better for you not to have any
 7 You should never marry
 8 You will be continually changing
 9 You will never gain his love
10 Tears and regret are reserved for you
11 If you make a hard bed, you must lie on it
12 You will die at a good old age, a widow
13 Very little, and very faintly
14 Yes, and they are apparently your friends
15 You could never do it too soon
16 Never, it is your destiny

Chart 69

1 No, it is impossible
2 No one marries his first love
3 Yes, in spite of your stupidity
4 If he is not rich now, he soon will be
5 Do not hope; it is impossible
6 Yes, if you behave yourself wisely
7 You will have more than one
8 He likes you, but will soon change his mind
9 If things go on so fast, they will not last
10 Great joy and very little sorrow
11 When your heart ceases to beat
12 He will never need to earn a living
13 Peaceful on the whole
14 You will inherit... debts
15 He does not believe you
16 No one escapes the necessary consequences

Chart 70

1 To the one you see first
2 A first love is always the strongest
3 It is impossible to hide things for long
4 Lively, obliging, and good
5 You will always have joy, health, and prosperity
6 It is already discovered
7 Household affairs will give you a taste of Hell
8 They wish to deceive you and succeed
9 What happened to Eve for eating the forbidden fruit?
10 You need a word of encouragement
11 Yes, but they fear you
12 Yes, if you take care to be cautious
13 In the country if you are wise
14 It will be a source of much happiness
15 Yes, but with much management
16 They are already thinking of parting

Chart 71

1 You will have to wait a long time for them
2 He is too well-off where he is
3 How can you know him? He is not born!
4 Love will embellish him
5 Ask the advice of others
6 Opinions on the subject are divided
7 Yes
8 He adores you and suffers
9 Yes – for pleasure, not honor
10 As they would regard a person of no importance
11 A little before sunrise
12 They are making fun of you
13 It would be better for you if it were
14 It is a fragile jewel
15 Real sorrow should always be unseen
16 Forgive now, or never

Chart 72

1 Very often
2 He is as truthful as you are
3 It ought to be eternal
4 He has a little, but it will last
5 The more you give, the less they will return you
6 It is a waste
7 No, he is blinded by love
8 You should give him up
9 The youngest are not always the best
10 Yes, but a child who wants to be thought a woman
11 A little after midnight
12 That you are as good as you really are
13 Yes, in changing some part of them
14 You are strong enough to fly alone
15 Loss of money is not what you must dread
16 It is a new trap

Chart 73

1 Enough to cause you deep regret
2 It is you alone who can stop it
3 It will bring happiness
4 You are surrounded by them now
5 To be happy in love, give way to others
6 Those who repent are easily forgiven
7 There is danger on both sides
8 Be constant
9 One for the day, another for the night
10 Soft
11 You are not strong enough
12 For a long time it has not been free
13 Regret will follow pleasure
14 More agreeable than productive
15 He is making grand plans, relinquished tomorrow
16 Choose a favorable time

Chart 74

1 It is now as it always should be
2 Better for you to be without it
3 The honeymoon cannot last
4 It was to try your self-esteem
5 As long as you deserve it
6 You will never cease to be one
7 Every year, and handsome like their father
8 When the first wrinkles appear on your forehead
9 You will have them and they will vary
10 Do not undertake impossibilities
11 They will mourn you for a long time
12 Yes, if you know how to provide for the future
13 You will die before your fourth husband
14 Much longer than necessary
15 Pretend they are not, and find there are lots
16 Yes, and you will not regret it

Chart 75

1 It will have the most natural outcome
2 Sooner than expected
3 Yes, the first he seriously loved
4 Success and failure
5 Riches will be his only good quality
6 Without a minister, you may
7 Fortune will come to you while you sleep
8 The first has given you a liking for them
9 You are beautiful, good, and charming
10 Yes, if you wish to reply to lies
11 There will be perfect compensation
12 You could never give up anything so sweet
13 He will grind you down
14 You will not get much rest
15 Yes, slowly
16 He knows what you have done

Chart 76

1 Promises like this are never kept
2 To the one who waits the longest
3 Not yet, but he may
4 Change of conduct and country
5 He will be a brute
6 Yes, it will be your only happiness
7 If not now, it never will be
8 He thinks more about himself
9 Take care not to be led astray
10 You gather sweet fruit which soon becomes bitter
11 As you now wish it, so you'll regret it
12 Of all colors and all sizes
13 Not if you keep calm
14 In the country if you can bear boredom
15 Do not refuse but remember reason
16 You will do better to leave him alone

Chart 77

1. Forgive if you would be forgiven
2. Do not count on it
3. He will return by Easter
4. From a known to an unknown one
5. Too handsome to be faithful
6. No, give him up now
7. They are obliged to, as you are so pretty
8. He loves you too much
9. He loves you as you deserve
10. Take care, he is artful
11. Not now, but he will with encouragement
12. By moonlight
13. They are discussing you
14. You have less than ever to fear
15. Yes, but some so-called friend will blame you
16. Walk upright, fear nothing

Chart 78

1. Only to play with you
2. You do not need them for perfection
3. He only tells the truth when he forgets
4. It could last forever, if you are wise
5. A little, perhaps
6. You know it is impossible
7. That you are deficient in this
8. He will be more jealous than loving
9. Yes, but he knows your love is shared
10. Yes, but that will be his only merit
11. You will always be thought of as wise
12. In silence and darkness
13. You are thought to have had more than one affair
14. Only accept them conditionally
15. This is bad advice
16. No, if you act sensibly and loyally

Chart 79

1 Whatever you do, do not rush
2 It cannot be
3 It depends how deep it is
4 It will bring joy, health, and prosperity
5 Several, but you will soar above them all
6 No doubt about it
7 They know all and forgive
8 A reconciliation is sure to follow
9 Do not appear agitated when with him
10 One you will govern, and one who will govern you
11 Yes, his heart beats only for you
12 The sooner the better
13 It will no longer be yours in eight days
14 It does not matter
15 More productive than agreeable
16 He is acting foolishly

Chart 80

1 Yes, if you wish to make it up quickly
2 It will change for the better but slowly
3 Many more months
4 His love is less lively, but more lasting
5 He has never been truthful
6 Yes, if you succeed in correcting yourself
7 That entirely depends on you
8 Several, but they will not resemble their father
9 What difference will that make?
10 Quality is preferable to quantity
11 Do not think about him, he is already engaged
12 That will depend on how you act
13 Yes, if you act uprightly
14 An old maid, but rich
15 It would be impossible to love you for long
16 Only fools envy you

Chart 81

1 He must be simple to think so
2 No, if you do not begin again
3 If it ends to your advantage, it has already ended
4 He had only loved a few dozen
5 Yes, if you do not discourage him
6 Rich, miserly, jealous, and slovenly
7 Neither him nor any other
8 A very large one
9 Yes, you will tread a tricky path
10 That you are the only woman for him
11 Wait at least for a second
12 As much of one as of the other
13 At midnight
14 He will be a tradesman
15 Folly is the enemy of peace of mind
16 Yes, and very soon

Chart 82

1 Yes, if you wish to ruin him
2 They promise, but never perform
3 To the one who talks least, and acts most
4 As much, yes... more, no
5 Avoid the world, and regret it
6 He will be grumbling, brutal, and sullen
7 Yes, if you do not spoil it
8 When it is, there will be no more danger
9 Yes, if love is enough for you
10 That would be the greatest mistake
11 That you will be cured of your mad passion
12 Yes, but it will not last long, though it will cost you
13 Yes, some very powerful ones
14 Yes, but not for long
15 In a town, if you are more than fifteen
16 Haven't you been tested?

Chart 83

1 To suffer and to enjoy is to live
2 You have no right to be severe
3 They are preparing them for you
4 He is going farther instead of returning
5 You know him better than he knows you
6 As ugly physically as morally
7 You never conceived a better one
8 Men say "yes" women say "no"
9 Fidelity is a virtue he possesses
10 His love is passing away
11 Do not be too hasty
12 He does not know how to be loved
13 At sunrise
14 Yes, they speak well of you
15 Be on your guard
16 It will always be as you make it

Chart 84

1 It is not your purse they want
2 Yes, perfectly sincere
3 Yes, if you do not dispense with them
4 For every lie you tell, he tells two
5 Still two days and three long nights
6 Yes, it shows in his eyes
7 You were one, but no longer
8 They know you are without any
9 If you are frank, he will forgive the past
10 Yes, and it makes him happy
11 He will be young, but masterful
12 Yes, and a terrible child
13 At midday, before witnesses
14 They think you kinder than you are
15 Do not accept any
16 You will lose nothing by following them

Chart 85

1 He is thinking of another
2 If you admit that, you will have to admit more
3 It will not last as long as it has
4 They are wondering how to rid you from it
5 Yes, if made by day. No, if made at night
6 Two, one of whom will dethrone you
7 It depends upon your conduct
8 Some faults can never be forgiven
9 If he loves you, do not worry
10 Abstain from habits that displease him
11 One tall, one short, one medium, and none too many
12 Never were two hearts more suited
13 Yes, if you wish to live long
14 You are too silly for that
15 The more you give, the more you receive
16 All your foresight will not help

Chart 86

1 Do you want them to envy you?
2 Certainly, as you are wrong
3 It will soon change for the worse
4 Slow progress
5 Men never love wives like sweethearts
6 They were lying and you knew it
7 As long as you love sincerely
8 Yes, but no one will know it
9 It will not be your fault if you have none
10 You will wish to be thought young
11 Three that will bring pleasure, and ten, grief
12 If you could do wonders, it would not help
13 No, if you stay as you are
14 Memories will make you happy
15 You will die maid or widow
16 Yes, if you are faithful

Chart 87

1 Wait for dead people's shoes, and go barefoot
2 He has known a long time
3 You are wrong to dread them
4 The longer it lasts, the better it will be
5 He had as many affairs as you had lovers
6 You lose at first, but gain later
7 He will be rich in good qualities
8 You may ask the same question in ten years
9 It would be hoping in vain
10 You will have many
11 Neither good nor bad; he looks and waits
12 You are in a great hurry to deceive him
13 Joy will surpass sorrow
14 When it is light at midnight
15 He will do nothing of any consequence
16 More peaceful than you wish

Chart 88

1 Always and everywhere
2 Do not meddle
3 They were soon forgotten
4 To one appearing uninterested at first
5 Not only as much, but more
6 Be more discreet than at present
7 Benevolent, credulous, and resigned
8 Do not sacrifice yourself to pleasure
9 Yes, you told an indiscreet person
10 Happiness is not for you
11 Yes, as they are sincere
12 That you will be laughed at and despised
13 Do not hurry to play with fire
14 Yes, but they can do no harm
15 Much sooner than you hope
16 In the country, if you have given up love

Chart 89

1 It has never has been good
2 Yes, but it will be followed by joy
3 You have already waited too long
4 Yes, but you will pay dearly
5 He will return as soon as possible
6 You have known him a long time
7 He will be charming in every way
8 Consult your friends, and act prudently
9 Yes, if you do not show two faces
10 He wishes to, but cannot
11 He has passed the test
12 Yes, it will only make one more
13 When he sees you, that is all
14 Early in the morning
15 They do not even think of you
16 It has never had any foundation

Chart 90

1 Think carefully
2 It is not money you would lose
3 Act more sincerely
4 Long and productive ones
5 For every two lies you tell, he tells three
6 It will finish when you choose
7 Too much to love you long
8 Not yet, but you will be
9 That you'd do well not to try for it
10 He cannot help having suspicions
11 He dared not hope for so much happiness
12 He was born in the same year as you
13 No children
14 On a dark night
15 They have an excellent opinion
16 Accept them by all means

Chart 91

1 Less than you hoped
2 He is thinking of your last meeting
3 If you confess it, you are lost
4 Bad acquaintances generally last
5 A friend is ready to console you
6 You will gain nothing by it
7 One that will cause you much grief
8 You would need what you have not
9 You will be forgiven eventually
10 Neither one nor the other
11 Be more loving when you meet
12 As many as you want, but you will be better without
13 Why should you worry? He will never matter to you
14 The world is poisoning you
15 It would be better for you if it did
16 Do not give away what you can sell

Chart 92

1 Not always as much as now
2 Those that you have are not dangerous
3 Do not rush to humiliate yourself
4 Yes, and you will regret it
5 You receive them too soon
6 Love is dying, friendship takes its place
7 You may believe them
8 As long as you hide your game
9 No, thanks to chance
10 Before, yes... after, no
11 You will not be wise
12 One only
13 Show yourself as you are
14 A little, not much
15 It will be very different from your youth
16 Widow and rich

Chart 93

1 No peace for you
2 It would be folly to hope so
3 He believes you're as good as most
4 Yes, but they will pass
5 It will last longer than it has
6 Before you, he changed partners each month
7 You have not enough perseverance
8 Do not look for happiness in riches
9 If you marry him today, you will weep tomorrow
10 You will gain a fortune, but not keep it
11 A few, early in the morning
12 That you amuse yourself by teasing him
13 You will be lost if you do
14 Your greatest sorrows are past
15 Never
16 He will be strikingly dreesed

Chart 94

1 Stay where you are
2 Yes, by night as well as day
3 Yes, if you are tired of being happy
4 They will keep them all, and will even do more
5 One is no better than the other
6 Not one, but many
7 Be reserved, and do not begin again
8 As good as yours is bad
9 That will depend upon your conduct
10 Yes, sooner or later
11 You will never know sorrow
12 You may believe it without danger
13 You know what generally happens
14 Not for several years
15 None to be really feared
16 It will be your own fault if it is not

Chart 95

1 Yes, it has a good foundation
2 The truth will soon be known
3 You will have more pleasure than sorrow
4 Should you not also be forgiven?
5 Yes, if you are not wise enough to refuse them
6 The later the better
7 You spoke to him only two days ago
8 He will be as handsome as a demon
9 Wait a little
10 Good-looking and a flirt
11 He is always seeking pleasure
12 Much too much; he frets you laugh at him
13 You granted it to others, why not him?
14 Yes, and you will soon have a proof of it
15 At the crowing of the cock
16 Yes, much more than they ought to

Chart 96

1 Accept them, if you have nothing to lose
2 Follow them, and ruin is certain
3 Give up, lose nothing
4 Regrets are frequently lies
5 Do not travel
6 He takes care not to do that
7 If it does not end today, it will tomorrow
8 Enough not to mistake chalk for cheese
9 They give you fifty for a hundred
10 They do not talk or think about it
11 Do not be too sure; he may
12 Yes, but he does not think it will last long
13 He will do many silly things to pretend
14 Yes, a child with teeth who wants to bite everybody
15 One fine day
16 You are thought happier than you are

FAMILY RELATIONSHIPS

Children, too, are particularly influenced by their
Soul Numbers, calculated by adding together the
numerical values of the vowels in the given name.
(See pages 96-97). This is why the choice of a name at
birth, in combination with a middle name(s) and
the surname, is so important. (See pages 113-119).
For valuable insight into how a parent-child
relationship is likely to develop during early years,
the Soul Number for the parent can be compared
with that for each child. The charts that follow
provide a basic guide to this.

Parental Soul Number 1
Child Soul Number 1
The adult with this Soul Number has a pioneering
spirit and is innovative in his/her approach to life.
The child with the Soul Number **1** may be equally
confident so that, at times, conflict can result.
Allowances need to be made for this.

Parental Soul Number 1
Child Soul Number 2
The adult with the Soul Number **1** forges ahead in
life and is as bold as brass in all sorts of
situations. The child with the Soul Number **2** may
be embarrassed by this at times but will come to
accept it in the end.

Parental Soul Number 1
Child Soul Number 3
The adult with the Soul Number **1** is full of vitality,
as is the child with the Soul Number **3**. In
adolescence, this can lead to an element of
competition, particularly between an adult and child
of the same sex.

Parental Soul Number 1
Child Soul Number 4
The child with the Soul Number **4** will be very
understanding of any family problems that arise.
The parent with the Soul Number **1**, meanwhile,
needs to be sure that the other adults do not take
advantage of this.

Parental Soul Number 1
Child Soul Number 5
The child with the Soul Number **5** is generally quick
to talk and is by nature an extrovert. The parent
with the Soul Number **1** may sometimes find such
constant chatter highly exhausting.

Parental Soul Number 1
Child Soul Number 7
A child with the Soul Number **7** is often stubborn and may lead the parent with the Soul Number **1** a merry dance, rarely taking "no" for an answer. This will call for a lot of patience.

Parental Soul Number 1
Child Soul Number 8
A child with the Soul Number **8** is usually very demanding of parental time and will sometimes indulge in dreadful behavior to get what he or she wants. A parent with the Soul Number **1** must take care not to spoil this child.

Parental Soul Number 1
Child Soul Number 9
A child with the Soul Number **9** will be full of fun. The parent with the Soul Number **1** will find this relationship particularly rewarding.

Parental Soul Number 2
Child Soul Number 1
The child with the Soul Number **1** will always be full of interesting but sometimes strange ideas. The parent with the Soul Number **2**, meanwhile, will need to learn not to dismiss these ideas automatically, so that the child does not lose confidence.

Parental Soul Number 2
Child Soul Number 2
The child with the Soul Number **2** is not naturally as considerate as he or she might be. The parent with the same Soul Number will need to be sure to encourage good manners from an early age.

Parental Soul Number 2
Child Soul Number 3
The parent with the Soul Number **2** tends to be very judgmental. This parent will therefore need to be sure to give the child with the Soul Number **3** sufficient freedom of expression and not to find fault unduly.

Parental Soul Number 2
Child Soul Number 4
The child with the Soul Number **4** is generally very reliant upon routine and harmony in the family circle. The parent with the Soul Number **2** will do well to ensure that this child does not become involved in any way with family squabbles.

Parental Soul Number 2
Child Soul Number 5
The child with the Soul Number **5** is enthusiastic about most things. The parent with the Soul Number **2**, however, may mistake this for unruly behavior.

Parental Soul Number 2
Child Soul Number 6
Most children with the Soul Number **6** will always try
to please and may be surprised to find that not all
children behave this way. The parent with the Soul
Number **2** will need to impart tolerance.

Parental Soul Number 2
Child Soul Number 7
The child with the Soul Number **7** will frequently
test the patience of a parent with the Soul Number
2, if only because of a reluctance to take adult
advice or guidance.

Parental Soul Number 2
Child Soul Number 8
Children with the Soul Number **8** do not react well to
criticism. The parent will need to be particularly
understanding if school results are not always up to
expectations, in spite of the child's efforts.

Parental Soul Number 2
Child Soul Number 9
The parent with the Soul Number **2** may need to
guide the child with the Soul Number **9** particularly
carefully. His or her creative talents need to be
nurtured right from a very early age.

Parental Soul Number 3
Child Soul Number 1
The parent with the Soul Number **3** will have to be wary of becoming bored when looking after a very small baby. Later, however, he or she will be delighted by the pioneering spirit of the child.

Parental Soul Number 3
Child Soul Number 2
The child with the Soul Number **2** may grow up to be highly critical of a parent with the Soul Number **3** if given the chance. The parent with the Soul Number **3**, meanwhile, needs to learn that the child is not a puppet but a strong individual.

Parental Soul Number 3
Child Soul Number 3
If parent and child with the same Soul Number, **3**, are to get on, they will have to be very open with each other. This does not come easily.

Parental Soul Number 3
Child Soul Number 4
The child with the Soul Number **4** will usually be a great source of comfort for the parent with the Soul number **3** who is rarely accepting of what life brings. The parent should listen to this child who may have wisdom beyond his or her years.

Parental Soul Number 3
Child Soul Number 5
A child with the Soul Number **5** will always be
aware of current trends and may seem rebellious at
times. The parent with the Soul Number **3** will
encourage this, even if unconsciously.

Parental Soul Number 3
Child Soul Number 6
The parent with the Soul Number **3** should take
special care when punishing the child with the Soul
Number **6** for any reason. This child has an innate
sense of justice and may respond unfavorably if he
or she thinks treatment is too harsh.

Parental Soul Number 3
Child Soul Number 7
Children with the Soul Number **7** are very much their
own people from the cradle onward. The parent with
the Soul Number **3**, however, has the right sort of
mentality to cope with such an independent streak
and will allow this child just enough leeway.

Parental Soul Number 3
Child Soul Number 8
Children with the Soul Number **8** often have it in mind
to go right to the top in a chosen field. The parent with
the Soul Number **3** will be very proud of what this
child achieves but should not push too hard.

Parental Soul Number 3
Child Soul Number 9
The child with the Soul Number **9** usually has a
particularly romantic view of his or her parents'
relationship. The parent with the Soul Number **3** will
need to be careful not to destroy this in any way, so
that the child does not develops a cynical view of
marriage and family life.

Parental Soul Number 4
Child Soul Number 1
The parent with the Soul Number **4** requires a very
orderly life, but the presence of children – particularly
one with the Soul Number **1** who is likely to be highly
energetic – can bring chaos to the family home.

Parental Soul Number 4
Child Soul Number 2
The parent with the Soul Number **4** excels at sorting
out problems. The child with the Soul Number **2** will
always be able to rely on parental support, in spite
of any major set-backs.

Parental Soul Number 4
Child Soul Number 3
If, at times, the child with the Soul Number **3**
is so boastful that friends come to resent him or her,
the parent with the Soul Number **4** will have the
wisdom to correct such behavior.

Parental Soul Number 4
Child Soul Number 4
Both parent and child, sharing the same Soul Number, **4**, are exceedingly practical. There will always be a strong bond between them, too. But the greatest love of all is a love that lets go.

Parental Soul Number 4
Child Soul Number 5
The child with the Soul Number **5** will keep the parent with the Soul Number **4** constantly amused. This parent will learn a lot from the offspring's sheer enthusiasm for life.

Parental Soul Number 4
Child Soul Number 6
The parent with the Soul Number **4** believes there is an unwritten law demanding that everything is kept in its place. The child with the Soul Number **6**, meanwhile, believes that people have to act correctly at all times. They will both have to strive not to overburden themselves with such demands.

Parental Soul Number 4
Child Soul Number 7
The child with this Soul Number is sometimes unwilling to share and this may cause problems with siblings. The parent with the Soul Number **4** will have to correct any such selfish behavior.

Parental Soul Number 4
Child Soul Number 8
Children with the Soul Number **8** often strive to be top of their grade at school in order to please their parents. Providing they can achieve this without overworking, all well and good.

Parental Number 5
Child Soul Number 1
The child with the Soul Number **1** is lucky to have a parent with the Soul Number **5** who is progressive in attitudes. Such parents always have an open mind when it comes to the latest fashions or gismos. The child loves to experiment, and so does the parent.

Parental Number 5
Child Soul Number 2
The parent with the Soul Number **5** excels at passing on information and has lots of patience. The child with the Soul Number **2** will benefit enormously from such instruction.

Parental Number 5
Child Soul Number 3
A child with the Soul Number **3** can be highly creative. The parent with the Soul Number **5** is bound to recognize such talent and encourage it at home. This child needs to be stimulated mentally at all times.

Parental Soul Number 5
Child Soul Number 4
The child with the Soul Number **4** may appear
withdrawn at times but this will change with age, as
the parent with the Soul Number **5** will know
instinctively how to bring out confidence.

Parental Soul Number 5
Child Soul Number 5
Both parent and child will enjoy their times together
enormously. However far apart in later life, they will
remain close because of shared values.

Parental Soul 5
Child Soul Number 6
This is an unusual relationship because it will
sometimes be the child with the Soul Number **6** who
keeps the parent with the Soul Number **5** in check.
Only later will the child learn that parents are
people, too, with innate needs.

Parental Soul Number 5
Child Soul Number 7
Children with the Soul Number **7** are frequently
those who have no second thoughts about
potentially dangerous activities. Fortunately, a
parent with the Soul Number **5** knows how best to
communicate and will be able to warn his or her
child of what might result from carelessness.

Parental Soul Number 5
Child Soul Number 8
The child with the Soul Number **8** is frequently
single-minded. Once he or she is determined to get
something, there is no letting go. The parent with
the Soul Number **5** is well able to cope with this sort
of behavior, however, and should be able to reason
with such a stubborn child.

Parental Soul Number 5
Child Soul Number 9
Children with the Soul Number **9** are often very
helpful at home and will sometimes take on
domestic tasks without even being asked. The
parent responds well to this, believing that everyone
in a family should play his or her part.

Parental Soul Number 6
Child Soul Number 1
Parents with the Soul Number **6** will have to be
careful not to treat the child with the Soul Number **1**
too strictly. Intelligence, remember, sometimes
shows itself in an inability to keep still.

Parental Soul Number 6
Child Soul Number 2
The child with the Soul Number **2** may be unduly
jealous of a sibling. The parent with the Soul
Number **6**, however, has an inborn sense of justice.

Parental Soul Number 6
Child Soul Number 3
As the child with the Soul Number **3** grows up, he or she may start to resent the family background and may want to rebel against it. The parent with the Soul Number **6** will need patience.

Parental Soul Number 6
Child Soul Number 4
The child with the Soul Number **4** is often shy but will go out of his or her way to be helpful to others. The parent with the Soul Number **6** is likely to encourage such kindness and must instill confidence.

Parental Soul Number 6
Child Soul Number 5
The child with this Soul Number will be very considerate towards younger siblings, encouraging them to develop all sorts of skills. The parent with the Soul Number **6**, meanwhile, has to remember not to ask too much of his or her children.

Parental Soul Number 6
Child Soul Number 6
A parent with the Soul Number **6** will have to make an effort to be less exacting as far as demands for good behavior are concerned if the child with the same Soul Number is not to become emotionally withdrawn. Spontaneity should be encouraged.

Parental Soul Number 6
Child Soul Number 7
Children with the Soul Number **7** do not readily stick
to rules. Parents with the Soul Number **6** may find
this very troublesome and need to learn that
intelligent children are often very lively.

Parental Soul Number 6
Child Soul Number 8
The parent with the Soul Number **6** may have to
learn not to be too reserved. The child with the Soul
Number **8** has an inner need to reach great heights
but risks being held back by the parent.

Parental Soul Number 6
Child Soul Number 9
The parent with Soul Number **6** needs to learn to keep
matters in proportion, something the fun-loving child
with the Soul Number **9** finds it far easier to do.

Parental Soul Number 7
Child Soul Number 1
The parent with Soul Number **7** will do well to listen
to the advice of family and friends about child-
rearing. They may have a wealth of experience to
offer, particularly when it comes to dealing with
such a very lively child.

Parental Soul Number 7
Child Soul Number 2
Parents with the Soul Number **7** may sometimes
feel that a child with the Soul Number **2** is unduly
sensitive and crying at nothing. Not everyone, this
parent needs to bear in mind, is as strongly spirited.

Parental Soul Number 7
Child Soul Number 3
A child with the Soul Number **3** is sometimes a
little embarrassed about his or her family. This may
be for any number of reasons – because they are
too rich, too poor, overweight, etc. The parent with
the Soul Number **7** needs to be aware of this and
talk about it.

Parental Soul Number 7
Child Soul Number 4
The child with the Soul Number **4** may be very
emotionally mature at an early age. He or she will
be able to give support to a highly-strung parent.

Parental Soul Number 7
Child Soul Number 5
The child with the Soul Number **5** may turn out to be
precocious, talking at an early age and with
boundless energy. The parent with the Soul Number
7 may not readily know how best to handle talent of
this kind and should not hesitate to seek professional
advice.

Parental Soul Number 7
Child Soul Number 6
A child with the Soul Number **6** may have a tendency to take life too seriously. The parent with the Soul Number **7** may need help with this.

Parental Soul Number 7
Child Soul Number 7
When parent and child both have the same Soul Number, **7**, each may sometimes find that the other's innate obstinacy is intolerable. They will have to learn to respect each other's viewpoints.

Parental Soul Number 7
Child Soul Number 8
This child will always prove supportive to every family member, even at his or her own expense. The parent with the Soul Number **7** risks being unaware of the child's selflessness.

Parental Soul Number 7
Child Soul Number 9
Even as a child, someone with the Soul Number **9** will be resourceful, something that the parent with the Soul Number **7** shares. Both will need to learn that there are times, however, when listening to the advice of reliable people will pay dividends.

Parental Soul Number 8
Child Soul Number 1
A parent with the Soul Number **8** risks being too ambitious for his or her children, even though the glory sought is for the child's own benefit. The child with the Soul Number **1**, in particular, should be allowed to develop at his or her own pace.

Parental Soul Number 8
Child Soul Number 2
The parent with the Soul Number **2** always wants the very best for his or her growing family but must become aware that the "best" for a child with the Soul Number **2** may lie elsewhere.

Parental Soul Number 8
Child Soul Number 3
The child with the Soul Number **3** will always try to achieve what the parent wants for him or her. This parent has the very best of intentions but risks that the child may find frustration at every turn.

Parental Soul Number 8
Child Soul Number 4
This parent is often over-ambitious, while the child with the Soul Number **4** is likely to be content with a quieter, stable life. The parent must take care that he or she does not use the child to fulfil his or her own unfulfilled ambitions.

Parental Soul Number 8
Child Soul Number 5
A child with the Soul Number **5** very often understands that a parent with the Soul Number **8** is only so demanding for the good of the family. Resentment therefore rarely occurs; but when it does, it will not remain unvoiced.

Parental Soul Number 8
Child Soul Number 6
The child with the Soul Number **6** may well feel that it is wrong for a parent with the Soul Number **8** to be so ruthlessly ambitious for the family.

Parental Soul Number 8
Child Soul Number 7
A child with the Soul Number **7** often wants to leave home as early as possible – not because he or she is unhappy as a rule, but where one or both parents have the Soul Number **8**, it could be because too many demands are being made.

Parental Soul Number 8
Child Soul Number 8
Parents with the Soul Number **8** are often very pushy. If the child is innately ambitious, too, this can sometimes lead to early burn-out. Within this relationship, if it is to remain stable, both parent and child need to take life more as it comes.

Parental Soul Number 8
Child Soul Number 9
Too much ambition on the part of a parent with the
Soul Number **8** could easily stifle all the natural flair
and creativity of a child with the Soul Number **9**.
Gentle encouragement is what is required.

Parental Soul Number 9
Child Soul Number 1
Right from the first few months of life, a child with
the Soul Number **1** often seems more alert and
confident than other children. A parent with the Soul
Number **9** will know instinctively how best to
communicate with such a bright baby.

Parental Soul Number 9
Child Soul Number 2
This parent will bring about a warm family
atmosphere. There will always be interesting things
to do for the child with the Soul Number **2** who will
come to develop confidence slowly but surely.

Parental Soul Number 9
Child Soul Number 3
The child with the Soul Number **3** will quickly
become irritable and often have a temper tantrum if
left to his or her own devices. Luckily the parent
with the Soul Number **9** has huge reserves of
energy to cope with this.

Parental Soul Number 9
Child Soul Number 4
The parent with the Soul Number **9** regards parenthood as the most creative profession of all. This is just as well for the child with the Soul Number **4** who will be constantly stimulated by all the effort this parent puts into providing an interesting daily program of activity. There is no risk that this child will not develop to his or her full potential.

Parental Soul Number 9
Child Soul Number 5
The child with the Soul Number **5** is one who loves communicating and will become distressed if boredom is allowed to set in. The parent with the Soul Number **9**, fortunately, is completely unselfish in this respect. However, he or she does need to reserve some personal time and space.

Parental Soul Number 9
Child Soul Number 6
These two personalities will bond right from the time they first set eyes on each other. The child with the Soul Number **6** will always try to please the parent, and the parent will always show great understanding – all this in spite of the fact that in many respects they differ so much.

Parental Soul Number 9
Child Soul Number 7
There may be a risk that a rift will develop if the child with Soul Number **7** does not realize by the time he or she reaches adolescence that even the most selfless parent has a breaking point and should be respected as an individual.

Parental Soul Number 9
Child Soul Number 8
On his or her way to the top, the child with the Soul Number **8** should be careful not to belittle the emotional needs of a parent with the Soul Number **9**. This child should be seen not to take the parent for granted.

Parental Soul Number 9
Child Soul Number 9
Providing that the child with the Soul Number **9** does not become too elitist, this parent and child relationship will certainly flourish and stand each of them in good stead as the years go by. Their bond will last beyond the grave.

NUMEROLOGY AND
THE ZODIAC

NUMEROLOGY AND THE ZODIAC

Ever since ancient times, astrologers have looked at the constellations in the heavens for clues concerning the life of individuals on earth. Fate and personality are said to be determined to some degree by the time and date of birth according to the western system of astrology; and each of us was born under one of twelve zodiac signs that form the astrological calendar.

Learning more about one's zodiac sign will help the individual to understand in greater depth the essence of his or her character and path in life – all the more so if this information is used in conjunction with the principles of numerology.

On pages 278-284, you will find charts listing lucky and unlucky dates under each sign of the zodiac. The dates for each sign are also given. The zodiac – or sign under which you were born – will also temper the characteristics of your Personality Number, achieved simply by taking the date of the month in which you were born.

The following chart shows how each Personality Number profile is modified by an individual's birth sign. In some instances, qualities are strengthened; in others, weakened.

Personality Number 1

Aries They will find that others consider them very opinionated and forceful.

Taurus This individual will be calm, but watch out if anger is roused!

Gemini The sign will make Personality Number 1 even more charismatic.

Cancer There will be signs of vulnerability at times. Moodiness is highlighted.

Leo Pride will be accentuated, and there is a marked sense of responsibility.

Virgo This person is far more practical than might be expected and far less selfish.

Libra One would never know what to expect from a Libran with the Personality Number 1.

Scorpio Most people will find him or her too blatant and indiscrete.

Sagittarius This person is likely to speak too freely at times.

Capricorn This social climber tries to rise to the top without attracting too much attention.

Pisces The individual becomes more grounded when born under this sign.

Personality Number 2

Aries This intrepid character will be prepared to take risks for others.

Taurus A careful approach to life and dependability are accentuated.

Gemini Charm and versatility come to the fore.

Cancer This personality will be sensitive and have a social conscience.

Leo Generosity and lavish hospitality become marked characteristics.

Virgo A painstaking nature and sensuality are highlighted.

Libra Clear opinions will be expressed in a refined way and with charm.

Scorpio This personality will be self-critical and unshockable.

Sagittarius A combination of sign and number that inspires optimism.

Capricorn High but realistic standards will be found, as will loyalty.

Aquarius This personality will show a lot of interest in others and be very caring.

Pisces A willingness always to help others in distress becomes more evident.

Personality Number 3

Aries This personality is sometimes surprisingly keen to defend the vulnerable.

Taurus An inner calm and great patience show themselves.

Gemini Manipulative and gossipy are adjectives that can frequently describe this individual.

Cancer There may be a risk that this personality is too easily hurt.

Leo This individual will have a very mature sense of responsibility.

Virgo Irritability and prudishness may be exaggerated characteristics.

Libra Flirtatious and manipulative, this personality is not influenced for the better.

Scorpio This personality becomes very tenacious and is at times unduly jealous.

Sagittarius Not often prepared to become committed, this individual is very happy-go-lucky.

Capricorn This personality firmly believes his or her way is always the best.

Aquarius A strong belief in human reforms becomes apparent.

Pisces Mystical and escapist interests become highlighted.

Personality Number 4

Aries Selfishness and an unwillingness to listen to others become marked.

Taurus This individual shows great resourcefulness and presence of mind.

Gemini A youthful approach to life and appearance are characteristic.

Cancer This individual may become too introspective for his or her own good.

Leo An unattractive stubbornness and propensity to sulking show themselves.

Virgo This personality may become dogmatic, irritable, and even cranky at times.

Libra The influence of this sign can make the Number **4** personality narcissistic.

Scorpio Vindictiveness may raise its ugly head if
Personality Number **4** is crossed.

Sagittarius This personality will always be prepared
to see the best in others.

Capricorn In a work situation, this personality may
become a slave-driver.

Aquarius This individual may have too much self-
interest at times.

Pisces There is a risk that this personality may take
the blame for everything.

Personality Number 5

Aries This personality tends to be very brash and and
may be disrespected for this.

Taurus A placid nature is instilled by this zodiac sign.

Gemini You will rarely find that this individual can be
accused of any sort of prejudice.

Cancer This individual knows instinctively when
someone needs help.

Leo If given half a chance, this personality will
always accept undue credit.

Virgo Untidiness commonly becomes a failing which
is surprising for this Personality Number.

Libra This personality can be lazy and sulky
sometimes.

Scorpio Very secretive, this individual is often
unnecessarily suspicious of others.

Sagittarius There is a risk that this personality does
not plan ahead sufficiently well.

Capricorn The organizational skills of this
  personality are exceptionally good.

Aquarius A great curiosity about other people and
  what motivates them comes to the fore.

Pisces There is a danger that in certain situations too
  much self-pity will have a negative effect.

Personality Number 6

Aries High energy levels become marked.

Taurus This combination may lead to an insensitivity
  to others.

Gemini There is every chance that this personality
  becomes easily bored.

Cancer This individual can readily become too
  inward-looking for his or her own good.

Leo Too much self-sacrifice has inherent dangers and
  may be resented later.

Virgo There is a risk that this personality may become
  a hypochondriac in middle age.

Libra Firmly held beliefs are greatly strengthened,
  perhaps to the extent of fanaticism.

Scorpio This personality is very kind and understands
  human failings.

Sagittarius The enthusiasm shown is inspiring to
  others at all times.

Capricorn Honest and cautious would best describe
  this personality.

Aquarius A marked lack of confidence may show itself.

Pisces This personality may spend too much time day-
  dreaming.

Personality Number 7

Aries An individual with this combination always likes to be the boss.

Taurus This personality generally ponders too much before acting.

Gemini Nervousness in most social situations may show itself.

Cancer Others will benefit from the protective nature of this individual.

Leo Others may find this personality brags too much and is smug.

Virgo This personality may have a very cold and undemonstrative side.

Libra Fun to be with and charming, this individual can nevertheless be overbearing every now and then.

Scorpio This is a very magnetic personality who, in spite of this, does not readily share his or her friends.

Sagittarius This personality will never hold a grudge against others, whatever they have done.

Capricorn Resentment will be long harbored if this person is driven to anger.

Aquarius This person has a very powerful intellect which should be carefully channelled.

Pisces There can be a tendency for this individual to be very temperamental for no obvious cause.

Personality Number 8

Aries This personality will not know the meaning of the word "failure."

Taurus When this personality is roused to anger, it is an exhausting experience for everyone within earshot, whether involved or not.

Gemini Inwardly, this personality often feels very alone and helpless.

Cancer This person develops a hard outer shell as protection against a feeling of insecurity.

Leo Love and recognition are craved by this seemingly confident personality.

Virgo In spite of a confident appearance, this individual may fear not being good enough for the job or for his or her partner.

Libra This personality is sometimes terrified of being left on his or her own,

Scorpio It will often be difficult for others to understand this intractable personality.

Sagittarius This personality may be a gambler at heart who likes to take risks.

Capricorn A respect for authority shows itself, whoever is in power.

Aquarius There may be an unwillingness to share ideas or knowledge of any kind.

Pisces A tendency to exaggerate and sensationalize may show itself.

Personality Number 9

Aries Whatever may be said of others, this personality will believe the best of them.

Taurus This personality risks losing self-esteem through too much self-indulgence.

Gemini risk of becoming too non-committal arises due to the influence of the sign of the twins.

Cancer This individual may be very easily hurt and tends to take umbridge when none is meant.

Leo No one has a sunnier disposition and more generous nature.

Virgo When the right partner comes along, a strong sexuality will show itself.

Libra This personality has a quick temper but the storm soon blows over.

Sagittarius There is a tendency for this individual to preach at everyone.

Capricorn This individual has a morbid fear of making a fool of himself and so does not act naturally for a lot of the time.

Aquarius Not one to be part of a crowd, this personality is somewhat perverse and eccentric.

Pisces This personality risks a sense of failure if any of the opportunities that present themselves are not taken up.

LUCKY AND UNLUCKY NUMBERS

LUCKY AND UNLUCKY DATES

Finding your lucky dates

These tables are organized in accordance with the twelve signs of the zodiac. They show which dates in each month are unlucky and lucky for you. For example, if you were born on April **5**, you can see that the lucky dates for you in the month of January are **1**, **5**, **9**, **23**, **27**, and **28**.

Birth dates

A birthday is never unlucky for anyone. So if you find your birth date listed in the unlucky column, simply transfer it to the lucky column. For example, if you were born on **April 17**, your lucky dates for April would be **1**, **5**, **14**, **15**, **17**, **19**, and **28**.

ARIES
March 21 – April 19

	Unlucky dates	Lucky dates
January	6, 16, 26, 29	1, 5, 9, 23, 27, 28
February	8, 15, 16, 23	2, 5, 10, 19, 25, 29
March	3, 6, 15, 21	4, 9, 10, 19, 20, 31
April	2, 3, 17, 30	1, 5, 14, 15, 19, 28
May	8, 14, 27, 28	3, 12, 13, 18, 21, 31
June	4, 5, 23, 26	3, 7, 17, 18, 25, 27
July	2, 4, 30, 31	1, 6, 14, 23, 28, 29
August	6, 12, 22, 23	2, 10, 11, 24, 25, 26
September	2, 23, 24, 26	7, 10, 11, 12, 21, 25
October	6, 14, 26, 27	3, 9, 13, 17, 19, 31
November	6, 18, 22, 29	1, 5, 8, 14, 20, 30
December	6, 12, 22, 28	1, 13, 25, 26, 27, 31

TAURUS
April 20 – May 20

	Unlucky dates	Lucky dates
January	2, 10, 24, 30	5, 7, 11, 15, 17, 25
February	19, 20, 22, 23	3, 5, 6, 7, 24, 28
March	3, 24, 25, 28	1, 10, 17, 19, 20, 29
April	14, 16, 19, 27	3, 7, 12, 24, 25, 29
May	11, 13, 24, 26	1, 5, 6, 9, 23, 27
June	3, 6, 18, 19	1, 5, 9, 14, 15, 27
July	5, 6, 18, 20	2, 7, 8, 17, 21, 31
August	1, 9, 28, 28	12, 13, 14, 22, 26, 31
September	5, 11, 25, 29	1, 12, 22, 26, 27, 30
October	10, 11, 24, 25	5, 6, 7, 20, 21, 26
November	5, 9, 20, 27	3, 7, 8, 13, 22, 29
December	1, 12, 22, 28	3, 5, 13, 20, 25, 31

GEMINI
May 21 – June 20

	Unlucky dates	Lucky dates
January	4, 5, 11, 26	1, 9, 19, 20, 27, 28
February	1, 2, 28, 29	5, 6, 11, 21, 23, 25
March	7, 19, 28, 29	6, 9, 15, 20, 30, 31
April	15, 19, 20, 22	1, 5, 7, 16, 17, 24
May	14, 21, 23, 26	3, 6, 7, 17, 24, 25
June	11, 16, 17, 27	3, 7, 9, 13, 25, 26
July	7, 8, 15, 20	2, 9, 10, 19, 23, 29
August	4, 11, 17, 22	7, 14, 21, 24, 25, 27
September	1, 6, 14, 22	3, 11, 12, 17, 21, 26
October	5, 8, 11, 27	1, 9, 17, 19, 23, 28
November	3, 7, 22, 28	5, 9, 15, 23, 24, 30
December	5, 6, 19, 27	1, 7, 11, 12, 21, 25

CANCER
June 22nd – July 22nd

	Unlucky dates	Lucky dates
January	6, 8, 27, 28	3, 9, 11, 13, 16, 29
February	3, 11, 24, 25	7, 8, 13, 14, 22, 27
March	1, 4, 22, 26	5, 7, 12, 20, 21, 25
April	5, 19, 20, 25	2, 7, 8, 12, 13, 29
May	3, 17, 23, 30	1, 5, 10, 11, 18, 19
June	13, 19, 20, 22	2, 7, 10, 15, 24, 28
July	10, 13, 23, 28	3, 4, 7, 20, 22, 25
August	7, 12, 19, 20	5, 8, 9, 21, 22, 30
September	3, 10, 16, 17	5, 12, 13, 19, 27, 28
October	7, 14, 27, 28	1, 3, 11, 15, 16, 30
November	8, 9, 18, 19	6, 7, 16, 17, 27, 30
December	6, 7, 18, 21	4, 9, 13, 24, 30, 31

LEO
July 23rd – August 21st

	Unlucky dates	Lucky dates
January	3, 8, 12, 30	1, 4, 13, 15, 18, 27
February	8, 12, 21, 28	1, 15, 20, 24, 25, 29
March	12, 22, 24, 25	9, 18, 19, 20, 21, 28
April	7, 8, 16, 22	1, 5, 10, 11, 18, 23
May	5, 18, 19, 24	2, 3, 6, 12, 13, 31
June	2, 14, 21, 22	3, 4, 13, 17, 26, 30
July	12, 13, 24, 25	2, 6, 9, 14, 23, 29
August	9, 14, 21, 22	3, 7, 10, 23, 25, 30
September	5, 17, 18, 19	3, 15, 16, 22, 26, 29
October	9, 14, 15, 29	1, 13, 17, 27, 28, 31
November	5, 12, 13, 17	9, 10, 15, 20, 23, 27
December	3, 9, 23, 28	7, 11, 16, 18, 22, 26

VIRGO
August 22nd – September 22nd

	Unlucky dates	Lucky dates
January	4, 11, 18, 19	1, 3, 9, 15, 20, 31
February	8, 15, 16, 29	3, 12, 13, 18, 23, 27
March	6, 7, 26, 27	1, 11, 20, 21, 28, 29
April	2, 3, 9, 29	7, 8, 15, 17, 24, 25
May	8, 21, 27, 28	4, 7, 10, 18, 22, 31
June	3, 9, 16, 24	1, 6, 7, 11, 15, 29
July	2, 14, 20, 22	4, 9, 10, 17, 25, 30
August	10, 17, 18, 23	3, 5, 12, 22, 28, 29
September	7, 8, 17, 21	4, 9, 10, 22, 23, 28
October	4, 8, 14, 20	1, 2, 11, 12, 25, 30
November	5, 7, 12, 21	17, 18, 22, 23, 25, 30
December	4, 5, 6, 14	9, 10, 18, 23, 26, 28

LIBRA
September 23rd – October 23rd

	Unlucky dates	Lucky dates
January	6, 7, 21, 23	1, 5, 9, 19, 20, 27
February	11, 17, 19, 22	2, 6, 15, 20, 24, 29
March	2, 9, 10, 28	4, 14, 18, 23, 27, 31
April	4, 5, 14, 26	1, 15, 19, 23, 24, 28
May	3, 9, 23, 29	7, 8, 12, 17, 21, 24
June	7, 19, 20, 27	8, 12, 13, 16, 22, 30
July	10, 17, 27, 29	4, 14, 19, 20, 23, 28
August	12, 13, 22, 27	1, 7, 10, 11, 15, 30
September	8, 16, 17, 24	3, 6, 11, 20, 22, 29
October	8, 12, 20, 21	4, 5, 17, 22, 24, 27
November	9, 17, 28, 29	1, 4, 6, 14, 19, 26
December	4, 7, 15, 19	3, 12, 13, 21, 25, 29

SCORPIO
October 24th – November 22nd

	Unlucky dates	Lucky dates
January	10, 16, 18, 24	2, 3, 7, 8, 22
February	1, 12, 14, 20	3, 9, 17, 18, 24, 27
March	3, 11, 19, 30	1, 6, 15, 20, 25, 29
April	7, 8, 26, 28	2, 3, 12, 17, 21, 29
May	4, 6, 24, 26	5, 10, 11, 15, 19, 27
June	2, 8, 26, 28	6, 11, 15, 19, 23, 25
July	3, 8, 19, 31	4, 7, 9, 17, 21, 30
August	2, 12, 22, 28	5, 9, 13, 17, 18, 27
September	11, 14, 18, 29	9, 10, 12, 23, 27, 28
October	8, 9, 22	2, 3, 11, 20, 25, 29
November	5, 12, 18, 29	2, 6, 16, 17, 23, 30
December	25, 12, 18, 29	2, 6, 16, 17, 23, 30

SAGITTARIUS
November 23rd – December 21st

	Unlucky dates	Lucky dates
January	6, 12, 18, 22	1, 9, 14, 15, 23, 24
February	8, 15, 16, 23	3, 5, 7, 19, 21, 28
March	6, 7, 15, 21	5, 8, 10, 19, 23, 31
April	3, 18, 22, 26	4, 14, 15, 19, 20, 28
May	7, 14, 15, 27	1, 12, 16, 20, 26, 31
June	3, 11, 23, 24	7, 8, 13, 17, 21, 25
July	7, 20, 23, 29	6, 11, 15, 21, 22, 25
August	4, 12, 18, 28	3, 6, 7, 14, 15, 29
September	13, 17, 20, 22	1, 10, 12, 15, 26, 29
October	11, 12, 18, 26	4, 5, 22, 23, 27, 31
November	6, 14, 15, 22	9, 19, 20, 23, 24, 28
December	6, 11, 18, 28	3, 7, 8, 17, 22, 25

CAPRICORN
December 22nd – January 20th

	Unlucky dates	Lucky dates
January	11, 14, 15, 28	2, 7, 8, 18, 26, 31
February	11, 18, 24, 25	3, 7, 9, 12, 13, 27
March	8, 16, 17, 23	1, 5, 7, 10, 24, 28
April	12, 13, 19, 20	2, 3, 7, 16, 25, 26
May	10, 16, 29, 30	5, 6, 14, 15, 27, 31
June	5, 13, 22, 26	1, 14, 15, 18, 24, 29
July	2, 11, 16, 24	9, 12, 13, 17, 20, 27
August	6, 18, 19, 29	3, 8, 9, 16, 21, 31
September	1, 3, 17, 23	5, 9, 14, 18, 19, 27
October	8, 12, 21, 27	10, 11, 16, 17, 25, 30
November	10, 17, 18, 25	6, 7, 8, 12, 13, 26
December	2, 6, 11, 30	3, 8, 9, 19, 24, 31

AQUARIUS
January 21st – February 19th

	Unlucky dates	Lucky dates
January	2, 19, 24, 31	1, 5, 9, 10, 15, 20
February	13, 20, 26, 27	2, 5, 6, 11, 16, 29
March	11, 19, 24, 25	3, 6, 7, 10, 17, 30
April	7, 14, 15, 24	4, 5, 10, 20, 23, 29
May	4, 12, 18, 19	7, 8, 16, 17, 25, 31
June	1, 2, 28, 29	5, 12, 17, 18, 25, 26
July	5, 12, 13, 26	10, 11, 19, 22, 23, 28
August	2, 22, 23, 27	10, 14, 19, 20, 24, 25
September	4, 5, 19, 25	10, 11, 12, 22, 29, 30
October	2, 8, 11, 26	1, 3, 9, 13, 27, 28
November	11, 18, 26, 27	4, 5, 10, 15, 23, 28
December	9, 16, 17, 24	7, 8, 13, 21, 25, 27

PISCES
February 20th – March 20th

	Unlucky dates	Lucky dates
January	8, 16, 23, 28	5, 7, 9, 21, 22, 27
February	5, 10, 22, 25	4, 7, 9, 20, 21, 26
March	11, 15, 18, 26	5, 6, 12, 13, 17, 29
April	9, 12, 20, 23	6, 8, 11, 15, 22, 30
May	4, 17, 20, 28	8, 14, 15, 19, 24, 29
June	6, 18, 24, 28	10, 11, 19, 21, 23, 27
July	8, 21, 25, 26	11, 15, 20, 22, 24, 31
August	4, 5, 19, 25	13, 16, 17, 20, 28, 30
September	3, 8, 18, 26	15, 17, 19, 24, 27, 28
October	4, 6, 8, 28	17, 19, 20, 21, 29, 30
November	1, 12, 18, 24	8, 9, 10, 14, 19, 21
December	11, 16, 20, 29	3, 7, 9, 13, 22, 28

UNLUCKY DAYS OF THE YEAR

It is considered unlucky to commence work, start a journey, fall ill, or get married on the following days:

January	1, 2, 4, 5, 10, 15, 17, 29
February	8, 10, 17, 26, 27, 28
March	16, 17, 20
April	7, 8, 10, 16, 20, 21
May	3, 6, 7, 15, 20
June	4, 8, 10, 22
July	15, 21
August	1, 19, 20, 29, 30
September	2, 4, 6, 7, 21, 23
October	4, 6, 16, 24
November	5, 6, 15, 20, 29, 30
December	6, 7, 9, 15, 22

SUPERSTITIONS

Many beliefs still surround certain numbers,
particularly most of those between **1** and **13**. The
following pages provide a guide to some of the most
curious of these. Note that some numbers have far
more beliefs surrounding them than others.

1

It is unlucky to walk about in just **one** slipper.

Only keep money in **one** pocket or you will lose it.

See **one** magpie and there will be sorrow.

Seeing **one** white horse will bring bad luck.

A **one**-eyed person has magical powers.

People with **one** hand are clairvoyant.

You will have bad luck if you give someone just
one primrose.

It is unlucky to take **one** violet indoors.

It is a good omen for a shepherd to have just **one** black
sheep in his flock.

Break **one** egg accidentally and you will break a leg.

2

Two people should never pour tea from the same pot.

If you place **two** teaspoons by mistake on the same saucer, there will soon be a wedding in the family.

If you get **two** holes in the same sock in a week, you will receive a surprise.

If **two** crows fly over a house, there will be a wedding.

If you see **two** white horses together, this brings very good luck.

Rub **two** horseshoes together for good luck.

If you catch **two** rats in the same trap, this is fortuitous.

If you see **two** ravens together, this brings happiness.

If **two** people sneeze at the same time, this brings good luck for both of them.

If a girl lets a man pour her a **second** cup of tea, she will succumb to his advances.

If you wear **two** odd socks in different colors, this protects against the evil eye.

If **two** letters cross in the mail, this is unlucky.

If **two** shoots grow from the single root of a cabbage, this brings good luck.

If you have a **two**-dollar bill, tear off a corner for good luck. Someone who gets it next should tear off another corner, as should the third recipient. The fourth person to receive it should tear it up to avoid bad luck.

It is unlucky for **two** people to kindle a fire.

Breaking **two** eggs accidentally is a sign that your love is true.

If you find an egg with **two** yolks, it is likely there will be a death in the family of the owner of the chicken that laid the egg.

If a girl puts a **two**-leaf clover in her right shoe, she will marry someone with the same name as the man she sees next.

3

If you break **three** eggs accidentally, bad luck is forecast.

If you see **three** butterflies on one leaf, this does not augur well.

Spit **three** times to prevent an audience with the devil.

Sneeze **three** times in quick succession and it is a sign that you have just told the truth.

The **third** finger of the left hand is said to be able to heal a wound.

If you see **three** ravens, there will be a wedding.

If an owl hoots **three** times, there will be misfortune.

It is unlucky for a smoker to light **three** cigarettes from the same match.

In Turkey, many people believe you should eat with **three** fingers as the devil is said to eat with two.

A **third** attempt at anything is said to be lucky.

The presence of a **three**-colored cat will help to protect a home from fire.

Three magpies seen together foretells a safe journey.

If a cat washes its ears **three** times, you can expect visitors from the direction it is facing.

To see an image of a future spouse, a man must eat a whole salted herring in **three** mouthfuls and go to bed silently, without drinking.

If a girl puts **three** carnations in her hair, she should note if the top one dies first. In this case, the last years of her life will be hard. If all **three** die together, she will have bad luck throughout her life.

4

If you find **four** streaks in a pansy petal, this means your wishes will come true.

A **four**-leaf clover is very lucky.

If **four** loaves fuse together while you are baking, there will be a wedding.

If you see **four** ravens together, there will be a birth.

A good hand of cards is said never to contain the **four** of clubs.

5

A **five**-leaf clover is thought by some to bring bad luck and by others to be a good omen.

An outstretched hand with **five** spread fingers is thought to turn away evil influences.

A **five**-pointed star or pentagram is said to be lucky.

The Greeks believed it was unlucky even to say the word for **five**.

If **five** loaves fuse together while baking, this is said to mean a funeral will take place.

6

Gambling before **6pm** on a Friday is said to be unlucky.

If you find **six** streaks in a pansy, this means you will get a surprise.

For the ancient Greeks, **six** was a talisman against storms.

7

If your date of birth is divisible by **seven**, you will have a particularly lucky life.

Do not sing before **7**am or you will cry before **11**am.

If a young woman is looking for a husband, she should stick **seven** needles into a candle and while it burns, she should pray to the Virgin Mary until the candle goes out.

Do not shatter a mirror or you will have **seven** years of bad luck.

If a woman wraps a belt **seven** times around a tree, she will be fertile.

The **seventh** son of a **seventh** son is said to have psychic powers.

8

If you get ill on the **eighth** day of a new moon, death may result.

The Chinese favor **eight** as it it the number of their traditional Immortals and the orientations of *Feng Shui*.

9

If you find **nine** peas in a pod, this is thought to be very lucky.

If you find **nine** streaks on a pansy petal, you will have a lot of changes in your life and, finally, riches.

If an unmarried girl finds **nine** peas in a pod, she should place the pod on the kitchen door. The first man who then comes into the kitchen will be her husband.

If a young man wants to marry, he should count **99** stars for **nine** days. On the morning of the tenth day, he will then see his bride.

The **nine** of diamonds is an unlucky card in Scotland.

13

Having **thirteen** letters in your name is said to be unlucky.

Having a house number **13** is widely thought unlucky.

Elsewhere, Friday **13th** of any month is said to be very unlucky.

It is unlucky to have **thirteen** people at a dinner party.

OTHER SUPERSTITIONS

For every falling leaf caught between September **29**
(Michaelmas) and Halloween (October **31**) there will
be a happy day in the coming year.

It will bring bad luck if you give an even number of
flowers in a bouquet.

According to one superstition, a man and his wife can
calculate which of them will die first by taking the
numerical value of each letter in their respective first
names and then adding them together. If the result is an
odd number, the woman will die first. If the result is an
even number, the man will die first. The table on page
102 can be used to make this calculation.

The number **666** is thought to be the number of Satan
and most people would try to avoid this as part of a
vehicle registration number or apartment.

UNLUCKY DAYS AND THE MOON

Unlucky days associated with the moon
This table shows unlucky days for each month of the year, dependent on how old the moon is at any particular time. For example, bad luck occurs in April, when the moon is five and eight days old.

Month	Number of days old the moon
January	Three or four days old.
February	Five or seven days old.
March	Six or seven days old.
April	Five or eight days old.
May	Nine days old.
June	Fifteen days old.
July	Thirteen days old.
August	Thirteen days old.
September	Eight or thirteen days old.
October	Five or twelve days old.
November	Five or nine days old.
December	Three or thirteen days old.

10 DAYS AFTER A FULL MOON

THE FIRST TEN DAYS AFTER A FULL MOON

Day	Superstitions
One	A good day to begin a new venture. Children born on this day will be happy, prosperous, and will live long. If you are sick you will have to endure much discomfort.
Two	A good day to sow seeds, plow, buy or sell anything, or take a sea voyage.
Three	An unlucky day. Children born on the third day will not live long. Criminals are likely to get caught in their undertakings.
Four	A good day for politicians to have been born. A good day to start building construction.
Five	A good day for a woman to conceive. The weather on this day will determine the weather for the rest of the month.
Six	A good day to go fishing or hunting.
Seven	A good day for partners to meet and fall in love.
Eight	A dangerous day to fall sick.
Nine	If the moon falls on your face on the ninth day, you may go mad or have your features distorted.
Ten	People born on this day are restless wanderers.

LUCKY DAYS TO GET MARRIED

WHEN TO MARRY

The day of the week

Monday for wealth,
Tuesday for health,
Wednesday the best day of all.
Thursday for losses,
Friday for crosses,
And Saturday no luck at all.

Lucky wedding days

January	2, 4, 11, 19, 21
February	1, 3, 10, 19, 21
March	3, 5, 13, 20, 23
April	2, 4, 12, 20, 22
May	2, 4, 20, 23
June	1, 3, 11, 19, 21
July	1, 3, 12, 19, 21, 31
August	2, 11, 18, 20, 30
September	1, 9, 16, 18, 28
October	1, 8, 15, 17, 27, 29
November	5, 11, 13, 22, 25
December	1, 8, 10, 19, 23, 29

Unlucky times to marry
- On your birthday.
- On the same day or in the same year as your sister.
- While you are still young.
- After sunset.

EVERYDAY LIFE

7

EDUCATION

The type of education to which a child might best be
suited and the subjects at which he or she may excel
can be assessed via the Personality Number, according
to some schools of numerology. This sort of indication
should not be taken as anything other than a pointer
toward possible natural talents, however. If spotted
early enough and then nurtured, these talents will
surely blossom. Again, you can find the Personality
Number by taking the day of birth in any month or
year. For example, someone born on August **4**th will
have the Personality Number **4**. The following charts
can then be consulted.

Personality Number 1
These children are such individuals that they will
benefit from learning how to be part of a team
from an early age. Having to wear a school
uniform may help with this. They may soon
show skills at writing stories and acting.
Teachers may need to use a strong hand at times
to keep them under control.

Personality Number 2

A child with the Personality Number **2** is often very sensitive and may be shy to ask about anything he or she does not understand. A teacher will need to keep an eye on progress, and the parent will do well to see that the child does not worry unduly about school work. This child will always try hard and needs to be rewarded with lots of praise for efforts made.

Personality Number 3

Full of fun and very communicative, the child with the Personality Number **3** will benefit from an education that permits lots of free expression. He or she will sometimes excel at reading and debating, as well as sports. They will find it hard to sit still unless they are given an outlet for their boundless energy. Math may often be a strong point, too, as well as music.

Personality Number 4
Children with this Personality Number are sometimes reluctant to start school and let go of the parental hand but they soon make friends. Then there is no stopping them – they thrive at school and cannot wait to get back after the summer vacations. Subjects they particularly enjoy include math, computer studies, and science. They usually make excellent students and are quick to grasp new concepts.

Personality Number 5
A child with this Personality Number often finds it hard to concentrate. This is probably a sign of a particularly lively and enquiring mind, however. This child is impatient for answers to his or her numerous questions. A strong interest in science, history, and geography is likely. Children with the Personality Number 5 also often go on to excel in technology.

Personality Number 6

Possibly one of the most popular in the class, a child with the Personality Number **6** will show great kindness towards others and usualy proves to be an excellent team member. This is a child who will benefit greatly from education that involves an element of competition. A parent should check that this child is not finding classwork too easy or boring.

Personality Number 7

Children with the Personality Number **7** may have very highly developed imaginations and show skills at writing stories. They may be quiet in class and will benefit from one-to-one tuition whenever possible. They may find it easy to learn a foreign language and have musical talents. They should be encouraged to take part in team sports and to have a wide circle of friends.

Personality Number 8
Full of confidence, this child is likely to become
a class leader and will be prepared to stand up
for his or her rights. Shyness is no problem.
Academically, too, the child with the Personality
Number **8** tends to forge ahead and get excellent
grades without too much effort. Work is always
well presented.

Personality Number 9
The child with this Personality Number will
thrive in an atmosphere that allows him or her
free rein. Too much discipline may prove stifling
to such an extravert. This child will readily take
to finding his or her own information, and will
enjoy doing research for school projects.
However, he or she will not thrive in a class
where any degree of unruly behavior is taken to
extremes. Liveliness is one thing; disobedience
and rebellion, another.

CAREERS

Choice of career is one of the most difficult decisions most people ever have to make. Those who are multi-talented find it particularly hard; and some may find themselves having to switch the type of work they do in middle life through personal circumstances. Linking the Life Number to particular professions is sometimes very helpful in this respect. The charts that follow provide a summary of the type of work best suited to each Life Number. (If you need to be reminded how to calculate this number from your date of birth, turn back to page 82).

Life Number 1
Those with this Life Number are blessed with tremendous creativity and leadership skills. Careers in the worlds of fashion, design, journalism, technology, the stage, and the film industry are all highlighted.

Life Number 2
Medicine, social work, and local or national government are all careers that may appeal to those with the Life Number **2** since they are frequently best employed in the service of others. This brings them far more satisfaction than substantial financial rewards.

Life Number 3
Those with the Life Number 3 are full of confidence and enjoy being in the limelight. They often make superb entertainers, models, tour guides, hoteliers, television presenters, professional athletes, or sportsmen. They rarely thrive in jobs where they would need to work in complete isolation.

Life Number 4
This Life Number endows an individual with very practical gifts and an eye for detail. This is why they would do well to choose a career path involving accountancy, banking, engineering, driving, building work, or computing. Those with the Life Number 4 prefer only to take calculated risks.

Life Number 5
Public relations executives, sales managers, politicians, photographers, television and radio presenters all require skills that frequently come with the Life Number 5. Those with this Life Number are essentially good communicators.

Life Number 6
Teaching, lecturing, the prison service, medicine, the law, nursing, the ambulance and fire services, the police – all will appeal to those with the Life Number **6** who enjoy working for the community at large and as part of a team.

Life Number 7
With a deep understanding of others' needs combined with remarkable intuition, those who have the Life Number **7** often make excellent therapists, counsellors, doctors, nurses, beauticians, housekeepers, personal trainers, cosmetic surgeons, dieticians, secretaries, or hairdressers.

Life Number 8
Such strongly individualistic personalities may find they succeed in the world of business. They make excellent chief executive officers of large companies, but may prefer to work in a smaller company where their innate financial acumen will also stand them in good stead. Even as a sole trader, they will show good business sense.

Life Number 9
Counselling, child guidance, interpreting, journalism, broadcasting, teaching – these are typical careers in which someone with the Life Number **9** may excel and which would be spiritually rewarding for them.

CAREER DIRECTORY

Consult the following list to see which careers are most likely to be suited to certain Life Numbers.

Accountancy	4	Journalist	1
Actor	1	Law enforcement	6
Architect	1	Lawyer	6
Banker	4	Model	3
Builder	4	Nurse	6
Business	8	Politics	2, 5
Chef	2	Real estate agent	5
Computing	4	Sales	5
Designer	1	Secretary	7
Doctor	2	Stockbroker	8
Engineer	4	Surgeon	2
Hairdresser	7	Teacher	6, 9
Hotelier	3	Television presenter	3, 9

You can find out more about the world of work in the section starting on page 356.

HEALTH

According to some schools of numerology, you may be prone to certain physical or emotional conditions according to your Life Number. Once you become aware of certain weaknesses, however, you may be able to do a lot to strengthen your immune system and general state of health. To find out your Life Number, turn back to page 82. The following charts provide a basic guide to the way in which a Life Number can affect your well-being.

Life Number 1
There may be so much concern over achieving ambitions that this individual risks neglecting his or her physical health. Those with the Life Number 1 should remember that physical exercise is often an excellent means of relieving high levels of stress.

Life Number 2
Those with this Life Number are often great worriers. Excessive anxiety may produce certain physical symptoms, too. Meditation may prove an excellent way of achieving a state of calm and produce all-round physical benefits.

Life Number 3
The sheer enthusiasm for life shared by people with this Life Number goes a long way toward keeping them healthy. They need to be wary, however, of cramming too much activity into their day on a regular basis so that they begin to tire easily.

Life Number 4
Taking on too much responsibility may wear this individual down so that he or she finds it difficult to sleep. Those with this Life Number need to pace themselves and must avoid becoming workaholics.

Life Number 5
Even when driven to distraction by an annoying situation, it is important for someone with the Life Number 5 to try to remain calm. High levels of stress bring with them risk of critical physical reactions.

Life Number 6
Prevention, this individual needs to remember,
is infinitely preferable to the need for a cure.
Overconcern for the welfare of others
sometimes means that those with the Life
Number **6** forget the principles of a healthy
lifestyle when it comes to themselves.

Life Number 7
Those with the Life Number **7** are usually very
much in tune with their bodies and can tell
immediately if something is not quite right.
They tend to know instinctively, too, which
foods to take to ensure maximum energy levels.

Life Number 8
Others may consider that those with the Life
Number 8 are physically very strong; but
reserves of energy may become severely
depleted in times of stress. Attention to
maintenance of a well-balanced diet is essential.
We are, after all, what we eat.

Life Number 9
These individuals are generally very unselfish
and therefore have a tendency to neglect their
own welfare while ensuring that their nearest
and dearest thrive. They need to remember to
stay well if others are to be able to continue to
rely on them.

FOOD PREFERENCES

The skilled numerologist may be able to assess an
individual's Personality Number simply by taking note
of his or her food preferences. This is also something
you could try after mastering the techniques outlined in
this book. Consult the following charts for an
indication of the sort of dishes favored by Personality
Numbers **1-9**.

Personality Number 1
Those with the Personality Number **1** often
enjoy trying foods that are entirely new to them
since their palates easily become bored. They
like food to be very well presented and will not
stint if it comes to paying a lot for exceptional
cuisine. Lobster, game, exotic fruits and
vegetables, and vintage wines please them most.

Personality Number 2
Comforting thick soups, rich desserts, creamed potatoes, and all sorts of milk dishes are certain to delight those with the Personality Number **2**. Home-made brown bread and cheeses of all kinds are enjoyed, as is pasta. This personality loves preparing nutritious meals just as much as partaking of them.

Personality Number 3
This personality likes to nibble throughout the day and prefers snacks to sitting down to an enormous, elaborate meal. A selection of *tapas* and good bottle of wine will suffice. Those with the Personality Number **3** rarely spend a lot of time in the kitchen even when they have a family, and mealtimes are always very relaxed affairs.

Personality Number 4
Throughout this book, you will have found how passionate and energetic those with the Personality Number **4** usually are. They are equally enthusiastic about food and regard it as a very important part of their lives. They relish the prospect of new culinary experiences and there are always interesting foodstuffs in the refrigerator. They cook with love.

Personality Number 5
Those with the Personality Number **5** are so energetic that they hardly sit down to eat and risk indigestion because they often survive on snatched meals. Most people would pile on the pounds if they survived on such a poor diet; but this personality is constantly on the go and burns up calories in no time. Chocolate is frequently a staple part of the daily intake, too.

Personality Number 6
Very sociable and giving, someone with the Personality Number **6** likes nothing more than to entertain and provide an impressive meal. The only trouble is that it may require days of preparation. But those with this Personality Number like to please their friends and to be praised for their hospitality.

Personality Number 7
Those with the Personality Number **7** are wizards in the kitchen. Give them just a few ingredients and they can whisk up something truly delicious and imaginative in less than no time. Their meals are simple but wholesome, and they usually have a considerable repertoire of dishes. The meals they prepare are always well seasoned and very tasty, but they rarely use a cookbook.

Personality Number 8
If you find that someone's kitchen is unusually well organized, the chances are he or she is has the Personality Number **8**. These people are confident cooks and will bravely experiment with exotic ingredients. They enjoy entertaining and expect their guests to be highly complimentary about what they serve. They may have a superb reputation for a particular dish; but then they may well have created this reputation themselves.

Personality Number 9
Inspired cooks who often make up their own recipes, those with the Personality Number **9** can sometimes be very critical of the culinary concoctions of others. They may also be fanatical about hygiene in the kitchen and strict about the table manners of a growing family. Spaghetti, risotto, kebabs, and desserts that require precise timing, such as meringues, are among their favorite dishes.

SEXUALITY

An individual's sexual needs and preferences are frequently influenced by the Personality Number, so some numerologists consider. Finding out a partner's Personality Number may therefore improve this aspect of the relationship. The chances are anyway that each partner will already be aware of the other's Personality Number because it is simply the day of any month in any year in which we were born. If, as demonstrated throughout relevant sections within this part of the book, you were born on May **5th**, for example, then your Personality Number will be **5**. Study the following charts if you would like to discover more about the sexuality of those you love.

Personality Number 1
Those with this Personality Number, whether male or female, usually like to take the initiative in a physical relationship. They will often go to considerable trouble to create a romantic atmosphere. Woe betide any unfaithful partner if he or she ever confesses or is found out! This personality does not readily condone disloyalty.

Personality Number 2

Very warm and caring by nature, those with the Personality Number **2** make very considerate lovers and go out of their way to please – once, that is, they feel entirely confident within a relationship. This is not the sort of individual who would enjoy a one-night stand. It takes time for trust to develop but the patient partner will find the wait worthwhile.

Personality Number 3

Those with the Personality Number **3** readily see the funny side of sex and are generally able to put a nervous partner at ease. They like to express their emotions physically, and hug at every opportunity. They rarely fail to greet their partner with a kiss and expect physical demonstrations of a partner's affection, too.

Personality Number 4

Passionate by nature and ardent lovers, those with the Personality Number **4** will be completely loyal providing there is no evidence of infidelity on the part of the life partner. Even after 40 years of marriage, they may still find excitement in the marriage partner's arms and will make that partner feel wanted.

Personality Number 5
Sometimes very demanding of a partner's
affections, particularly physically, this
personality may soon become bored with his or
her love life if some element of variety is not
introduced. They tend to be as adventurous in the
bedroom as they are in every other aspect of life,
and as energetic.

Personality Number 6
Physically very demonstrative, those with the
Personality Number **6** enjoy showing their
partners just how attractive they find them and
excel at boosting sexual confidence in those
who might otherwise be a little shy. If the
partner so much as even admires anyone else,
however, jealousy will raise its ugly head.

Personality Number 7
Those with this Personality Number have very
good imaginations and can find comfort in the
arms of even the clumsiest of lovers. But they are
easily hurt and will become very resentful if they
suspect a wandering eye. If they become moody
or withdrawn, a partner will do well not to
complain but should wait for this phase to pass, as
it will soon enough.

Personality Number 8
This is another personality that often likes to take control of love-making, not only at the beginning of the relationship. The partner will have to fall in with his or her needs if this couple are to remain together. When two people with this Personality Number become involved, sparks may fly, but the relationship will be all the more exciting as a result.

Personality Number 9
Highly creative, the partner with the Personality Number **9** will always try to extend this gift to love-making. However, those with the Personality Number **9** are known to be very critical of others on many fronts and any behavior deemed too unconventional or bizarre will not be tolerated. A very adventurous sexual partner might even consider a slightly less imaginative partner with the Personality Number **9** to be prudish.

BIORHYTHM

Definition

Using three human energy cycles – physical, emotional, and intellectual, collectively known as biorhythm – to predict the times of high and low energy.

History

Dr. H. Swoboda and Dr. W. Fliess in Vienna and Berlin respectively, developed the theory of biorhythm.

How does it work?

Beginning at birth, our emotional, physical, and mental activities follow cycles of slightly different length. These can be printed out on a graph and indicate days of high and low energy and times when we are most vulnerable, say, to accidents. Using an on-going biorhythm chart, problems can be avoided by taking advantage of high-energy periods and resting during low-energy periods.

Biorhythm charts do not determine what will happen; they only indicate your probable disposition and can be useful when planning ahead.

The cycles

The creation and discharge of energy by living things is a fundamental of biological theory. Early this century three human energy cycles were observed, lasting 23, 28, and 33 days. These were named the physical, emotional, and intellectual cycles and are known collectively as biorhythm.

A biorhythm cycle can be shown graphically as a wavy line called a sine curve. Starting from the baseline on the day of birth, the wave represents the energy available for physical, emotional, or intellectual activities. In the first part of the cycle, available energy rises to a peak; then it falls below the baseline to a trough. As energy is replenished it rises again to the baseline to complete the cycle.

Positive and negative periods

A positive period occurs when the cycle is above the baseline; this is favorable for inspiration and high energy activities. The negative energy period occurs when the cycle is below the baseline; this time is favorable for slower and more pedantic activities.

A triple critical day occurs when all three cycles cross, even if they are not in the same phase. On these days, which happen once a year, prudence is the best policy when planning demanding activities.

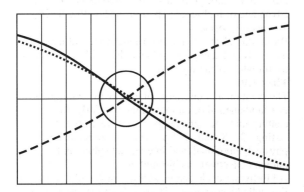

SECTIONS FROM A BIORHYTHM CHART

1 Physical cycle
Length   23 days
Peak day 6th
Trough day   17th
Critical days   11th, 23rd

Affects a broad range of physical factors such as
fitness, coordination, speed, adaptability, resistance
to disease, healing, and all basic body functions.

2 Emotional cycle
Length   28 days
Peak day 7th
Trough day   21st
Critical days   14th, 28th

Affects emotional factors such as perceptions,
attitudes, prejudices, sensitivity, moods, and general
mental health.

3 Intellectual cycle
Length   33 days
Peak day 8th
Trough day   24th
Critical days   16th, 33rd

Affects intellectual abilities such as memory,
alertness, learning, generation of ideas, and the
analytical function of the mind.

Physical cycle: 23 days

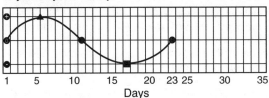

Emotional cycle: 28 days

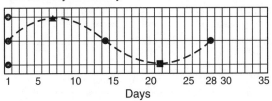

Intellectual cycle: 33 days

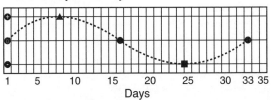

MONEY MANAGEMENT

Some people are very astute when it comes to finances. Others always seem to squander what they have or do not put much store by financial gain. Could it have something to do with their Life Number? Some numerologists believe that Life Numbers have considerable influence over the part that money plays in our lives but that awareness of how Life Numbers can affect our outlook can often help to put us on the right track. Consult the following charts to see how your Life Number may be weakening or strengthening your financial acumen. Once again, you can find out how to calculate Life Numbers on page 82.

Life Number 1
Those with Life Number **1** are usually concerned with keeping up appearances and like to be seen to have the very best of everything. They insist upon designer labels and would overlook a cheaper item of equal quality simply because they want to be thought of as chic or up-market.

Life Number 2
Highly intuitive by nature, those with the Life Number **2** rarely take risks when it comes to money. This is of course a sensible approach but there may well be times when these individuals miss out on the opportunity to make a quick profit – perhaps on the stock market – because they would not chance their luck.

Life Number 3
An individual with the Life Number **3** is frequently very generous with his or her money. A good part of any capital may therefore be spent on giving a helping hand to those less well off. There is little financial acumen, nor much interest in money for all the trappings it can bring.

Life Number 4
Those with the Life Number **4** are highly creative as a rule but also very practical. They will generally put something aside for a rainy day, but may invest in a more creative way by collecting antiques, for instance. Sometimes they give the impression of being tight-fisted or materialistic.

Life Number 5

Always the first to try out something new on the market and highly adventurous by nature, those with the Life Number **5** will freely spend on expensive nights out and the very latest fashions. They soon come to tire of any new items for their wardrobe, however, and frequently make mistakes in what they purchase. It sometimes seems they were born to shop, whatever their income level.

Life Number 6

Those with the Life Number **6** are very charitable and like to be seen to help a worthy cause, so the motive is not entirely altruistic. They are highly sociable and will not stint on entertaining. Money, they believe, is for using, not stashing away. Old age will look after itself. Right now, they intend to enjoy every penny.

Life Number 7

Saving is no easy matter for those with the Life Number **7** because, by nature, they are highly impatient. They can also be moody and when this happens, they may not be able to control their spending. The happiness that unnecessary purchases bring, however, is only momentary.

Life Number 8
Those with the Life Number 8 have a very
independent streak and are highly organized.
Right from the time they start work, they will
set aside something for the future and express
concern about an adequate pension for their
retirement years. They are also always careful to
compare prices and interest rates, and have a
good eye for a bargain.

Life Number 9
Whether or not they are schooled in financial
planning, those with the Life Number 9 always
check the ins and outs of any policy or savings
plan they are considering. With an open
approach to life, they will be happy to share any
particularly useful information they come across
and could never be accused of being acquisitive
or greedy on the financial front.

STYLE

Some people have excellent dress sense that seems to
come completely naturally. Others are much more
uncoordinated in their appearance. Of course we can
all seek advice about how to make ourselves look our
best or decorate our homes with flair. But it is
interesting to consider how some numerologists relate
our taste to our Personality Numbers. To find out
someone's Personality Number, simply take the day
of the month in which they were born. Someone with
the birthday June **21**st will therefore have the
Personality Number **3**. (Take **21** as the day of birth
and then reduce this to **2 + 1 = 3**). Then consult the
charts that follow.

Personality Number 1
Those with the Personality Number **1** love to
show off and frequently do this by wearing
something that immediately attracts the eye –
either because it is in a very bright color or
because it is not generally available in the
shops. They like their homes always to look a
little different, too, and will enjoy picking up
unusual items and putting them to entirely
novel uses.

Personality Number 2

Rather conventional in dress and tending to choose garments that could be classed as classical so that they rarely go out of fashion, those with the Personality Number **2** tend to take considerable time over making a purchase. The decor in their homes will also tend to be traditional. They like to play it safe.

Personality Number 3

Those with the Personality Number **3** prefer to dress casually most of the time and cannot cope with daily life unless they feel comfortable. They have a down-to-earth approach to dress and like natural fibers, not synthetics. They have a preference for earthy colors, too; and for the home, tend to go for pale, relaxing schemes.

Personality Number 4

Often described as being exceedingly chic, those
with the Personality Number **4** may not have
many items in the wardrobe but what they do have
could be counted as elegant in every respect.
Their clothes always make a statement, and that
statement usually points to their creativity and
innate confidence. Their homes, too, will be
imaginatively but sparsely furnished, and all the
more interesting for this.

Personality Number 5

Because those with the Personality Number **5** are
so dynamic and usually on the move, they tend
to opt for very comfortable garments and like to
have a lot of changes of clothes. These are
people who firmly believe that you are judged by
what you wear. They like to appear as natural as
possible, while conveying their great sense of
adventure. When it comes to interior decoration,
they will enjoy frequent changes of the
arrangement of furniture and will experiment
with color schemes, too.

Personality Number 6
A love of sensual fabrics, such as silk or satin,
is usually shared by those who have the
Personality Number **6**. They appreciate
traditionally sensual colors, too, such as red and
black. Even if these shades do not suit them,
they may try to incorporate them into a room
setting. They are very sociable, and never try to
outdress their friends. Their personalities come
over readily enough.

Personality Number 7
Those with this Personality Number are not too
concerned about their appearance and do not
overspend on clothes, yet somehow they will
always be able to find soemthing suitable in the
wardrobe or a bargain to suit every occasion.
They do not seem to need a lot of money either
in order to furnish their homes in an interesting
way. What to others may seem junk will be
polished up and recycled to superb effect.

Personality Number 8
Always very tidy in appearance and hardly the
type to wear anything outrageous, those with the
Personality Number **8** have a very independent
spirit and do not feel they need to follow the
herd by dressing in anything that is the latest
vogue. Their clothes are never allowed to take
over from their personalities, and their homes are
not furnished in any style that could be called
"loud" or "ostentatious."

Personality Number 9
Those with the Personality Number **9** are
essentially fun-loving and will sometimes dress
in an extrovert way, choosing to wear bright
colors and perhaps using flamboyant accessories.
In their homes, too, you may find a few eccentric
items, reflecting an appreciation of the comic or
bizarre. They are sometimes very critical of
others, and this may extend to what friends and
colleagues choose to wear, even if they do not
actually voice their true opinions.

LEISURE TIME

Sensible use of time not spent working does not mean wasting it but choosing activities that will be beneficial both physically and mentally. According to our Personality Number, we all have differing needs when it comes to making the most of our leisure hours, so numerologists hold. Consult the charts that follow to find out which type of sport, vacation, and hobby might suit you best. Again, to find your Personality Number, simply take the day of the month in which you were born, regardless of the year. If you were born, for example, on February 5th, your Personality Number will be **5**.

Personality Number 1
Because those with the Personality Number **1** like to be thought of as "different," they may well take up a very esoteric form of hobby and collect unusual items of some sort – books by a particular author, perhaps; or fossils, or butterflies. They like to take very exotic holidays, and will travel far afield independently, rather than joining a tour group, unless they choose to organize a trip themselves, inviting close friends.

Personality Number 2
Those with the Personality Number **2** are as
reserved in their choice of recreational activities
as they are in everyday life. They tend to enjoy
relaxing country walks or visits to museums and
art galleries, and beachcombing may also appeal.
Any exercise they take will not be physically
demanding, and they may choose to take up
meditation or yoga through which they can
further their sense of calm. They do not enjoy
group vacations, nor crowded resorts, and would
far rather spend time alone or with the family, or
just one close friend. Many enjoy painting or
pottery, and spend a good deal of their free time
reading or listening to music.

Personality Number 3
If you have the Personality Number **3**, you are
likely to enjoy team sports such as baseball, soccer,
or basketball. Alternatively, you may find it fun to
join a gym where you can exercise with others. As
you are so outgoing, you may well enjoy dancing,
and might choose to join a choir, too. Visits to the
theater and cinema are likely to be frequent, and as
much enjoyment will be gleaned from comedies as
from high drama. A good vacation for this
personality might center around some form of
exercise.

Personality Number 4

There is nothing someone with this Personality Number likes better than an evening spent with old friends, reminiscing over past times. Very practical hobbies usually appeal, so that dressmaking, woodwork, jewelry, and cake-making may become strong points. Whatever hobby is taken up, it will be done with tremendous enthusiasm. As for holidays, those with the Personality Number 4 do not enjoy taking luxury tours and may disdain first-class hotels. They would far prefer to rent an apartment or to go camping, and rarely spend lavishly on vacations. If friends can join them, so much the better.

Personality Number 5

Those with the Personality Number 5 generally love dancing and also like to travel. They revel in change, and so frequently choose to go touring for a vacation but will try to stay at resorts where there is a lot of nightlife. Weekends away may appeal, as will hobbies that involve going out and about – treasure-hunting with a metal-detector, for example, hiking, cycling, climbing, or ballooning. Staying at home with his or her feet up is no form of relaxation for this personality.

Personality Number 6
Highly sociable and sensual by nature, those with
the Personality Number **6** find eating out and
experimenting with ethnic cuisines an excellent
way of spending their free time. They enjoy
group visits to cultural centers, and never refuse
a party invitation. Rather than staying in more
economical accommodation, they would always
prefer a luxury hotel. A cruise would be an ideal
vacation. Suitable sports include skiing, golf, and
gymnastics.

Personality Number 7
Those with the Personality Number **7** often find
they need to spend time alone if they are to
recharge their batteries. Sporting activities that
provide an opportunity for this include walking,
cycling, swimming, and some of the martial
arts, as well as meditation. Vacations are never
spent at crowded resorts. Quiet spots will appeal
– the heart of unspoilt countryside, for example,
or a deserted beach. Interests are also often
those that do not require the participation of
others – painting, reading, creative writing, or
caring for pets, perhaps.

Personality Number 8

Because they love their independence so much,
those with the Personality Number **8** will
usually choose a sport they can enjoy alone –
riding, perhaps, or jogging. If they do engage
in team sports, they will want to take on the
role of manager or captain as soon as they can.
If they collect objects for a hobby, you can be
sure the display will be kept in perfect order
and be catalogued. As for the ideal vacation,
this would probably be spent touring the sites
of a major city.

Personality Number 9

Those with the Personality Number **9** enjoy
exploring and would generally like to spend
their vacation somewhere new to them. They do
not like to stay in first-class hotels but would
prefer to stay somewhere more modest, eating
and mixing with the locals as much as possible.
They really like to get the feel of a place and
may put a lot of effort into getting all the
information they can from guide books. They
will also always make an effort to experiment
with a foreign language. A good sense of fun,
combined with the desire to find balance in their
lives, means that sports such as skating, polo, or
skateboarding may be taken up.

MAXIMS

The following maxims and proverbs have been
selected according to their suitability for each
Personality Number from **1-9**. Personality Numbers,
remember, are simply the number of the day in the
month in which you were born.

1 *Look before you leap.*
Take care not to act too impetuously.

2 *Many hands make light work.*
Do not be too proud to let others help you.

3 *Charity begins at home.*
Do not overlook your own needs.

4 *Friends in need are friends indeed.*
Be wary of those who might take advantage of you.

5 *Live and let live.*
Try to respect other people's opinions.

6 *Laugh and the world laughs with you.*
A good sense of humor will see you through.

7 *Patience is a virtue.*
Try to bear with those less quick-witted.

8 *Never judge a book by its cover.*
Try not to make decisions by appearances.

9 *A pot should not call the kettle black.*
Be wary of becoming over-critical.

DREAMS ABOUT NUMBERS

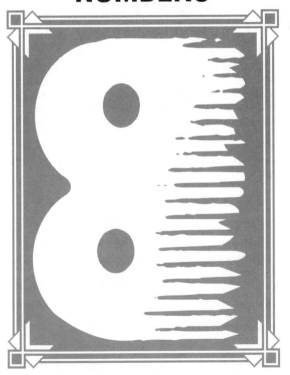

DREAMS ABOUT NUMBERS

If you sometimes dream about a certain number, there is likely to be a significance that may not correspond at all to the way in which it is featured in the dream. In other words, the numbers that feature in dreams are sometimes symbolic in content.

The pages that follow give examples of actual dreams with numerical content from **0-10** and possible explanations. Once you start to recognize the presence of such symbolism in dreams, you should be able to turn what you discover to good advantage and also help others to analyze their dreams.

0   Oblivion
    Forgetfulness
    Failure

"I dreamed that I was floating in the air while flat on my back, and that all around me were lots of empty circles. They looked a bit like bubbles. I felt nervous at first but eventually sensed a most remarkable calm."

This dreamer may well have been unnecessarily concerned about the possibility of being made redundant because there was so little for her to do at work. Perhaps, though, deep inside she knew it might be a blessing in disguise and that she would soon find another job.

1
God
Loneliness
Self

*"A recurring dream that I have often had involved
me searching for an address that is No. 1 Bloom Street.
However, try as I might, I can never find it. Finally I
do locate Bloom Street but No. 1 has been
demolished."*

This repetitive dream could well be a sign of the
dreamer's extreme anxiety about self-identity. He has
not found his true path in life as yet, and may be
worried that others are taking advantage of him.
Possibly he spends too much time worrying about his
family, rather than looking after number **one**.

2
Partnerships
Opposition
Jealousy

*"I have been dreaming a lot recently about two
black cats who seem to get on well but suddenly start
to fight. There is nothing I can do to stop them. After
this dream, I always find I wake with a jolt."*

Dreams that involve two people or animals fighting
are often about the dreamer and someone towards
whom he or she feels antagonistic, even though the
dreamer does not actually star in the dream. Only the
dreamer would be able to identify the object of this
secret resentment or jealousy with any accuracy.

3 The Trinity Wishes

*"I had a very strange dream as a teenager, since when it has recurred a few times. I would dream I was getting dressed in the morning and when I went to put on my bra, there were **three** cups instead of two I remember feeling terrified."*

This dream clearly reflects doubts about sexuality and doubts about developing in a normal way during adolescence.

4 Order Family Security

*"I dreamed that I was out in the countryside on a bright, sunny day in a meadow full of buttercups when I noticed an airplane drawing out a huge figure **4** high above me. The pilot threw out the longest rope I had ever seen and I started to climb it I could not reach the top, however, as it got longer and longer the higher I climbed."*

Since **four** is representative of order, this dream could indicate a desire for security that, for the moment, is beyond the dreamer's reach.

5 Wholeness
Love
Life force

*"I once dreamed that I was playing in a group. Our manager, however, told us he would not work with us any longer unless we let another guitarist join us, so that we formed a quintet. He also wanted us to change our name to **Five Live**. We did this and soon made a recording that took us to the top of the charts."*

Dreams that contain the number **five** are often a reflection of the dreamer's desire to experience life more fully and to be loved not only by individuals but by the public at large.

6 Sexual relationships
Evolution
Danger

*"One of the strangest dreams I ever had involved trying to ring the operator but repeatedly getting the number **666**. Each time I would put down the phone and then the same thing happened. I apologized for bothering them but the person who answered invited me to continue the conversation, saying he was pleased to hear from me."*

The number **666** occurs in the *New Testament* as the mark of the devil. A dream such as this may well reflect feelings of guilt.

7 Luck
Heaven
Wholeness

"In one dream, I gave birth not to one baby but **seven.** *There had been no prior warning but I was delighted to have these septuplets. They seemed to grow remarkably quickly and always went around, hand in hand.*

Since the number **seven** refers to "wholeness," there seems to be a feeling on the dreamer's part that she will not be "whole" as a woman unless she has a large and close (joined together) family.

8 Soul
The sacred
Reward

"My 16-year-old daughter dreamed she was forced to eat 8 hamburgers in succession. But try as she might, she could not swallow them all."

This could be a sign that the 16-year-old is doing some soul-searching. Perhaps she is anxious about all the temptations that teenage society puts before her.

9 Suitability
Achievement
Pregnancy

*"I have a repeated dream that I have to catch the last train home at **9pm** and rush to get it, only to see it pulling out of platform **9**. I keep looking up at the clock but it still says **9pm** and has obviously stopped."*

As the number **9** frequently symbolizes achievement, this dream seems to indicate a fear of under-achieving, either at work or in a social situation. The fact that the clock has stopped at **9pm** points to likely doubts that a current situation will improve in the short term.

10 Marriage
Obedience
Discipline

*"On several occasions recently I have dreamed that I lose **10** pounds in weight in one day. I do not want nor need to lose weight. It surprised me, too, that in each dream the weight loss was the same."*

When the number **10** occurs in a dream, it may relate to a marriage. It could be that the dreamer is anxious about infidelity – either her partner's or her own – or their relationship generally.

12 Time
Learning
Christianity

*"I dreamed on Christmas Eve that I had **12** dogs and had to train them all at once. Amazingly they were very obedient and did exactly as I said. They then went off to train other dogs themselves and had somehow gained the gift of speech. It was very peculiar."*

This dream seems to have a religious content and may refer to the **12** disciples of Jesus who spread the Christian teachings, as it was dreamed by someone of this faith. Alternatively this dream may relate to the **12** days of Christmas in view of when it was dreamed.

100 Growing old
Completion
Success

*"I dreamed recently that I was given a box of chocolates and counted them - there were exactly **100**. However when I went to choose one later in the day, there were none left. Curiously, I started to weep in my dream."*

This dream clearly reflects a fear of ageing and the feeling of having missed out on so much in life for whatever reason. Some dreams featuring the number **100**, however, point to imminent success.

CELEBRITY CHARTS

CELEBRITY CHARTS

The Life Number, as outlined on page 82, is calculated by adding together all the digits in the full date of birth. In the charts that follow, you will find the Life Numbers **1-9**, followed by a list of several celebrities whose birth dates give each Life Number. This will enable you to see who shares your own Life Number, and the Life Numbers of family and friends. You will also be able to assess for yourself the extent to which the life of each of these personalities has indeed been influenced by the total of the digits in the date of birth.

Yves St Laurent
Couturier
Born August 1, 1936

Ringo Starr
Drummer
Born July 7, 1940

Rupert Murdoch
Newspaper magnate
Born March 11, 1931

Sean Connery
Actor
Born August 25, 1930

Sophia Loren
Actress
Born September 20, 1934

Placido Domingo
Opera singer
Born January 21, 1941

Billy Graham
Preacher and evangelist
Born November 7, 1918

Edmund Hillary
Mountaineer
Born July 20, 1919

Charles, Prince of Wales
Heir to the British throne
Born November 14, 1948

Jacqueline Onassis
Widow of President John
Kennedy
Born July 28, 1929

Henry Kissinger
Statesman
Born May 27, 1923

Bob Hope
Comedian
Born May 29, 1903

Bill Clinton
42nd American President
Born August 19, 1946

Henry Kissinger

Bill Clinton

Gina Lollobrigida
Actress
Born July 4, 1927

Salvador Dali
Artist
Born May 11, 1904

Indira Gandhi
Former Prime Minister
  of India
Born November 19, 1917

Andy Warhol
Film-maker and artist
Born August 8, 1931

Tom Stoppard
Playwright
Born July 3, 1937

Audrey Hepburn
Actress
Born May 4, 1929

Alec Guinness
Actor
Born April 2, 1914

Salvador Dali

Indira Gandhi

Paul McCartney
Former Beatle, guitarist
and singer
Born June 18, 1942

Woody Allen
Writer and
actor/producer/director
Born December 1, 1935

Luciano Pavarotti
Opera singer
Born October 12, 1935

Robert Maxwell
Newspaper magnate
Born June 10, 1923

Clint Eastwood
Actor
Born May 31, 1930

Frank Sinatra
Singer and actor
Born December 12, 1915

Frank Sinatra

Woody Allen

Ravi Shankar
Musician
Born April 7, 1920

Billie-Jean King
Tennis player
Born November 22, 1943

Lord Snowdon
Photographer
Born March 7, 1930

Christiaan Barnard
Surgeon
Born October 8, 1922

Mick Jagger
Singer
Born July 26, 1943

Robert Mitchum
Actor
Born August 6, 1917

Saul Bellow
Author
Born June 10, 1915

Irving Berlin
Composer
Born May 11, 1888

Irving Berlin

Christiaan Barnard

Greta Garbo
Actress
Born September 18, 1905

Isaac Asimov
Scientist and writer
Born January 2, 1920

James Galway
Flautist
Born December 8, 1939

Roman Polanski
Film director
Born August 18, 1933

Peter Ustinov
Actor and writer
Born April 16, 1921

Alexander Solzhenitsyn
Writer and political
activist
Born December 11, 1918

Danny Kaye
Comedian and actor
Born January 18, 1913

Greta Garbo

Alexander Solzhenitsyn

Queen Elizabeth II
British monarch
Born April 21, 1926

Leonard Bernstein
Conductor and composer
Born August 25, 1918

Margot Fonteyn
Ballerina
Born May 18, 1919

Arthur Ashe
Tennis-player
Born July 10, 1943

Margaret Thatcher
Former British Prime
Minister
Born October 13, 1925

Harold Robbins
Author
Born May 21, 1916

Muhammed Ali
Boxer
Born January 17, 1942

Margaret Thatcher

Muhammed Ali

Willy Brandt
Politician
Born December 18, 1913

George Solti
Conductor
Born October 21, 1912

Neil Armstrong
Astronaut
Born August 5, 1930

Paul Newman
Actor
Born January 26, 1925

Laurence Olivier
Actor and director
Born May 22, 1907

Barbra Streisand
Actress and singer
Born April 24, 1942

Neil Armstrong

Paul Newman

Brigitte Bardot
Actress
Born December 28, 1934

Jimmy Carter
39th American President
Born October 1, 1924

David Hockney
Artist
Born July 9, 1937

Henry Fonda
Actor
Born May 16, 1905

Desmond Morris
Zoologist
Born January 24, 1928

Henry Moore
Sculptor
Born July 30, 1898

WORLD
OF WORK

WORLD OF WORK

When applying for a job, it can be very useful, according to practicing numerologists, to be aware of your Soul Number, and also to calculate the Soul Number of the potential supervisor or director under whom you may be working. Similarly, a manager may find it useful to check your Soul Number against his or her own to assess compatibility. Soul Numbers are calculated as outlined on pages 96-97. Then consult the following tables for insight into possible strengths and weaknesses in the world of work.

Manager with Soul Number 1
Employee with Soul Number 1
Both are very enterprising. Providing no element of competition arises, they will make an excellent team and work together for the company's benefit.

Manager with Soul Number 1
Employee with Soul Number 2
Those with the Soul Number 2 will need to become particularly understanding of the manager with the Soul Number 1 when difficulties arise. The manager will come to rely on his or her support when problems arise.

Manager with Soul Number 1
Employee with Soul Number 3
Those with the Soul Number **3** are often highly ambitious. The manager with the Soul Number **1** will need to realize this and provide scope for promotion so that the employee does not quickly become bored.

Manager with Soul Number 1
Employee with Soul Number 4
Very reliable and well organized, the employee with the Soul Number **4** will soon become a highly valued member of staff who is extremely loyal to the company. The manager will soon come to wonder how they could have managed without him or her.

Manager with Soul Number 1
Employee with Soul Number 5
Those with Soul Number **5** are very good communicators and will usually excel at explaining systems to other staff. The manager with the Soul Number **1** will benefit enormously from this exceptional talent.

Manager with Soul Number 1
Employee with Soul Number 6
The employee with the Soul Number **6** sets very high standards and therefore makes an extremely useful second-in-command. He or she may even keep the manager in check at times, something for which the manager should give credit.

Manager with Soul Number 1
Employee with Soul Number 7
Because those with the Soul Number **7** are so independent of spirit, they do not like taking advice. The manager with the Soul Number **1** may find this difficult at first, but in the long run he or she will come to value the fact that this employee can indeed manage to cope if left to his or her own devices.

Manager with Soul Number 1
Employee with Soul Number 8
Those with the Soul Number **8** are generally very stubborn and can be so ambitious that they may become a rival for the manager's job. The manager will need to make it clear right from the start that he or she alone is in command.

Manager with Soul Number 1
Employee with Soul Number 9
Someone with the Soul Number **9** will be very kind toward other staff and will be lively in the workplace. The manager must be careful not to take advantage of his or her good nature.

Manager with Soul Number 2
Employee with Soul Number 1
This manager is not always fair in decision-making and will need to come to terms with the novel approaches to work often adopted by an employee with the Soul Number **1** who may be critical of existing systems at times.

Manager with Soul Number 2
Employee with Soul Number 2
This is not an ideal combination as both might come to be resented by other members of staff. They are not as understanding of other people's problems as they might be.

Manager with Soul Number 2
Employee with Soul Number 3
The employee with the Soul Number 3 can be
very talkative, which is something the manager
may not appreciate. It will be best to accept this
fact and for the manager to be sure that little of
the working day is wasted in this way.

Manager with Soul Number 2
Employee with Soul Number 4
This employee will make an excellent staff
representative, encouraging the manager with
Soul Number 2 to view any tricky staff problems
more impartially. In this respect they make an
excellent team.

Manager with Soul Number 2
Employee with Soul Number 5
Often aware of a problem before it arises, the
employee with this Soul Number will make the
manager's life far easier than it would otherwise
be. Staff problems will be minimal as a result.

Manager with Soul Number 2
Employee with Soul Number 6
This employee will come to understand the
manager's personality very quickly and will
always see that other companies they deal with are
treated with respect and fairly. Their own
company's reputation will blossom as a result.

Manager with Soul Number 2
Employee with Soul Number 7
This employee could become the backbone of the
company and is not easily replaceable. The
manager may come to resent this fact but would
be wrong to dismiss him or her. The employee's
strengths are a company asset.

Manager with Soul Number 2
Employee with Soul Number 8
The single-mindedness of this employee will
benefit the company if the manager encourages
him or her to take regular vacations and not to
work too much overtime. A fresh mind is
important if any difficulties are to be overcome.

Manager with Soul Number 2
Employee with Soul Number 9
These two will get on well together and quickly
come to appreciate that they have complementary
talents. The manager will come to rely on this
employee in many respects, and they will be able
to resolve any problems that arise in the company
by mutual consultation.

Manager with Soul Number 3
Employee with Soul Number 1
This manager is sometimes easily bored and will
welcome the pioneering spirit of the employee
with the Soul Number 1 who will keep him or her
alert as to possibilities for the company.

Manager with Soul Number 3
Employee with Soul Number 2
If the employee has a lot of previous experience,
he or she will be aware that a manager with the
Soul Number 3, who at times seems very pushy,
needs to be treated with kid gloves.

Manger with Soul Number 3
Employee with Soul Number 3
Both tend to be very ambitious and have a lot of
pride. Neither will readily take any criticism from
the other. Both will need to tread warily if they
are to get on.

Manager with Soul Number 3
Employee with Soul Number 4
The employee with the Soul Number **4** soon
becomes a prized member of staff. He or she is
highly practical and understands that this manager
may sometimes want to take the credit for
suggestions and improvements made by others.

Manager with Soul Number 3
Employee with Soul Number 5
This employee is very versatile and will be able to
turn his or hand to any tasks that the manager
requires. However, this manager may come to
resent such skills if he or she does not share them.

Manager with Soul Number 3
Employee with Soul Number 6
This manager will need to understand that the
employee with the Soul Number **6** has an innate
need to succeed and may feel dreadful if at times
things do not run as smoothly as they might. A
sympathetic hand is required.

Manager with Soul Number 3
Employee with Soul Number 7
There may be a need for this employee to
appreciate that the manager is a human being, too,
who may be upset from time to time. An
employee with this Soul Number should
remember that a manager with the Soul Number **3**
needs to feel wanted, too.

Manager with Soul Number 3
Employee with Soul Number 8
This employee has good intentions but they may
be misinterpreted by the manager with the Soul
Number **3** who does not appreciate stubbornness.
It is this very stubbornness, however, that may at
times keep the company or department going.

Manager with Soul Number 3
Employee with Soul Number 9
Because the employee often lacks a sense of
humility, the manager with the Soul Number 3 can
sometimes resent this and will want to keep this
employee in his or her place at all times.

Manager with Soul Number 4
Employee with Soul Number 1
Because this manager is very conventional, the
employee with the Soul Number 1 may find him
or her very restricting when it comes to trying out
entirely new systems or products.

Manager with Soul Number 4
Employee with Soul Number 2
This manager will know instinctively how to
handle an employee with the Soul Number 2 who
may not always excel at dealing with a difficult
situation. The manager will always try to be
helpful and will never let the employee down.

Manager with Soul Number 4
Employee with Soul Number 3
This manager is very realistic in his or her
approach to life and will appreciate that the
employee with the Soul Number 3 needs an outlet
for creative talent.

Manager with Soul Number 4
Employee with Soul Number 4
Both like to create a stable environment and will
make an excellent team. Others in the company or
organization will benefit from this and will come
to respect them because of this.

Manager with Soul Number 4
Employee with Soul Number 5
The manager with the Soul Number 4 may come
to see that the employee with the Soul Number 5
is more skilled at speaking on behalf of the
company or department and will do well to hand
over such responsibility.

Manager with Soul Number 4
Employee with Soul Number 6
Together they will ensure that all staff are
looked after well. Their offices or factory will
be very orderly. However both share a
reluctance to try out new systems unless they
are convinced of the benefits.

Manager with Soul Number 4
Employee with Soul Number 7
This employee is fun to work with, but the
manager with the Soul Number 4 may find him or
her a little too unconventional for the company or
department. However, everyone would probably
benefit from the presence of an employee with
this Soul Number.

Manager with Soul Number 4
Employee with Soul Number 8
It could be that a manager with the Soul Number
4 comes to resent an employee with the Soul
Number 8 because of his or her obvious desire to
achieve promotion within a short period of time.
They may need to talk this through early on.

Manager with Soul Number 4
Employee with Soul Number 9
The manager with the Soul Number **4** is very
understanding, and the employee with the Soul
Number **9** is equally compassionate. Both will
want to provide support for other members of
staff but must be wary of becoming too
involved with others' difficulties or the
department may suffer.

Manager with Soul Number 5
Employee with Soul Number 1
The manager with the Soul Number **5** is a good
communicator, which is just as well since the
employee with the Soul Number **1** is very
enterprising and the manager will need to
exercise a degree of control.

Manager with Soul Number 5
Employee with Soul Number 2
The employee with this Soul Number may find
it difficult to cope with the driving force of this
manager. This employee may find new methods
difficult to accept but fortunately the manager
with the Soul Number **5** is a good teacher.

Manager with Soul Number 5
Employee with Soul Number 3
The employee with this Soul Number sometimes
has a tendency to exaggerate his or her abilities,
but the resourceful manager with the Soul Number
5 will soon be able to assess him or her and give
any necessary instruction.

Manager with Soul Number 5
Employee with Soul Number 4
This manager has very progressive attitudes and
excels in installing enthusiasm in others. He or she
will really appreciate the organizational abilities of
the employee with the Soul Number **4**, even if this
employee is very conventional in comparison.

Manager with Soul Number 5
Employee with Soul Number 5
These two make an excellent team and together
will relate very well to other staff. Working with
these Soul Numbers should never be boring, and
they will both do everything to make sure that
colleagues are fully aware of what they are trying
to achieve.

Manager with Soul Number 5
Employee with Soul Number 6
This employee is very conscientious and expects
everyone else to be equally hard-working.
Fortunately, he or she will get on well with the
manager with the Soul Number 5 who makes a lot
of demands that the employee enjoys fulfilling.

Manager with Soul Number 5
Employee with Soul Number 7
The employee with the Soul Number 7 has a very
independent streak and often does not listen to
advice from others. The manager with the Soul
Number 5 does not react favorably to this and will
expect the employee to take instruction.

Manager with Soul Number 5
Employee with Soul Number 8
This employee is very ambitious not only
personally but also for the whole company or
organization. The manager with the Soul Number
5 also has a driving force, and together they could
conquer the world.

Manager with Soul Number 5
Employee with Soul Number 9
This manager is very good at stimulating creativity, and the employee with the Soul Number **9** will therefore very much enjoy working with such a very special boss.

Manager with Soul Number 6
Employee with Soul Number 1
This manager has very exacting standards, both personally and for his or her staff. The employee with the Soul Number **1** may have to learn to subdue a spirit of enterprise and be less individualistic.

Manager with Soul Number 6
Employee with Soul Number 2
The manager with the Soul Number **6** is a perfectionist, while the employee with the Soul Number **2** is also exacting in some respects. They may expect too much of one another.

Manager with Soul Number 6
Employee with Soul Number 3
This employee may try too hard at times to prove
himself or herself as an exceptionally talented
worker. Anyone other than a manager with the
Soul Number **6** would readily come to dislike such
concern with the self.

Manager with Soul Number 6
Employee with Soul Number 4
Both are very practical and reliable, with high
standards. Each will appreciate the other's
contribution to the working day, and praise will be
heaped upon this employee.

Manager with Soul Number 6
Employee with Soul Number 5
The employee with the Soul Number **5** knows
instinctively what the manager with the Soul
Number **6** expects. They will probably both
work long hours, but the results will be
rewarding on all fronts.

Manager with Soul Number 6
Employee with Soul Number 6
Both are so exacting in their requirements that
they may soon get on each other's nerves unless a
mutual respect exists right from the beginning.
They may both be too demanding of themselves
and others.

Manager with Soul Number 6
Employee with Soul Number 7
The manager with Soul Number **6** will tend to be
critical of the employee with Soul Number **7**
because this employee is too opinionated and
often makes decisions without taking the
manager's advice.

Manager with Soul Number 6
Employee with Soul Number 8
This manager admires the ambition shown by the
employee with the Soul Number **8** and will not be
slow to praise his or her efforts. The employee
with the Soul Number **8**, however, may need to be
more attentive to the manager's requirements.

Manager with Soul Number 6
Employee with Soul Number 9
The manager with the Soul Number **6** is
demanding, while this employee can be
exceedingly proud and resents any criticism. The
manager will need to understand that the standards
he or she sets can sometimes be too high.

Manager with Soul Number 7
Employee with Soul Number 1
The manager with this Soul Number does not
readily delegate, while the employee with the Soul
Number **1** is very assertive. There could be
problems in the workplace.

Manager with Soul Number 7
Employee with Soul Number 2
This manager is not as sensitive as the employee
would like. But the employee, too, will have to
learn not to be too critical if this working
relationship is to thrive.

Manager with Soul Number 7
Employee with Soul Number 3
This manager may find the employee with the
Soul Number **3** becomes too competitive with
other staff. The manager will have to be sensitive
to everyone's needs.

Manager with Soul Number 7
Employee with Soul Number 4
The employee with the Soul Number **4** has strong
organizational abilities and may resent the fact
that this manager does not give free rein as far as
office systems are concerned. The manager must
learn to be more trusting.

Manager with Soul Number 7
Employee with Soul Number 5
Both are so independent of spirit that there is a
risk they might clash and frequent confrontations
could result. Each will need to develop greater
sensitivity toward the other.

Manager with Soul Number 7
Employee with Soul Number 6
The employee with the Soul Number **6** will have
to be particularly patient with this manager who is
so masterful that the opinions of others are rarely
taken into consideration.

Manager with Soul Number 7
Employee with Soul Number 7
These two are both so strong-willed that they
may have frequent arguments about how the
company or organization should be run. One will
have to be prepared to give way, not necessarily
the employee.

Manager with Soul Number 7
Employee with Soul Number 8
These two personalities are both too independent
and ambitious to survive together in the same
working environment. The relationship will rarely
be a relaxed one.

Manager with Soul Number 7
Employee with Soul Number 9
The employee with Soul Number **9** will readily see the funny side of such a strong-willed manager. He or she may even have the skill to tease this manager about being too independent.

Manager with Soul Number 8
Employee with Soul Number 1
There may be an element of rivalry that develops between these two personalities, both of whom are very ambitious. The employee may be far too big for his or her boots as far as the manager is concerned.

Manager with Soul Number 8
Employee with Soul Number 2
This employee easily gets upset and may not be able to cope with the singlemindedness of the manager with the Soul Number **8**. The employee may need to toughen up in order to be accepted.

Manager with Soul Number 8
Employee with Soul Number 3
This employee may not be able to cope with the
stubborn nature of the manager with the Soul
Number **8**. Ideas put forward by this employee
may not be found acceptable most of the time.

Manager with Soul Number 8
Employee with Soul Number 4
This employee may be inclined to grumble at the
manager with Soul Number **8**. The employee's
approach to work is far more regimented, and the
manager with this Soul Number may find his or her
attitude overpowering.

Manager with Soul Number 8
Employee with Soul Number 5
The employee with this Soul Number will back
the manager to the hilt and has a shared
enthusiasm for the work that they do. Together
they form a mutual appreciation society.

Manager with Soul Number 8
Employee with Soul Number 6
If the manager with this Soul Number is too demanding of staff, the employee with the Soul Number **6** will try to intervene and see that there is a fair result for both sides. In this respect, the employee is an excellent moderator.

Manager with Soul Number 8
Employee with Soul Number 7
The employee with Soul Number **7** is very headstrong and has very definite opinions, something that this manager does not readily accept. They may find that they cannot reach a mutually satisfactory method of working together.

Manager with Soul Number 8
Employee with Soul Number 8
These two both take work very seriously and are highly ambitious. If each sticks to his or her duties and does not interfere with the other's responsibilities, no trouble will arise in spite of this.

Manager with Soul Number 8
Employee with Soul Number 9
The manager with Soul Number **8** is so
dedicated to his or her work that the sparkle of
an employee with the Number **9** will help to
keep this manager on an even keel. They are
likely to become firm friends.

Manager with Soul Number 9
Employee with Soul Number 1
Fortunately the manager with Soul Number **9** is
easy-going, and so all the ambition and drive of an
employee with the Soul Number **1** is not upsetting
to the daily routine in any way.

Manager with Soul Number 9
Employee with Soul Number 2
This employee probably needs to be more
diplomatic if the manager with the Soul Number **9**
is to be tolerant of attitudes displayed. Luckily,
this manager does not take things too seriously.

Manager with Soul Number 9
Employee with Soul Number 3
This employee is frequently boastful and impatient
if not kept busy. The manager with the Soul
Number **9**, however, naturally takes such behavior
with a pinch of salt and makes allowances.

Manager with Soul Number 9
Employee with Soul Number 4
The Manager with the Soul Number **9** values an
employee with the Soul Number **4** because
everything will be kept in apple pie order, allowing
the manager time and space for creativity.

Manager with Soul Number 9
Employee with Soul Number 5
The employee with this Soul Number is right
behind the manager at all times, ever ready to
discuss new ideas and to encourage others to back
special projects or ventures. This is in many
respects a dream team.

Manager with Soul Number 9
Employee with Soul Number 6
If this manager fails to look after his or her own interests, the employee with the Soul Number 5 will endeavour to see that others do not take advantage of the manager's kindly attitude to staff and customers.

Manager with Soul Number 9
Employee with Soul Number 7
This employee may become over-emotional if faulted in any way. It is therefore just as well that the manager with the Soul Number 9 has infinite patience and does not become too angry if this employee makes mistakes through not bothering to take advice.

Manager with Soul Number 9
Employee with Soul Number 8
The employee with Soul Number 8 is very ambitious. Fortunately the manager with the Soul Number 9 makes allowances for this and recognizes the employee's efforts – as long as there is no attempt to take over the manager's position.

Manager with Soul Number 9
Employee with Soul Number 9
This highly creative pair should get on really well and will have a lot of fun in the course of work. The hierarchy does not affect their companionship, and each is always ready to help the other.

MOST UNFAVORABLE WORKING RELATIONSHIPS

Manager with Soul Number **1**
Employee with Soul Number **8**

Manager with Soul Number **2**
Employee with Soul Number **2**

Manager with Soul Number **3**
Employee with Soul Number **9**

Manager with Soul Number **5**
Employee with Soul Number **7**

Manager with Soul Number **6**
Employee with Soul Number **6**

Manager with Soul Number **7**
Employee with Soul Number **1**

Manager with Soul Number **7**
Employee with Soul Number **8**

Manager with Soul Number **7**
Employee with Soul Number **7**

Manager with Soul Number **8**
Employee with Soul Number **1**

Manager with Soul Number **8**
Employee with Soul Number **7**

MOST FAVORABLE WORKING RELATIONSHIPS

Manager with Soul Number **1**
Employee with Soul Number **4**

Manager with Soul Number **1**
Employee with Soul Number **5**

Manager with Soul Number **2**
Employee with Soul Number **6**

Manager with Soul Number **2**
Employee with Soul Number **9**

Manager with Soul Number **5**
Employee with Soul Number **8**

Manager with Soul Number **5**
Employee with Soul Number **9**

Manager with Soul Number **6**
Emplyee with Soul Number **4**

Manager with Soul Number **8**
Employee with Soul Number **5**

Manager with Soul Number **8**
Employee with Soul Number **9**

Manager with Soul Number **9**
Employee with Soul Number **4**

Manager with Soul Number **9**
Employee with Soul Number **5**

Manager with Soul Number **9**
Employee with Soul Number **9**

DIVINING BY
DOMINOES AND DICE

DIVINING WITH DICE

Dice are, of course, used today as a form of gambling, but their use as a means of divining the future goes back to ancient times. The *Old Testament* talks of "casting lots," and some very early dice from Iraq, dating back to 3000BCE, have also been discovered. However, it was not until around 1400BCE that the pattern of spots on dice that we recognize today (adding up to **7** if you total the spots on opposite sides of the cube shape) was developed.

When using this or any other form of divination, be sure to remember that a certain amount of intuition is required if making a reading for yourself or anyone else. Clearly, no two people will have an identical reading. The information in the tables provided is therefore only intended as a starting point and as an aid to concentrate the mind.

ON THE SPOTS

When divining with dice, it is usual to have three of different colors – red, white, and green or blue perhaps – and always to throw them in a set sequence – perhaps red first, then white, and then green or blue. The querent (the person seeking guidance about the future) first draws a large circle approximately 10 inches in diameter. This circle is then divided into 12 equal segments and labelled as shown. Each number corresponds to an aspect of life.

1 Home life
2 Health and well-being
3 Finances
4 Love/romance
5 Travel
6 Work

7 Difficulties
8 Friendships
9 Adversaries
10 Aspirations
11 The present
12 The past

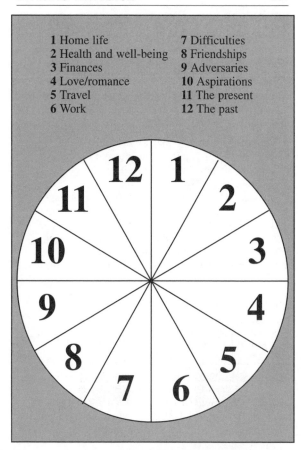

Each of the three dice is then thrown into the circle and note taken of the section into which each falls. Throw the dice again if they land across two sections. The number of spots on the upturned side can then be interpreted for the subject of each segment.

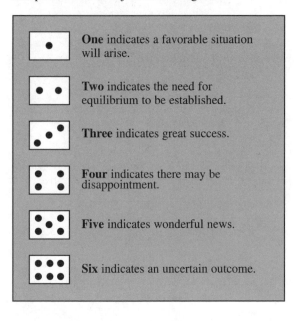

One indicates a favorable situation will arise.

Two indicates the need for equilibrium to be established.

Three indicates great success.

Four indicates there may be disappointment.

Five indicates wonderful news.

Six indicates an uncertain outcome.

If two or three dice land in the same segment of the circle, the number of spots showing on each should be totaled to give the following indications:

Two: the need for a more balanced lifestyle

Three: surprising success

Four: arguments will arise

Five: wishes come true

Six: depletion

Seven: a problematic situation

Eight: trouble may lie ahead

Nine: a renewed relationship

Ten: promotion at work

Eleven: a journey will be undertaken

Twelve: worries will be assuaged

Thirteen: regrets

Fourteen: help from a friend

Fifteen: be wary

Sixteen: the road to happiness starts here

Seventeen: weigh up options carefully

Eighteen: great fortune

Symbols and their key

More complex and potentially revealing readings can
also be made using dice. Analysis not only by the
number of spots also by specific symbols is required.

Your first die (perhaps you have chosen a red one
always to be thrown first) should be cast to give a
figure that will be placed in a hundreds column of a
three-figure number. It will also have a symbolic name
and meaning, as in the table *on the next page*. Now get
a number for the tens column by throwing your second
die (a white one, maybe). Then, with the third die (a
green or blue one, say), find a number for the units
column.

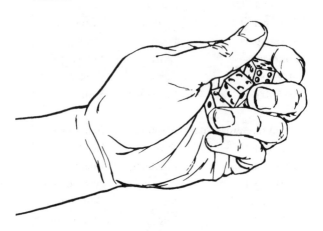

First die (red)	Symbol	Key word
One spot	Web	Confusion
Two spots	Skull	Destruction
Three spots	Ship	Exploration
Four spots	Horseshoe	Great luck
Five spots	Beetle	Ambition
Six spots	Bat	Warning

Second die (white)	Symbol	Key word
One spot	Sun	Success
Two spots	Stork	Beginnings
Three spots	Heart	Love
Four spots	Knife	Vulnerability
Five spots	Cat	Family circle
Six spots	Crossroads	Surprises

Third die (green/blue)	Symbol	Key word
One spot	Snail	Health
Two spots	Lightning	Anger
Three spots	Ladder	New horizons
Four spots	Key	Opportunity
Five spots	Cup	Celebrations
Six spots	Orchard	Wealth

Sample readings

The following are sample readings provided by a highly intuitive numerologist working with dice.

Subject: 40-year-old woman, working as a journalist. She is unmarried but has a long-term partner. She has asked for a reading about this relationship.

Dice thrown: 6/4/2, corresponds to

Bat/Knife/Lightning

Reading: There seems to be terrific tension within the relationship at home, and dreadful arguments could well arise unless both parties do everything to control their tempers and are more understanding of each other's needs. The querant feels very vulnerable to her partner's mood swings, and they might do well to try a temporary separation. The querant needs more stability in her life.

Subject: 22-year-old man who has just graduated from university and is seeking career guidance. He feels he would like to set up home on his own.

Dice thrown: 1/5/3, corresponds to

Web/Cat/Ladder

Reading: The querant should try to be his own man and not let the family confuse him. He should listen to advice but weigh it up carefully and then make his own decisions. It would be advisable to stay at home for a while, at least until he has a regular income. The "Ladder" shows he will soon find the right post and quickly gain promotion.

Subject: 63-year-old retired grandfather, a widower, who has recently come out of hospital after a minor operation. He is finding life a trifle boring and lonely.

Dice thrown: **6/6/1**, corresponds to
Bat/Crossroads/Snail

Reading: The querant should take great care when it comes to health. He should eat sensibly and get as much rest as he can. He may be feeling low right now but he is at a crossroads in his life and should soon be a lot better. He might even be able to find a part-time job. It may take him a while longer to come to terms with the loss of his wife, but he has many years of happiness ahead with his children and grandchildren who value his participation in their lives.

Subject: 30-year-old woman who has recently discovered that her husband has been unfaithful. She is undecided as to whether she should leave him after only two years of marriage.

Dice thrown: **3/3/4**, corresponds to
Exploration/Love/Opportunity

Reading: The querant should give thought to exploring with her husband, and possibly together with a counselor, what may have been going wrong with their partnership that infidelity arose.

Their love may be strong enough to help them both weather this storm; and if she does agree to forgive the transgression, it may provide the opportunity to strengthen their bond.

DIVINING WITH DOMINOES

Even though most familiar to us in the West as a game
rather than a means of fortune-telling, dominoes are
thought to have first evolved as an augury in the Far
East. There, to this day, they commonly have both
functions. The first record of them dates from the 12th
century, and they seem to have become popular in
Europe six hundred years later.

The domino set
Usually comprising 28 tiles – each divided into two
sections with 0-6 pips – dominoes are made from
plastic, wood, or ivory. A standard set dominoes with
features all possible number combinations between
double zero and double six.

In China, however, dominoes sometimes have red
spots and there are 32 riles. They are also popular in
India and Korea.

The reading
To use a domino set to give a reading about the future,
first turn all the tiles upside down and shuffle them
around on the surface of a table so that they are in no
particular order. You will now have to choose *three*
tiles in order to carry out the reading for yourself. If,
however, you are reading for someone else, he or she
should pick the tiles.

Always try to pick a tile instinctively, exponents recommend. Do this by running your hand over all the tiles until you feel you are drawn to a particular one. Choose one tile first, and then give the reading for that tile. Next proceed likewise with each of the two tiles that remain to be picked. On pages 397-400 you will find the traditional meanings for each of the number combinations on the tiles.

Blank: blank You will need to fight against any negative forces that might arise, but perseverance should see you through.

Blank: one Be wary of confidence tricksters and do not be taken in by promises of great wealth.

Blank: two You should find you win more friends, but one might lead to a tricky relationship.

Blank: three Difficulties arise, but don't lose heart.

Blank: four If there have been quarrels, try to make up. It will pay dividends.

Blank: five Be helpful to a friend in need.

Blank: six Not everyone is as straightforward as you are, or as discreet.

One: one You will enter into a valuable relationship and should be confident about any decision you make.

One: two Friends stand by you in times of hardship.

One: three Beware of advice from strangers.

One: four Be sure to settle your bills promptly.

One: five Romance lies on the horizon but the outcome is uncertain.

One: six A marriage or some other form of alliance may take place.

Two: two You should be successful with your plans.

Two: three Do not overspend, in spite of temptations.

Two: four Someone may not be as honest or generous as he/she seems. There could be a catch involved.

Two: five There is a lot of fun ahead since you are about to become part of a very lively circle of friends.

Two: six Be as open as you can about things and you should find that a huge piece of luck comes your way.

Three: three Problems may arise on the emotional front due to envy on someone's part.

Three: four Happiness lies around the corner.

Three: five Life will proceed on an even keel.

Three: six You will enjoy an interesting journey and perhaps receive a most surprising gift from an unexpected source.

Four: four It's time to relax and enjoy life to the full.

Four: five There could be a win in store for you.

Four: six There could be a legal dispute in the offing.

Five: five Changes occur that herald good fortune.

Five: six Be as patient as you can, and you will be rewarded with promotion at work.

Six: six Tremendous happiness lies ahead. This domino augurs most favorably of all.

SIMPLE PROCEDURES

A simplified method of predicting with dominoes
involves placing a whole set in a drawstring bag and
selecting a single domino instead of three as required
for a complete reading. The total number of spots on
this single domino should then be noted so that the
following chart can be consulted.

Total number of spots
Prediction

0
Difficulties may soon arise

1
Do not trust anyone too
readily

2
A new friendship will
soon be formed

3
Your friends will help you

4
Put quarrels behind you

5
Watch your finances
carefully

6
Someone is jealous of you

7
Enjoy yourself to the full

8
Try to relax more

9
You will win a lottery or
competition

10
Good fortune lies ahead

11
Great success at work

12
Tremendous happiness lies
in store

DIVINING WITH CARDS

Tarot

Definition Divination using a set of specially
decorated cards.

History Some occultists claim that the origins of tarot
lie with the priests of ancient Egypt, or ancient
Babylon, or ancient Tibet. The exact origins of tarot
are not clear, although its first recorded appearance
was in medieval France, in about 1390. In medieval
times people used the cards to play quite ordinary
games, often for money, although practitioners today
suggest that the tarot must be taken seriously. Some
practitioners insist that the tarot is a repository for a
special kind of lore, and the cards have always been
associated with a slightly sinister mystery. The
numbers and names of the cards play an important part
in a reading.

Modern methods The method of reading the tarot has
changed little, but requires considerable practice.
Provided here is a description of the tarot cards and an
explanation of how to use them for divination.

Equipment Although the European kind of tarot cards
were more or less standardized in the 18th century, and
their central figures remain the same, they have been
constantly redesigned. As a consequence, sets of tarot
cards can now be bought in a huge variety of styles, in
shops specializing in the "occult," or via mail order
through fortune-telling magazines. Some readers like
to deal the cards onto a silk cloth.

Tarot cards

There are **78** cards in a tarot set, divided into two groups: the major arcana and the minor arcana.

The major arcana (sometimes known as the greater trumps) contains **22** cards representing stages in an individual's progress through life.

The minor arcana contains **56** cards and is divided into four suits: cups, swords, pentacles, and wands. Each suit contains 14 cards, and these are numbered sequentially.

General guidelines

- Handle your own tarot cards as much as possible.
- Study your cards, think about them, and attune them to your own intuitive awareness.
- Do not use tarot cards frivolously.
- Practice using tarot cards until you become familiar with their symbolism.

THE MAJOR ARCANA

The **22** cards of the major arcana are numbered from **0-21** and named. Traditionally numbered, each is attributed with significant meaning. The first **11** cards represent the first half of life and tend to be outward-looking, oriented toward the world of positive action and development. The second **11** reflect a more meditative, quiet, inward-looking time that is focused on inward development. Because tarot cards are not double-headed, they can be reversed when laid out and meanings differ accordingly.

LE MAT

I

LE BATELEVR

0 The Fool
Unnumbered, this card is often used as the significator, to represent the subject of the reading. Symbolizing new beginnings, potentiality, and fresh challenges, it is the most complex of the cards—"holy innocent," a wise man, and trickster, with all of humanity's contradictions (good/evil, angel/devil, male/female, etc.).
Reversed Beware of foolish lack of forethought.

1 Magician (or Jester)
A fortunate card indicating decisions to be made, progress in worldly understanding, and progress toward success. Only one step away from the Fool (as jester), it relates more to a stage magician—an entertainer—than to a master of magical lore.
Reversed Warns against an unwillingness to confront the real world, or against hesitation.

LA PAPESSE

L'IMPERATRISE

2 High Priestess
Indicating a female
influence and the prospect
of light being shed on a
secret or problem, this card
suggests an element of
creativity, intuition, special
knowledge, the non-
rational, natural side of
wisdom and understanding
(including the psychic
sort).
Reversed Warns against
irrationality, insufficient
use of rational thought and
over-emotionalism.

3 Empress
A fortunate card
suggesting a solid stability
and a natural growth and
creativity (perhaps a new
baby, material prosperity,
or just general well-being).
It represents the fertility
principle, the caring,
loving, enriching, bountiful
symbol of the Earth
Mother.
Reversed Domestic
trouble and insecurity,
perhaps career setbacks or
sexual difficulties.

4 Emperor

For women, this card can mean achievement of ambition through forcefulness and controlled aggression, or a dominating male influence. For men, it is a fortunate card. A male symbol, the father figure to the Empress's mother, this card indicates energy, strength of will, success, authority, power, and the triumph of rationality.
Reversed Warns against weakness, submission.

5 High Priest

The male counterpart of the High Priestess, this card suggests spiritual rather than worldly power and authority; the gaining of understanding, not necessarily religious; intelligence, rational knowledge, inspiring perceptions, and wisdom. It can also refer to the influence of an important teacher or advisor.
Reversed Beware of misleading advice, lies.

6 Lovers
Relating to love relationships, this card involves choices made between attractions of the flesh and of the spirit. It suggests a rewarding relationship or a good marriage and indicates generally positive decisions.
Reversed A wrong choice will be made, perhaps involving sexual infidelity. Also warns of sexual difficulties.

7 Chariot
A card indicating progress, achievement, and travel and which represents an important stage in the advance through worldly life, with obtacles overcome and success gained through personal dynamism.
Reversed Beware of too much dynamism leading to ruthlessness.

8 Justice

This card suggests the person is to be judged—a positive sign, unless they are found wanting. A useful balance to the Chariot, this is a reminder of the need for balance and sound judgment, that a complete person needs more than material triumphs—that the heart and spirit must also be served.

Reversed Injustice, unfair or harsh judgment by others.

9 Hermit

A card indicating a need for inner growth and development, reevaluation, and perhaps counsel about the future. Like Justice, it shows the tarot moving away from outward advance toward less worldly and material considerations.

Reversed Warns against a refusal to think things out or to take notice; against imprudence and stubbornness.

10 Wheel of fortune

A fortunate card implying destiny will work itself out positively. A clear sign of a new stage or beginning, it alludes to the mystic idea of karma, individual inner growth toward wholeness and harmony (symbolized by the circular mandala); that without change life will stagnate, and luck will play a part in decisions to be made.

Reversed Ill luck, decline, adversity, changes for the worse.

11 Strength

Implies difficulties and setbacks overcome by inner resources. Indicates the need to face developments with fortitude, courage, and moral fiber. Some experts prefer to transpose the positions of this card with justice.

Reversed Obstacles will not be overcome, owing to lack of spiritual or moral strength.

16 Tower

An unfortunate card suggesting the shattering of hopes and ambitions, of ruin and destruction. However, out of suffering can come understanding; out of destruction can come rebuilding.
Reversed Ruin and calamity needlessly brought upon oneself.

17 Star

A fortunate card of enlightenment and enhanced awareness, this indicates hope and renewal after calamity, and promises new and rich horizons, perhaps in previously unforeseen directions, once you have come through the bad times.
Reversed Warns against spiritual blindness that prevents seeing or taking advantage of new horizons.

18 Moon

An unfortunate card for the rational person, this indicates a time when only intuition, the nonrational side, can overcome obstacles. It suggests the nonrational must be used with care as it can lead toward a dangerous fantasy world.
Reversed Warns against fearing the nonrational and settling for a life of stagnation and sterility.

19 Sun

A card signifying a triumphant reward for coming through hardships. The goal is visible: it suggests illumination in every sense, adversity overcome, wholeness and harmony achieved.
Reverse Failure, the collapse of hopes, or at best, a superficial, dubious success.

20 Judgment
This is a fortunate card
signifying new beginnings.
It concerns the day when
you pause to weigh up
what you have done and
what you have become in
your passage through life.
It indicates the attainment
of inner development, that
your achieved goals are
worthy, and you are now
entering a time of serenity
and happiness.
Reversed Regrets,
recriminations, remorse.

21 World
The ultimate circular
mandala, this card
symbolizes triumph,
fulfillment, and
completion. The cycle of
the major arcana begins
again with the Fool, but
perhaps with greater goals
and on a higher plane.
Reversed A bleak
immobility, the inability to
progress on and up,
ultimate failure rather than
ultimate fulfillment.

THE MINOR ARCANA

The minor arcana contains **56** cards divided into **four suits**, each with its own sphere of influence. When cards are dealt upside down, the meaning is reversed. There are **14** cards in each suit.

Spheres of influence

Suit	Spheres of influence
Cups	• Emotional matters • Love • Sex • Marriage • Fertility • Creativity
Pentacles	• Wealth • Finance • Commerce • Prosperity • Economic security
Swords	• Activity • Progress • Opposition and conflict • The need to impose order on chaos
Wands	• The mind • The world of ideas • Deep thought • Intellectual strength • Range • Purposefulness

Suit of cups

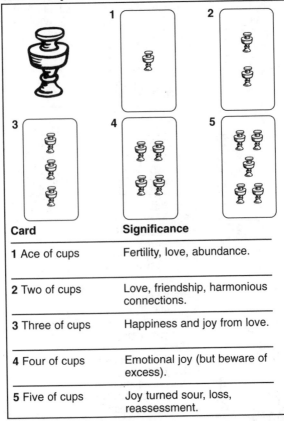

Card	Significance
1 Ace of cups	Fertility, love, abundance.
2 Two of cups	Love, friendship, harmonious connections.
3 Three of cups	Happiness and joy from love.
4 Four of cups	Emotional joy (but beware of excess).
5 Five of cups	Joy turned sour, loss, reassessment.

Card	Significance
6 Six of cups	Happy memories, the past reawakened.
7 Seven of cups	Ambition, hope (with forethought).
8 Eight of cups	Disappointment, search for new paths.
9 Nine of cups	Peace, contentment, fulfillment.
10 Ten of cups	Peace, happiness, achievement.

Suit of cups (continued)

Card	Significance
11 Knave of cups	A thoughtful, helpful youth.
12 Knight of cups	A fair, cheery youth, a lover.
13 Queen of cups	A bright, loving, creative woman.
14 King of cups	An intelligent, successful, worldly man.

Suit of swords

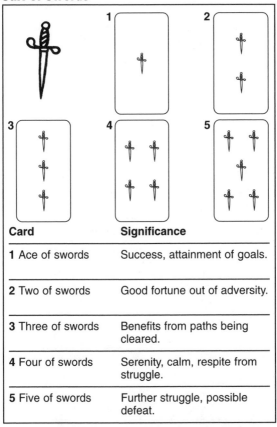

Card	Significance
1 Ace of swords	Success, attainment of goals.
2 Two of swords	Good fortune out of adversity.
3 Three of swords	Benefits from paths being cleared.
4 Four of swords	Serenity, calm, respite from struggle.
5 Five of swords	Further struggle, possible defeat.

Suit of swords (continued)

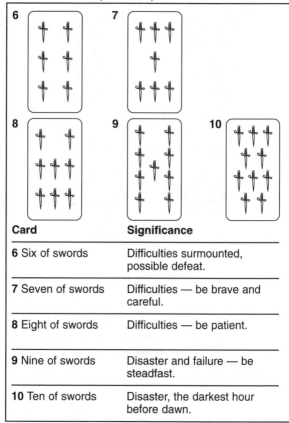

Card	Significance
6 Six of swords	Difficulties surmounted, possible defeat.
7 Seven of swords	Difficulties — be brave and careful.
8 Eight of swords	Difficulties — be patient.
9 Nine of swords	Disaster and failure — be steadfast.
10 Ten of swords	Disaster, the darkest hour before dawn.

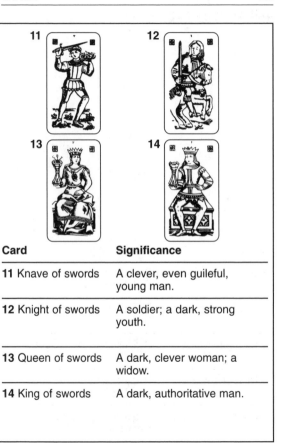

Card	Significance
11 Knave of swords	A clever, even guileful, young man.
12 Knight of swords	A soldier; a dark, strong youth.
13 Queen of swords	A dark, clever woman; a widow.
14 King of swords	A dark, authoritative man.

Suit of pentacles

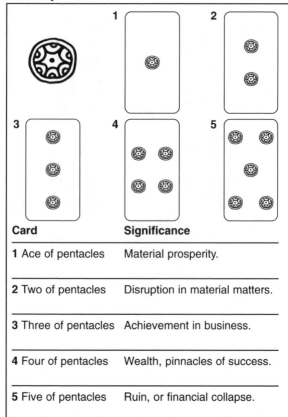

Card	Significance
1 Ace of pentacles	Material prosperity.
2 Two of pentacles	Disruption in material matters.
3 Three of pentacles	Achievement in business.
4 Four of pentacles	Wealth, pinnacles of success.
5 Five of pentacles	Ruin, or financial collapse.

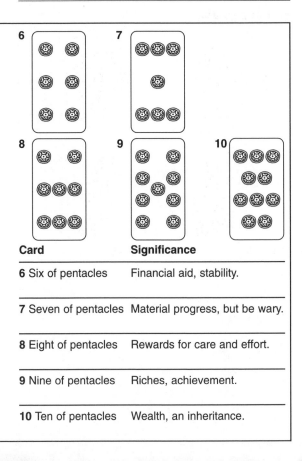

Card	Significance
6 Six of pentacles	Financial aid, stability.
7 Seven of pentacles	Material progress, but be wary.
8 Eight of pentacles	Rewards for care and effort.
9 Nine of pentacles	Riches, achievement.
10 Ten of pentacles	Wealth, an inheritance.

Suit of pentacles (continued)

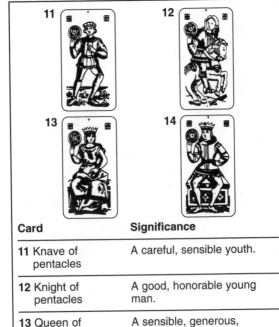

Card	Significance
11 Knave of pentacles	A careful, sensible youth.
12 Knight of pentacles	A good, honorable young man.
13 Queen of spentacles	A sensible, generous, wealthy woman.
14 King of spentacles	A careful, practical, successful man.

Suit of wands

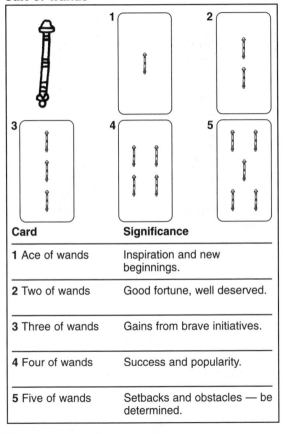

Card	Significance
1 Ace of wands	Inspiration and new beginnings.
2 Two of wands	Good fortune, well deserved.
3 Three of wands	Gains from brave initiatives.
4 Four of wands	Success and popularity.
5 Five of wands	Setbacks and obstacles — be determined.

Suit of wands (continued)

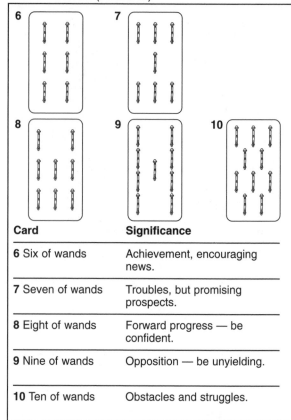

Card	Significance
6 Six of wands	Achievement, encouraging news.
7 Seven of wands	Troubles, but promising prospects.
8 Eight of wands	Forward progress — be confident.
9 Nine of wands	Opposition — be unyielding.
10 Ten of wands	Obstacles and struggles.

Card	Significance
11 Knave of wands	A dark, lively youth, an employee.
12 Knight of wands	A dark, energetic man, a journey.
13 Queen of wands	A practical, dominant woman.
14 King of wands	A powerful, determined man.

Choosing a significator

When using the minor arcana, you may choose a
significator — a card that represents the subject of the
reading. Choose this from among the court cards,
trying to ensure that it corresponds with your subject in
terms of age, sex, complexion, and (where possible),
personality. The following chart should help.

Subject	For significator use:
WOMEN	
Fair-haired young woman	**Queen of cups.**
Fair-haired mature woman (especially if well-to-do)	**Queen of pentacles.**
Dark and perhaps dangerous woman	**Queen of wands.**
Dark and sad woman	**Queen of swords.**
MEN	
Fair young man, or any young man in love	**Knight of cups.**
Wealthy young man	**Knight of pentacles.**
Dark young man	**Knight of wands.**
Dangerous young man	**Knave of wands.**
Fair-haired mature man	**King of cups.**
Wealthy mature man	**King of pentacles.**
Mature man in a position of power	**King of swords.**
Dark and/or dangerous mature man	**King of wands.**

Reading the tarot

The reader and *querant* (the person whose fortune is to be told) should concentrate throughout the reading.

1 Place the deck in order, checking to ensure that every card is the right way up.
2 Choose the spread you are going to use.
3 Select the significator if one is needed for the spread you have chosen.
4 Shuffle the cards thoroughly. In so doing, make sure that you turn some cards from top to bottom to ensure that some reversed cards will appear in the spread.
5 Hand the cards to the querant and ask him or her to repeat the shuffle.
6 Deal the cards, following any guidelines laid out in your chosen spread.

Horseshoe spread

This spread is useful for answering specific questions and is the most straightforward of the tarot spreads. You do not need a significator. Using the major arcana only, deal the first **seven** cards face up in the order shown *below*.

Positions and their meanings
1 Past influences
2 Present circumstances
3 General future prospects

4 Best course of action
5 The attitudes of others
6 Possible obtacles
7 Final outcome

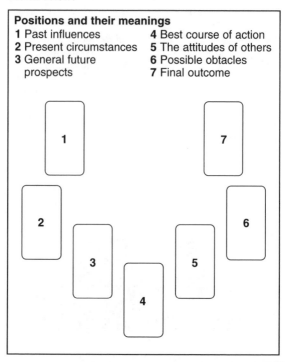

Seven-pointed star spread

This spread is useful for predicting events on the **seven** days after it is used. It can be used on any day of the week. Deal the first **seven** cards face down in the order shown. Place the significator face up in the center. Turn up the cards in order and interpret them.

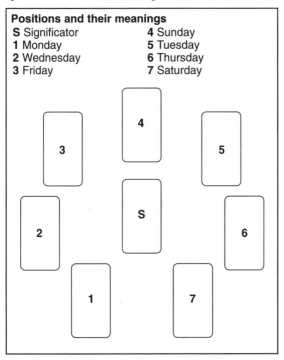

Positions and their meanings

S Significator	**4** Sunday
1 Monday	**5** Tuesday
2 Wednesday	**6** Thursday
3 Friday	**7** Saturday

Celtic cross spread

Some readers believe this to be the most useful of the spreads as it can be used to answer general or specific questions, or to give a picture of the year ahead. You can use the whole tarot deck, or just the major arcana.

Card, phrase to be repeated, and meaning
1 "This covers you."   The querant's present situation or state of mind.
2 "This crosses you."   Influences or events in the very near future.
3 "This crowns you."   The best course of action and the results of ignoring it.
4 "This is beneath you."   An event or matter in the past relevant to the present situation.
5 "This is behind you."   A more recent relevant event.
6 "This is before you."   The state of the querant's affairs in about six months' time.
7 "This is yourself."   Influences or events in the querant's main sphere of work.
8 "This is your house."   Influences or events in the querant's home or social life.

Choose a significator (**S**) and place it face up. Deal out
the first **10** cards face down, in the order shown. As
you set them out, repeat the phrases described **below**.

9 "Your hopes and fears."
Reflects the querant's feelings and influencing the
likely outcome of events.

10 "This is what will come."
The final outcome: the accumulative statement of
the whole spread.

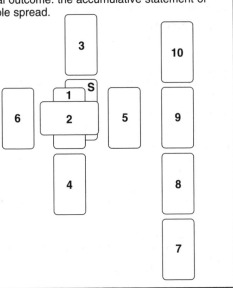

21 card spread

This is an in-depth yet easily-interpreted tarot spread. By giving each aspect of the reading **three** cards, more information can be gathered than in, say, the horseshoe spread, where just one card is used. Deal **21** cards face down in the order shown. Place the significator (**S**) face up to the right. Turn over the cards and interpret them in columns of **three**.

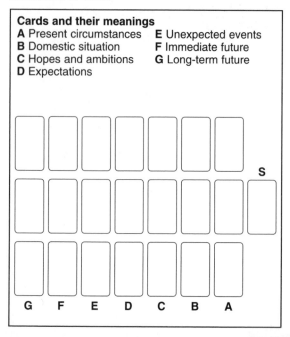

Cards and their meanings
A Present circumstances   **E** Unexpected events
B Domestic situation   **F** Immediate future
C Hopes and ambitions   **G** Long-term future
D Expectations

S

G   F   E   D   C   B   A

Circular spread

Use this spread to give a general impression of the coming year, starting from the time of the reading. You do not need a significator. Deal the first **13** cards face down in the order shown. Interpret the thirteenth card first.

Positions and their meanings
- The first card refers to the coming month, the second to the month after that, and so on
- The thirteenth card provides the main emphasis of the reading

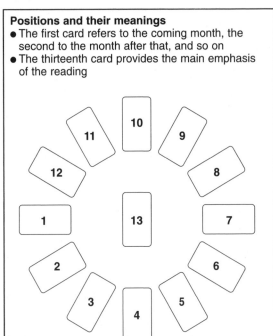

CARTOMANCY

Modern playing cards evolved from the tarot deck, so
it is not surprising that they are often used to predict
the future. The 52 cards in a standard deck are derived
from the tarot's minor arcana; and four court cards –
the knights – have been dropped. The only trace
remaining of the 22 cards of the major arcana of the
tarot is the Fool, who has become the joker of the
modern deck. Lords were originally made to be viewed
from one direction only (as tarot cards still are). The
double-headed playing card was not introduced until
the late 19th century.

The interpretations of the individual cards in predicting
the future probably also derive from the tarot. Until
comparatively recently, these interpretations were
preserved only in the oral tradition, and so can vary
from source to source. The interpretations given here
are those that are most generally accepted today.

Divination using playing cards

You can use the full deck of 52 playing cards when
trying to read the future – or, if you prefer, you can
discard all the **twos**, **threes**, **fours**, **fives** and **sixes**, and
use only the remaining 32-card deck. Both decks will
give you equally good results. Use whichever you
prefer, but make sure not to confuse the two: the
meanings of the individual cards in the 52-card deck
are *not* the same as those in the 32-card deck, and the
methods of laying out the cards also vary. But the areas

of influence of the four suits do not change whichever deck is used, nor does the choice of client card, nor your general preparation before laying out the cards.

The influence of the suits

When you are laying out the cards for a reading, you may find that one suit is more strongly represented than the others. As each suit is said to have its own particular area of influence, you must take this into account in your reading, and allow the atmosphere conveyed by the prominent suit to modify your interpretation of the other cards.

Hearts are considered lucky. Your emotions and your domestic life – love, affection, friendship, marriage, the family – are all said to be under their influence. They also stand for ambitions that will be successfully realized.

Clubs are the cards of success and are connected with money, business, and loyalty. But they can also be associated with failure, betrayal, and financial worries.

Diamonds influence your life outside your home. They also suggest that ambitions can only be realized and money made through determination and hard work.

Spades warn of dangers ahead. Your misfortunes – loss, suffering, enemies, treachery, failure – are all said to be under the influence of this suit.

Client card

The "client card" is a king or queen selected to
represent the person who is the subject of the reading.
As far as possible, choose a card that corresponds with
your subject's age, sex, and hair color.

- For a fair-, gray- or auburn-haired older man, use the
  king of diamonds.
- For a fair-, gray- or auburn-haired older woman, use the
  queen of diamonds.
- For a fair- or auburn-haired younger man, use the
  king of hearts.
- For a fair- or auburn-haired younger woman, use the
  queen of hearts.
- For a dark-haired older man, use the **king of spades**.
- For a dark-haired older woman, use the **queen of spades**.
- For a dark-haired younger man, use the **king of clubs**.
- For a dark-haired younger woman, use the **queen of clubs**.

Preparing to read the cards

Choose the client card for your subject, and place it in
the center of the table. Ask your subject to shuffle the
cards thoroughly, and then cut them with the left hand.
You should both concentrate fully on the cards,
clearing your minds of all other thoughts. Arrange the
cards around the client card in your chosen layout (see
pages 429-34), and begin the reading.

Note that it is traditionally considered unlucky to read
your own future in the cards, or to read the cards when
you are alone.

DIVINATION WITH THE 52-CARD DECK

When you use a full deck of 52 cards for divination, whether a card is upright or reversed, its meaning will be the same.

The basic significance of each numbered and court card in each suit follows on pages 439-40, but it will be for the person giving the reading to use his or her intuition to provide an accurate forecast.

HEARTS

Ace The home. Love, friendship, and happiness.
King A good-natured, impetuous, fair-haired man.
Queen A trustworthy, affectionate, fair-haired woman.
Jack A close friend.
Ten Good fortune and happiness.
Nine The "wish" card that makes dreams come true.
Eight Invitations and festivities.
Seven False hopes and broken promises.
Six An overgenerous disposition, unexpected good fortune.
Five Jealousy, indecisiveness.
Four Changes, delays, and postponements.
Three Warns of a need for caution.
Two Success and prosperity.

CLUBS

Ace Wealth, health, love, and happiness.

King An honest, generous, dark-haired man.

Queen An attractive, self-confident, dark-haired woman.

Jack A reliable friend.

Ten Unexpected money, good luck.

Nine Friends being stubborn.

Eight Opposition, disappointment, the taking of reckless chances.

Seven Prosperity – provided a member of the opposite sex does not interfere.

Six Business success.

Five A new friend or a successful marriage.

Four Fortunes changing for the worse.

Three Marriage bringing money. May indicate several marriages.

Two Opposition and disappointments.

DIAMONDS

Ace Money, a letter or a ring.

King A stubborn, quick-tempered, fair-haired man.

Queen A flirtatious, sophisticated, fair-haired woman.

Jack A relative, not altogether reliable.

Ten Marriage or money, a journey, changes.

Nine Restlessness. A surprise connected with money.

Eight A marriage late in life. A journey leading to a new relationship.

Seven Heavy losses.

Six A warning against a second marriage.

Five Prosperity, good news, a happy family.

Four An inheritance, changes, troubles.

Three Legal or domestic disputes.

Two A serious love affair.

SPADES

Ace Emotional conflict, an unfortunate love affair.
  Sometimes regarded as the "death card."
King An ambitious dark-haired man.
Queen An unscrupulous dark-haired woman.
Jack A well-meaning but lazy acquaintance.
Ten Misfortune and worry.
Nine Bad luck in all things.
Eight Trouble and disappointment ahead.
Seven Sorrow, loss of friendship.
Six Some improvement in circumstances.
Five Reverses and anxieties, but eventual success.
Four Jealousy, illness, business worries.
Three Faithlessness and partings.
Two Separation, scandal, deceit.

SPECIAL COMBINATIONS: USING 52 CARDS

Some combinations of cards have special meanings when the deck of 52 cards is used. These meanings apply only when the cards are immediately next to one another in the layout.

Ace of hearts next to any other heart Friendship.

Ace of hearts with another heart on each side
Love affair

Ace of hearts with a diamond on each side Money

Ace of hearts with a spade on each side Quarrels

Ace of diamonds/eight of clubs A business proposal

Ace of spades/king of clubs A politician

Ace of spades/ten of spades A serious undertaking

Ace of spades/four of hearts A new baby

Ten of hearts Cancels adjacent cards of ill-fortune; reinforces adjacent cards of good fortune

Ten of diamonds/two of hearts Marriage/money

Ten of spades Cancels adjacent cards of good fortune; reinforces adjacent cards of ill-fortune

Ten of spades next to any club Business troubles

Ten of spades with a club on each side Theft, forgery, grave business losses

Nine of hearts next to any card of ill fortune Quarrels, temporary obstacles

Nine of hearts/five of spades Loss of status

Nine of clubs/eight of hearts Gaiety

Nine of diamonds next to any court card Lack of success, an inability to concentrate

Nine of diamonds/eight of spades A bitter quarrel

Nine of spades/seven of diamonds Loss of money

Eight of hearts/eight of diamonds A trousseau

Eight of hearts/five of hearts A present of jewelry

Eight of diamonds/five of hearts A present of money

Eight of spades on the immediate right of the client card Abandon your current plans.

Four of hearts next to any court card Many love affairs

Four of clubs next to any court card A loss, injustice

Two of clubs/two of diamonds An unexpected message

EXAMPLES OF READINGS USING 52 CARDS
Seven triplets

This spread, also known as the *seven packs*, is used to give a general picture of the client's future. Use the full 52-card deck, and place the client card face up in the middle of the table. After shuffling, deal the first 21 cards face down in the order shown by the numbers on the diagram. Beginning on the left, turn up each pack of **3** cards and interpret them.

The client is a dark-haired young woman; her client card is the queen of clubs (**C**).

POSITIONS ON THE SEVEN TRIPLETS SPREAD

Pack **a** Personality and state of mind.
Pack **b** Family and home.
Pack **c** Present desires.
Pack **d** Hopes and expectations.
Pack **e** The unexpected.
Pack **f** The immediate future.
Pack **g** The more distant future.

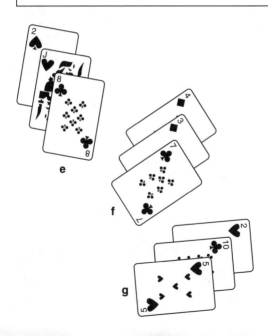

DIVINATION WITH THE 32-CARD DECK

The 32-card deck is formed by discarding the *twos*, *threes*, *fours*, *fives*, and *sixes* from a standard 52-card deck. You will need to mark the top of each card in a 32-card deck: the meanings of the individual cards differ, as shown in the charts that follow, depending on whether they are *upright* or *reversed*.

HEARTS

Ace Good news, love, domestic happiness.
Reversed A move, changes, short-lived happiness.
King An affectionate, generous, fair-haired man.
Reversed A deceitful person.
Queen An affectionate, dependable, fair-haired woman.
Reversed A widow, divorcee, or woman unhappy in love.
Jack A friend or lover.
Reversed An untrustworthy lover.
Ten Good fortune and happiness.
Reversed A surprise, a birth.
Nine The "wish" card that makes dreams come true.
Reversed Temporary troubles.
Eight An invitation, a journey, a wedding.
Reversed Unrequited love.
Seven Contentment.
Reversed Boredom.

CLUBS

Ace Good luck, good news, financial letters or papers.
Reversed Unpleasant letters, short-lived happiness.
King A friendly, honest, dark-haired man.
Reversed Minor worries and troubles.

CLUBS continued

Queen An affectionate, helpful, dark-haired woman.
Reversed An unreliable woman.
Jack An amusing, dark-haired lover.
Reversed An insincere lover.
Ten Luck, luxury, prosperity.
Reversed Business troubles, a journey.
Nine Unexpected money.
Reversed A small gift, or a slight problem.
Eight Good fortune, brought by a dark-haired person.
Reversed An unhappy love affair, a legal dispute, a divorce.
Seven Minor money matters.
Reversed Financial problems.

DIAMONDS

Ace A letter, money, or a ring.
Reversed Bad news.
King A powerful fair-haired or gray-haired man.
Reversed Treachery, deception.
Queen A spiteful, talkative, fair-haired woman.
Reversed Malice.
Jack A messenger, employee or person in uniform.
Reversed A trouble-maker.
Ten Moving house, a journey, a major change.
Reversed Changes for the worse.
Nine News, surprises, anxieties.
Reversed Domestic disputes, lovers' quarrels.
Eight A love affair, a short journey.
Reversed A separation, affections ignored.
Seven Teasing, criticism, a small gift.
Reversed Minor scandal, gossip.

SPADES

Ace Emotional satisfaction, business propositions.
Reversed Bad news, disappointments, death.
King An untrustworthy dark-haired man, possibly a lawyer.
Reversed An enemy.
Queen An older, dark-haired woman.
Reversed A cunning, treacherous woman.
Jack An ill-mannered young person.
Reversed A traitor.
Ten Grief, a long journey, confinement.
Reversed Minor illness.
Nine Loss, failure, misfortune.
Reversed Unhappiness for a close friend.
Eight Bad news, impending disappointments.
Reversed Quarrels, sorrow, separation, divorce.
Seven New resolutions, a change of plan.
Reversed Bad advice, faulty planning.

SPECIAL COMBINATIONS: USING 32 CARDS

Some combinations of cards have special meanings
when the deck of 32 cards is used. These meanings
apply only when the cards are immediately next to one
another in the layout.

Ace of clubs with a diamond on each side Money's
coming your way.

Ace of clubs/nine of diamonds Legal affairs.

Ace of diamonds/eight of clubs Unexpected money.

Ace of diamonds with a diamond on each side
Financial prosperity.

Ace of diamonds/seven of diamonds Quarrels.

Ace of diamonds/seven of diamonds/jack of diamonds A cable or telegram.

Ace of diamonds/nine of spades Illness.

Ace of spades/queen of clubs A tiresome journey.

Ace of spades/nine of spades Business failure.

Ace of spades/eight of spades Betrayal.

King of hearts/nine of hearts A happy love affair.

King of clubs/ten of clubs A proposal of marriage.

King of diamonds/eight of spades An unexpected journey lies ahead.

King of spades/seven of clubs Be cautious with your investments.

Queen of hearts/seven of diamonds Unexpected delights await you.

Queen of hearts/ten of spades Danger, adventure.

Queen of clubs/seven of diamonds Uncertainty.

Queen of diamonds/seven of hearts Happiness tainted by jealousy.

Queen of diamonds/seven of spades Success in the village rather than in the city.

Queen of spades/jack of spades Great evil.

Jack of hearts/seven of clubs Beware a lover who is motivated by greed.

Jack of clubs/jack of spades Business difficulties, financial losses.

Jack of diamonds/nine of spades Beware of taking bad advice.

Ten of hearts/nine of clubs Show business.

Ten of hearts/ten of diamonds A wedding.

Ten of clubs next to any ace Large sums of money.

Ten of diamonds/eight of clubs A honeymoon.

Ten of diamonds/seven of spades A delay.
Ten of spades/seven of clubs An unfortunate future.
Nine of hearts/nine of clubs A fortunate legacy.
Nine of clubs/eight of hearts Celebrations, festivities.
Nine of diamonds/eight of hearts Long-distance travel.
Eight of hearts/eight of diamonds New and important
work to be done.
Eight of clubs/eight of diamonds True love.
Eight of diamonds next to any club A prolonged
journey will be taken.
Eight of spades/seven of diamonds Help needed.
Seven of diamonds next to any club Money problems.
Seven of spades/king, queen, or jack of spades Look
out for a traitor.

QUARTETS, TRIPLETS, AND PAIRS

It is considered to be very significant when two, three, or
four cards of the same value are placed immediately next
to one another in the layout. These groups of cards
should be interpreted first, as they have an influence on
the layout as a whole.
Four aces Separation from friends or from money.
The more *aces* reversed, the greater the separation.
Three aces Flirtations, foolishness, and temporary
anxieties. The more *aces* reversed, the greater the folly
and anxiety.
Two aces A marriage. Two red *aces* – a happy
marriage; a red *ace* and a black *ace* – an unhappy
marriage; one *ace* reversed – potential marriage
breakdown; both *aces* reversed – divorce.
Four kings Good fortune, which lessens with each *king*
that is reversed.

Three kings A new venture. The more *kings* reversed, the less successful it will be.

Two kings A business partnership. One *king* reversed –partially successful partnership; *both kings* reversed – the partnership will fail.

Four queens A party or some other social gathering. The more *queens* reversed, the less successful it will be.

Three queens Visitors and conversation. The more *queens* reversed, the greater the degree of scandal.

Two queens Friendship. *One queen* reversed – rivalry; *both queens* reversed – betrayal.

Four jacks Quarrels. The more *jacks* reversed, the more violent the quarrel.

Three jacks Family disagreements. The more *jacks* reversed, the greater the disagreement.

Two jacks Loss or theft, with each *jack* reversed bringing it nearer.

Four tens Unexpected good fortune, which lessens with each *ten* reversed.

Three tens Financial and legal problems, which lessen with each *ten* reversed.

Two tens Changes at work bringing good fortune. Each *ten* reversed delays them.

Four nines A pleasant surprise. The more *nines* reversed, the sooner it will happen.

Three nines Health, wealth, and happiness. The more *nines* reversed, the longer they will be delayed.

Two nines Small financial gains. Each *nine* reversed delays and lessens the gain.

Four eights Success and failure mixed. The more *eights* reversed, the higher the proportion of failure.

Three eights Love and marriage. The more *eights* reversed, the less the degree of commitment.

Two eights A brief love affair. One *eight* reversed – a flirtation; both *eights* reversed – a misunderstanding.

Four sevens Enemies, mischief-makers. The more *sevens* reversed, the less successful they will be.

Three sevens A new enterprise, or a new baby. Each *seven* reversed delays it.

Two sevens A new and happy love affair. One *seven* reversed – deceived in love; both *sevens* reversed – regrets in love.

EXAMPLES OF READINGS USING 32 CARDS
The fan

This spread is used to give a general reading of the client's future. Shuffle the 32-card deck and spread it out face down. Ask your client to choose any **18** cards and to set them out face up in the order shown. If the client card is not among cards **1-13**, look for the **seven** of the same suit.

If neither card is there, the reading should be left to another day.

Cards **1-13** are read first. Considering the client card as the first card, count *five* cards to the right and interpret the **fifth** card.Use that card as the first card of the next set of *five*, and continue reading every **fifth** card until you have returned to the client card. Then read cards **14-18**: interpret cards **14** and **18** together, then cards **15** and **17**, and finally card **16**. Summarize all your interpretations into a coherent reading.

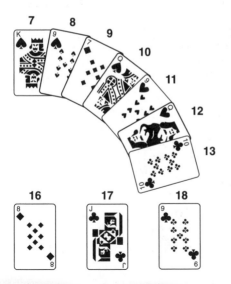

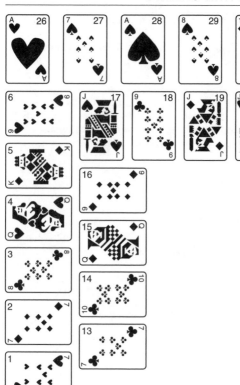

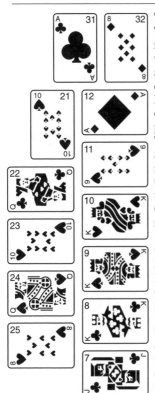

The temple of fortune

This spread dates from the middle of the 18th century, when it was developed by a famous French cartomancer called Etteilla. It gives a complete reading of the client's life – past, present and future. The 32-card deck is used; a client card is not required. After shuffling, the cards are laid out face up in the order shown. Cards **1-6** and **13-16** represent the past; cards **17-21** and **26-32** represent the present; cards **7-12** and **22-25** represent the future. In each case the outer row of cards gives the primary indications of the reading, which are then modified by the inner row. Some cartomancers also consider that the outer rows refer to events in the client's outer, worldly life, while the inner rows refer to his or her inner, mental, and spiritual life.

Grand star

The popular star spreads are found in a number of traditional forms. Of these, the grand star is probably the most useful for a general reading. The 32-card deck is used. Place the client card (C) face up in the center, and deal the first *21* cards of the shuffled deck face down around it in the order shown. Turn up and interpret the cards in pairs, in the order **13, 15; 20, 18; 14, 16; 19, 17; 9, 5; 11, 8; 10, 6; 12, 7; 3, 1; 4, 2**. Read the final card, **21**, on its own. Cards *above* the client card represent success and achievements to come; those *below* refer to the past, and to things already accomplished. Cards to the *left* of the client card represent obstacles and opposition; those to the *right* refer to the future, and to help and assistance to come.

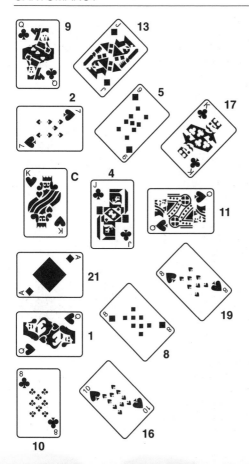

Great star

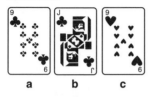

a   **b**   **c**

This is the most detailed of the
traditional star spreads. The 32-card
deck is used, and the client card (**C**) is
chosen and placed face up on the table. The
client then shuffles the
deck and divides it into
three. Turn each of these
piles face up and read the
three cards exposed, first
singly and then in
combination. These cards (**a**, **b**, **c**) are called the
indicators and give the general tone of the
reading. Remove them from the deck
and place them to the *left* of the table.
Reshuffle the deck and deal the
star in the order shown **1-24**.
Interpret each group of *three*
cards in conjunction,
beginning with the group
immediately above the client card
and continuing in a counterclockwise direction.
Finally, study the spread as a whole and
summarize your interpretation.

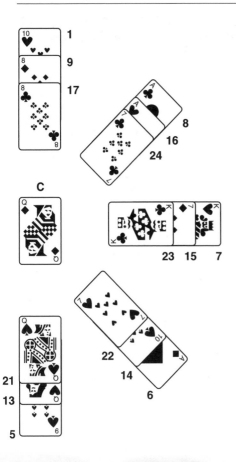

FORTUNE-TELLING CARDS

A certain Mlle Lenormand from Paris, France, was
well-known for divinations produced by reading
special cards during the l9th century. She had designed
a unique pack comprising **36** cards for this purpose.
You could perhaps make a similar set for yourself from
stiff paper and even decorate them according to the
name of each card, giving them plain or patterned
backs. Each card has a different name and significance,
as in the chart that follows. The image on each relates
to the name but the Clouds card (number **6**) should
feature both stormy and light cards.

The layout
The *querant*, or the person doing the reading, should
first shuffle the cards. The cards are then dealt left to
right, face up, in four rows with eight cards in each,
leaving four cards for a fifth row to be placed below
the others and centrally.

Card number **28** (Gentleman) is the master card if
the querant is a man. Card number **29** (Lady) is the
master card if the querant is a woman. The position of
the other cards in relation to number **28** or **29** is
important. The querant or diviner must then consider
the significance of those cards closest to either number
28 or number **29**, as appropriate, and should intuitively
produce a prediction.

The cards

1	**Knight**	Wonderful news
2	**Clover**	Good fortune
3	**Ship**	New horizons
4	**House**	Good results
5	**Tree**	Good health
6	**Clouds**	A good or bad omen
7	**Serpent**	Beware of treachery
8	**Coffin**	Financial loss
9	**Flowers**	Happiness
10	**Scythe**	Difficulties ahead
11	**Whip**	Family problems
12	**Birds**	Short-term problems
13	**Child**	You will be admired
14	**Fox**	A trickster at large
15	**Bear**	Someone envies you
16	**Stars**	Efforts are rewarded
17	**Stork**	You may move
18	**Dog**	True friendship

19	**Tower**	A long life
20	**Garden**	A new friendship
21	**Mountain**	Opposition
22	**Roads**	Problems ahead
23	**Mice**	An unfortunate robbery
24	**Heart**	Romance in the offing
25	**Ring**	Happy family circle
26	**Book**	A secret worries you
27	**Letter**	Good news by mail
28	**Gentleman**	A master card
29	**Lady**	A master card
30	**Lilies**	Contentment
31	**Moon**	Great honors
32	**Sun**	A wonderful future
33	**Key**	Life will run smoothly
34	**Fish**	Good fortune around the corner
35	**Anchor**	Success in business
36	**Cross**	Difficulties

THE
I CHING

THE I CHING

One of the world's most ancient systems of divination, the *I Ching* is in some ways related to numerology since it involves use of a combination of randomly chosen numbers, represented by broken and unbroken lines, that form a six-line figure or hexagram from which a reading can be made.

It is a system that originated in China at least 5,000 years ago and relates closely to Taoism, providing a philosophical framework for life.

Method
Yarrow sticks were once used, but these have now been replaced by coins. Ideally old Chinese coins should be used. These are round in shape but have a square hole in the center. A serious question of any kind should first be thought up but not spoken. This oracle is not to be taken lightly, exponents strongly recommend. If you cannot find any Chinese coins, others may be used as an alternative.

Three coins are required. The side of each coin to be counted as "heads" has the value **3**. The other side, equivalent to "tails," has the value **2**. The coins are thrown **6** times in all. On each throw, a value of **6**, **7**, **8**, or **9** will be allocated. With each throw, a hexagram (or group of six lines) can be started from the bottom up.

A single unbroken line is used for results that are *yang* – **7** and **9**; and a broken line is used for results that are *yin* – **6** and **8**. It should also be noted that: **6**

equates to *Old Yin*; 7 equates to *Young Yang*; **8** equates
to *Young Yin*; **9** equates to *Old Yang*. The "***Old***" in the
above signifies that resulting lines in the hexagram will
need to be changed, as described later.

The table that follows should then be consulted.
Take the first three lines of the hexagram (the lower
three) and see where they meet with the pattern of the
upper three. (These groups of three lines are known as
trigrams). This will give the number of the hexagram
to be consulted.

Trigrams Upper ▶ Lower ▼	Ch'ien	Chen	K'an	Ken	K'un	Sun	Li	Tui
Ch'ien	1	34	5	26	11	9	14	43
Chen	25	51	3	27	24	42	21	17
K'an	6	40	29	4	7	59	64	47
Ken	33	62	39	52	13	53	36	31
K'un	12	16	8	23	2	20	35	43
Sun	44	32	48	18	46	57	50	28
Li	13	55	63	22	36	37	30	49
Tui	10	54	60	41	19	61	38	38

Example

If a **7**, **6**, **8** , **7**, and **9** are thrown in that order, the result
is, starting from the bottom, a hexagram comprising
Young Yang, *Old Yin*, *Young Yin*, *Young Yang*, *Old
Yang*, and *Young Yin*, written as follows:

A circle has been placed on two lines as a reminder
of which lines are "*Old*." (Note that this will not
always be necessary – for example, when only **7s** and
8s are thrown).

The earlier table on page 464 can then be consulted.
From this it can be seen that the bottom trigram is
Chen and the top trigram is *Tui*, leading to hexagram
17. The reading for this hexagram can then be made,
and summaries for this purpose are provided on pages
466-481.

But there were two changing or "*Old*" lines,
remember – *Old Yin* (second from the bottom) and **Old
Yang** (second from the top). These lines are then
changed to *Yang* and *Yin* respectively, forming a new
hexagram, as *below*.

The table on page 464 is again consulted.

The trigrams *Tui* (lower) and *Chen* (upper) lead to hexagram **54** this time. This hexagram reading will provide guidance as to the outcome of the questioner's predicament.

The hexagrams
To provide an idea of the insight to be gleaned from consulting the *I Ching*, a basic, highly abridged interpretation of the meaning of each of the **64** hexagrams follows. But for a full explanation of their content, a complete translation with annotations will be required, and these are readily available. They include analyses known as *The Judgment* and *The Image*, as well as further insight into lines making up each hexagram. Interpretation always requires an open mind since the content is highly enigmatic and in verse. Practice will be essential.

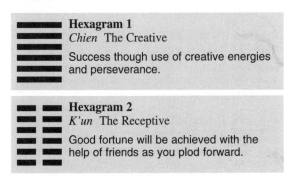

Hexagram 1
Chien The Creative
Success though use of creative energies and perseverance.

Hexagram 2
K'un The Receptive
Good fortune will be achieved with the help of friends as you plod forward.

Hexagram 3
Chun Difficulty at the start

Do not act too quickly. You need to strive for the success you will ultimately achieve.

Hexagram 4
Meng Youth

Remember to take heed of the advice of those who have a lot to teach you, and you will surely benefit.

Hexagram 5
Hsu Contemplation

Proceed with care, considering carefully each step that you take in life. Patience is a virtue.

Hexagram 6
Sung Conflict

Be prepared to compromise in an attitude or decision for a happy outcome, or seek advice.

Hexagram 7
Shih The Army

Act fairly if those around you are to continue to have respect for you. If difficulties arise, a good reputation will pay dividends

Hexagram 8
Pi Union

Commitment to a project or to a friend or colleague will bring about goodwill and prosperity. Honesty is the best policy.

Hexagram 9
Hsiao ch'u The Restraining

A new venture or, alternatively, someone who appears strong, may meet with difficulties because of what appear to be trivialities.

Hexagram 10
Lu Treading

Take care in what you do and you should find that you will be able to overcome almost any potentially dangerous situation.

Hexagram 11
T'ai Peace

There are indications of a strong force that will bring about harmonious relationships and a sense of equilibrium.

Hexagram 12
P 'i Discord

Things may appear to be on an even keel
but inwardly there may be confusion.
Only by slowing down will good fortune
be maintained.

Hexagram 13
T'ung jen Sociability

True friendship and cooperation will lead
to tremendous achievements. A shared
goal will be reached all the more
speedily.

Hexagram 14
Ta yu Wealth

Whether you are wealthy by virtue of your
possessions, or in your degree of
happiness, or in wisdom, proceed with all
due modesty.

Hexagram 15
Ch'ien Modesty

Life will have its ups and downs. In
periods of success, remember not to
disregard those less fortunate and do not
become conceited.

Hexagram 16
Yu Enthusiasm

This may be the right time to start a new venture. Proceed enthusiastically, but with all due care.

Hexagram 17
Sui Following

Be prepared to adapt to circumstances and to the demands of others if the status quo is to be maintained.

Hexagram 18
Ku Mending

Some damage may have been done, or a loss may have occurred. It is time for a new beginning. Think carefully about this.

Hexagram 19
Lin Behavior

One should watch one's conduct and either give or accept appropriate examples of behavior. Do so and good fortune will result.

Hexagram 20
Kuan View

Someone in a position of responsibility must act with sensitivity towards others if the matters are to succeed.

Hexagram 21
Shih ho Biting

Obstacles may stand in the way. Hence the necessity to bite through them. However, do not act too vigorously. Instead use grim determination.

Hexagram 22
Pi Grace

Do not take beauty for granted as it may fade. Acting with grace and having beauty around you will lift your spirits.

Hexagram 23
Po Decay

You will do well to try and assist others while you bear your own difficulties with dignity and fortitude.

Hexagram 24
Fu Returning

New opportunities arise. Success is in the offing as you experience renewed creative energies for some special undertaking.

Hexagram 25
Wu wang Simplicity

Act as you feel is right and in a natural way, and the results this will bring about will be in tune with nature and highly rewarding.

Hexagram 26
Ta ch'u Restrained power

Conserve your energies until the moment seems right. You will go on to better things if external forces are in tune with your own energies.

Hexagram 27
I Nourishment

Take care of others, and yourself, in both spiritual and material ways. Even those who at present do not seem worthy of your attention will benefit, and so in turn will you.

Hexagram 28
Ta kuo Overwhelming greatness

Troubles may loom, but you will manage to overcome them. The very shape of this hexagram (three solid lines centrally) seems to indicate you can hold things together.

Hexagram 29
K'an Depth

Danger may threaten, but with a clear, deep understanding of the situation, it will be possible to win through and avoid disaster.

Hexagram 30
Li Fire

The fiery personality should try as far as he or she can to control this trait. It may bring benefits but can also be destructive.

Hexagram 31
Hsien Support

A strong union between partners is indicated, the one giving to the other valuable support.

Hexagram 32
Heng Consistency

Keep striving and do not give up with what you are trying to achieve. This will ensure your success.

Hexagram 33

Tun Retreat

The two broken lines at the base of this hexagram are taken to signify that there is risk of hostility of some kind and that retreat is the best policy.

Hexagram 34

Ta chuang Great Power

You will come to have influence over others but this new status should not be abused. Act with fairness and do not use your power to anyone's detriment.

Hexagram 35

Chin Progress

There will be great achievements if you stick to your aims and do not try to overtake others on the way.

Hexagram 36

Min I The light dims

Bide your time and wait until the right opportunity presents itself. Do not act to arouse feelings of envy or resentment in others.

Hexagram 37
Chia jen Family

It may seem to the outside world that the man holds a marriage together, but in fact it is the woman who does so, and a strong family unit promotes a stable society.

Hexagram 38
K'uei Disharmony

Do not be swayed by the behavior or opinions of others if they are at variance with your own principles. Maintain your own standards, but do not judge others too harshly.

Hexagram 39
Chien Obstacles

Trying to fight against difficulties that arise in the course of life is not always the best solution. It can be wiser to keep one's composure and consider a novel approach to solving the problem.

Hexagram 40
Hsieh Freedom

There may have been great difficulties and confusion but soon you will see the light. Do not rest on your laurels, however.

Hexagram 41
Sun Lessening

Sometimes with loss comes a lesson. Misfortune may cause one to reassess one's values so that one thereby becomes a better and stronger person.

Hexagram 42
I Increase

Seize the moment and act now. The time will not always be right. All the signs are that you will be successful. Enjoy such good fortune but do not forget others in times of plenty.

Hexagram 43
Kuai Determination

After continous effort over a long period, a breakthrough lies ahead. Share the benefits with others.

Hexagram 44
Kou Facing temptation

Be careful about the way in which you judge people. They are not always what they seem. Do not be led astray.

Hexagram 45
Ts'ui Agreement

This is the moment for establishing peace and equilibrium. Everyone will benefit if you try to do this. On the way, you may have to influence someone else.

Hexagram 46
Sheng Rising

Remain determined and you will rise to great heights. But avoid selfishness at all costs since it may bring about a downfall.

Hexagram 47
K'un Oppression

When problems come our way, only strength of character will see us through. Be sure to learn from your experiences. You will have a lot to overcome.

Hexagram 48
Ching The well

Use your knowledge for everyone's benefit, not only your own. Draw on your experiences to good effect. Think deeply about matters and avoid a flippant attitude.

Hexagram 49
Ko Revolution

Things may seem settled but you may need to change with the times and adapt accordingly. Wait for the right moment. Success is certain if you act unselfishly.

Hexagram 50
Ting The cauldron

The cooking pot symbolizes nourishment. Good fortune is indicated by this hexagram, as is spiritual comfort.

Hexagram 51
Chen Thunder

Even in a seemingly disastrous situation you may find inner strengths which enable you to accept what transpires and move other things.

Hexagram 52
Ken Stillness

Keeping still can help one to preserve a valuable inner calm. Composure is a valuable quality when dangers threaten.

Hexagram 53
Chien Development

This is an auspicious hexagram, indicating that the very best of relationships are often formed over time and with concentrated effort.

Hexagram 54
Kuei mei The young bride

Do not expect too much of others. They may be making use of you for their own ends. People enter into relationships for all sorts of reasons.

Hexagram 55
Feng Greatness

Prosperity often brings with it a certain complacency, but the wise, successful individual puts something aside for the future and is not ostentatious.

Hexagram 56
Lu Stranger

People who are constantly on the move may be taken advantage of by others at times, just as strangers may occasionally be taken in by the traveler. This hexagram may not augur well for any permanent arrangement.

Hexagram 57
Sun Gentle wind

Sustained gently effort wins out in the end. Prepare for the future by putting your affairs in order and gaining the confidence of others.

Hexagram 58
Tui Joy

If you can show joy to the world and remain steadfast in your efforts, this will bring you enormous success and recognition.

Hexagram 59
Huan Dispersal

This hexagram is sometimes taken to mean that there may be benefits in moving on or away. Self-sacrifice may sometimes be necessary for success at a later stage.

Hexagram 60
Chieh Limits

Learn to recognize your limits and realize where your true talents lie. This is the surest route to happiness and success.

Hexagram 61
Chung Fu Understanding

If you can be gentle with those who are less confident than yourself, they will respond and become stronger as a result of your empathy.

Hexagram 62
Hsiao kua Small successes

Do not expect always to achieve great things. Continue to strive, but be satisfied with smaller accomplishments, too.

Hexagram 63
Chi Chi Completion

If you have some unfinished task, however small, it will be as well to complete it before too long. Be aware that success may not last.

Hexagram 64
We chi Prior to completion

Look carefully at your circumstances and make preparations for the future. Take precautions and your success will be assured.

MISCELLANY OF NUMBERS

WINNING NUMBERS

There is no way of guaranteeing that everyone can buy
a winning ticket for a lottery or sweepstake, of course,
nor that we could all be sure to back a winning horse.
Nevertheless numerologists frequently recommend that
there are certain things we can do to increase the
chances of causing what are thought to be "lucky
vibrations."

Gambling on a lucky day, calculated according to
your sign of the zodiac, may helps towards success.
The tables you will find on pages 279-285 will help
you to identify lucky days on which to gamble.
Importantly, there may be more chance of scooping the
jackpot if both the day on which the bet is placed and
the date on which the draw, race, or game takes place
are deemed "lucky days."

Other means of influencing a lucky outcome include
the following:

Predictive dreams
Claims are sometimes made that, if notice is taken of a
number occurring in a dream, this may sometimes turn
out to be the number of a winning horse or greyhound.

Life numbers
Some people opt to use their Life Number, calculated
according to the instructions on pages 82-84. When
gambling in this way, it is not always necessary to
reduce the calculation to a single digit.

Square of Venus

On page 31 you will find the layout of this ancient magic square that includes all the numbers from **1-49**. By coincidence many countries operate national lotteries that involve choosing six numbers in this range. You might therefore choose to draw out an enlarged Square of Venus and then, with eyes closed and mind cleared, to point to six numbers in succession and at random.

Another way of selecting six numbers from the Square of Venus is first to find your birth number, calculated according to the instructions on pages 82-85. Then find the date number for the lottery using the method *below*. If the date *number* (not the actual date) for the day on which the lottery is to take place is *odd* (**1,3,5,7,** or **9**), look at the *vertical* line in which your birth number appears. Then use the other six numbers in that vertical line for your lottery selection.

If, however, the date *number* (again, not the actual date) for the day on which the lottery is to take place is *even*, look at the *horizontal* line in which your birth number appears and use the other six numbers in that row for your lottery selection.

Calculating the date number

You can work out the date number (remember, this is not the date itself) as follows. Say the date on which a lottery takes place is **September 9, 2001**.
First take the day and the number of the month.
Add these digits:
9 + 9 = 18

Then take the year and add together all the digits:
2 + 0 + 0 + 1 = 3
Now add the two results: **18 + 3 = 21**
Finally reduce **21** to **2 + 1 = 3**
The date number for **September 9, 2001** is therefore
3. This is an *odd* number so the querent would need to
look along the *vertical* line in which his or her birth
number appears in the Square of Venus.

Changing luck

Thirteen may sometimes have been lucky for you, but
there are few who would claim they can always rely
upon it, or any other number, for that matter. On
Friday, September **13**, 1991, the wife of a private
hospital managing director drew the winning prize –
number **13**. Thinking it would seem unfair to everyone
present if his wife accepted the prize, the managing
director insisted that the draw should be repeated.
Amazingly, his wife drew the same ticket. At the third
attempt, however, Friday the **13th** proved unlucky.

ELEMENTS AND NUMBERS

In the West, there are traditionally four elements: Fire, Water, Earth, and Air. (In the East, however, the elements Wood and Metal are added, and air does not apply.) Some numerologists believe that certain Personality Numbers are influenced by particular elements. The following chart shows how such influences may become apparant. The Personality Number is calculated by taking the date of the month in which you were born.

Personality Number 1
Air
Ambition becomes
  exaggerated

Personality Number 2
Water
Sensitivity is marked

Personality Number 3
Fire
A passionate nature rules

Personality Number 4
Earth
Practicality comes to the
  fore

Personality Number 5
Air
Creative talents are
  characteristic

Personality Number 6
Water
Intuition is appreciated by
  others

Personality Number 7
Water
There is a tendency to be
  over-emotional

Personality Number 8
Earth
The facility for hard work
  is marked

Personality Number 9
Fire
A bad temper becomes a
  trait

WEIRD NUMBERS

This is an actual term used by mathematicians and refers to a number which cannot be written as the sum of any of its factors. For example, **36** is not a weird number. Its factors are **1, 2, 3, 6, 12, 18, 9**; and **18 + 12 + 6 = 36**. **Seventy**, however, is classed as a weird number because no combinations of any of its factors will add together to give **70**. Other so-called weird numbers include **836**; **4,030**; **5,830**; and **7,192**.

Even stranger
5,040 was said by Plato, the Greek philosopher, to be the ideal number of inhabitants for a city. Interestingly, it can be divided by all numbers from **1-10**.

Multiply the number **142,857** by **1, 2, 3, 4, 5,** or **6** and you will see that each time you get a different arrangement of the figures it contains. The answers are **142,857**; **285,714**; **428,517**; **571,428**; **714,285**; and **857,142** respectively.

A number is always divisible by **9** if the sum of its digits is divisible by **9**.

2 is the only *even* prime number.

NUMEROLOGY
CHARTS

NUMEROLOGY CHARTS

On the pages that follow, you will find 10 blank
charts. If you collect the relevant data of selected
family members, friends, and colleagues, you will be
able to draw up a profile of each using the information
contained in this book. As a result, you will be able to
assess the personality traits of each individual, major
trends in the life of each, how they are likely to relate
to one another, and when they are likely to be at their
most fortunate.

We have filled in a sample chart on the page
opposite, so that you can see how each should be
completed.

Once you have the given name as on the birth
certificate, the nickname (if relevant), the current name
by which the subject is known and any pseudonym
used, as well as the date of birth, you will be able to
calculate the Personality, Life, Soul, Karmic, and
Expression Number for each person, as well as his her
her lucky color, lucky flower, and lucky gemstone.

Make sure that you have the correct spelling of each
name as this can affect the resulting numerical
calculations.

We trust that the practice of numerology will bring
you much valuable insight and many hours of
fascinating discoveries.

KEEPING RECORDS (example chart)

Given name (in full) .Alison Helen Gibbs.............

Nickname (if relevant) .Alli.............................

Current name .Alison Barnard..........................

Any pseudonym used ..Rose Clark (for writing).

Date of birth ..January 14th 1967...................

Personality Number .14...............................

Life Number ..2..

Soul Number ..8..

Karmic Number .9......................................

Expression Number .1..................................

Lucky colors ..Orange, gold, tangerine, peach.....

Lucky flowers .Freesias, orange roses, orange lilies

Lucky gemstones ..Gold, coral............................

Given name (in full) ....

Nickname (if relevant) ....

Current name ....

Any pseudonym used ....

Date of birth ....

Personality Number ....

Life Number ....

Soul Number ....

Karmic Number ....

Expression Number ....

Lucky colors ....

Lucky flowers ....

Lucky gemstones ....

Given name (in full) ....

Nickname (if relevant) ....

Current name ....

Any pseudonym used ....

Date of birth ....

Personality Number ....

Life Number ....

Soul Number ....

Karmic Number ....

Expression Number ....

Lucky colors ....

Lucky flowers ....

Lucky gemstones ....

Given name (in full) ....

Nickname (if relevant) ....

Current name ....

Any pseudonym used ....

Date of birth ....

Personality Number ....

Life Number ....

Soul Number ....

Karmic Number ....

Expression Number ....

Lucky colors ....

Lucky flowers ....

Lucky gemstones ....

Given name (in full) ....

Nickname (if relevant) ....

Current name...

Any pseudonym used ....

Date of birth ....

Personality Number ....

Life Number ....

Soul Number ....

Karmic Number ....

Expression Number ....

Lucky colors...

Lucky flowers ....

Lucky gemstones...

Given name (in full) ....

Nickname (if relevant) ....

Current name ....

Any pseudonym used ....

Date of birth ....

Personality Number ....

Life Number ....

Soul Number ....

Karmic Number ....

Expression Number ....

Lucky colors ....

Lucky flowers ....

Lucky gemstones ....

Given name (in full) ....

Nickname (if relevant) ....

Current name ....

Any pseudonym used ....

Date of birth ....

Personality Number ....

Life Number ....

Soul Number ....

Karmic Number ....

Expression Number ....

Lucky colors..

Lucky flowers ....

Lucky gemstones ....

Given name (in full) ....

Nickname (if relevant) ....

Current name ....

Any pseudonym used ....

Date of birth ....

Personality Number ....

Life Number ....

Soul Number ....

Karmic Number ....

Expression Number ....

Lucky colors ....

Lucky flowers ....

Lucky gemstones ....

Given name (in full) ....

Nickname (if relevant) ....

Current name ....

Any pseudonym used ....

Date of birth ....

Personality Number ....

Life Number ....

Soul Number ....

Karmic Number ....

Expression Number ....

Lucky colors ....

Lucky flowers ....

Lucky gemstones ....

GLOSSARY

Alchemist
Medieval magicians who practiced the art of alchemy. This science involved trying to turn base metals into gold or silver through use of the *Philosopher's stone*.

Astrology
Study of the influence of the stars and planets upon life on Earth, according to the time of birth of an individual.

Biorhythms
Three distinct cycles starting from the day of birth that are said to affect everyone physically, emotionally, and intellectually. The three cycles only rarely coincide.

Cartomancy
Divination involving use of playing or Tarot cards in order to predict future events in an individual's life and to advise about conduct.

Deity
A god or other supreme figure of divine status. The ancient Greeks and Romans had a whole pantheon of deities, but the Jews, Christians, and Moslems have one God only.

Divining
The art or science of trying to find out about the future by intuition, magic, or special calculations, as in numerology, astrology, cartomancy, or palmistry, for example.

Elements

The Chinese speak of five elements when divining. These are Earth, Fire, Water, and Wood. According to the year in which you were born, you will by influenced by one of these elements. In the West, however, Earth, Air, Fire, and Water apply.

Expression Number

A number obtained by adding together the numerical equivalents of all the consonants in the full (including surname) name that was given at birth.

Feminine Numbers

These are the even numbers that occur between 1 and 9 in numerology, but they also occur from 10 upwards. They are 2,4,6,8, etc.

Feng shui

This branch of Chinese philosophy involves using correct placing and measurements in order to ensure greater happiness and prosperity. Its literal meaning is "wind and water."

Gematria

An ancient Hebrew system of equating letters with numerical values and the basis of modern use of numerology. It was widely used by the medieval Kabbalists.

I Ching

An ancient Chinese oracle used for obtaining advice about the future. It involves the throwing of yarrow sticks or

coins to build up a pattern or hexagram to provide an
answer.

Kabbalah

A system of mysticism and occult lore still used today but
originally developed by the medieval Hebrews as an aid to
finding out more about God's purpose.

Kabbalist

A student of the Kabbalah, both in medieval times and
today. Not all such students today are of the Jewish faith.

Karmic Number

A number obtained by adding together all the numerical
equivalents of the full name that was given at birth,
including both vowels and consonants.

Kiology

An eastern philosophy/science that, through three numbers
and complex charts, provides a key to greater self-
awareness and future trends in an individual's life.

Life Number

A number obtained by adding together all the digits that
occur in the full date of birth of an individual.

Magic squares

Talismans traditionally made in special colors and
featuring numbers which add up to the same figure
whether added vertically, horizontally, or diagonally.

Masculine Numbers

These are the odd numbers that occur between 1 and 9 in
numerology, but they also occur from 10 upwards. They
are 1,3,5,7,9, etc.

Oracle

Any system that can be consulted in order to find out about the future. It was also the name of the place at Delphi where the ancient Greeks consulted their gods

Pentateuch

This is the Greek name for the first five books of the *Old Testament* – *Genesis*, *Exodus*, *Leviticus*, *Numbers*, and *Deuteronomy*.

Personality Number

To obtain this number, simply take the number of the day on which an individual was born in any month or year. Someone born on June **3** or September **3**, for example, has the Personality Number **3**.

Perfect Number

This type of number is one that can be achieved by adding together its factors. **Six**, for example, is a perfect number $(1 + 2 + 3 = 6)$.

Philosopher's stone

A mysterious item that alchemists of medieval times believed could be used to turn base metals into either gold or silver, but never identified.

Philosophy

The seeking after wisdom or knowledge, particularly in connection with principles for life, ideas, and also ethics.

Prime Number

A prime number cannot be divided by any other number except for **1** and itself. The numbers **1**, **3**, **5**, **7**, and **11**, for instance, are all *prime* numbers.

Psyche
This is another word, taken from the ancient Greek for "*breath*," for the soul or mind, or the very essence of a human being.

Pythagoras
An ancient Greek mathematician and philosopher who worked extensively with numbers and put forward the theory that they pervade our lives, as the later Kabbalists also thought.

Querent
This is someone who seeks an answer to a question about the future through any one of various methods of divining.

Sikhism
An Indian monotheistic sect founded in the 16th century. Male Sikhs always carry with them five special and highly sacred items.

Soul Number
One of the calculations of numerology involving addition of the vowel numbers only in the full birth name of an individual.

Superstition
Something believed by an individual, but for which there is no real evidence. It remains to be proven, for example, that **7** is always a lucky number.

Talisman
A lucky charm of any sort, worn or carried to ensure the well-being and prosperity of the individual, or to ward off the evil eye or devil.

Tarot
 A special set of highly illustrated cards used in order to predict the when used by a diviner in particular layouts.

Torah
 This is another word for the Pentateuch, the first five books of the *Old Testament*, and said to contain the will of God, as revealed by Moses.

Triskaidekaphobia
 A technical term for morbid fear of the number **13**, thought to be unlucky in many societies because it was the number of people present at the *Last Supper*.

Yin
 The passive, feminine, principle of Chinese philosophy; and the opposite of *yang*.

Yang
 The more active, male, principale of Chinese philosophy, and the opposite of *yin*.

INDEX

FURTHER READING

Arnold, M. *Love Numbers*. Llewellyn, 1997

Crawford, S. and Sullivan, G. *The Power of Birthdays, Stars, and Numbers*. Ballantine, 1998

DiPetro, S. *Live your Life by Numbers*. Penguin, 1991

Duce, S. *The Complete Illustrated Guide to Numerology*. Element, 1999

Lagerquist, K. and Lenard, L. *The Complete Idiot's Guide to Numerology*. Alpha, 1999

Line, J. *Discovering Numerology*. Sterling, 1993

Pierson, G. *What's in a Number?* Abbeville, 1996

USEFUL ADDRESSES

Marina D. Graham
888 Prospect Street, Suite 200
La Jolla, Ca. 92037, USA

Connaissance School of Numerology
8 Melbourn Street
Royston, Herts SG8 7BZ, UK

Christian Gilles School
17 rue Pirel
93200 St Denis, France

Character Analysis and Numerology
23 Flinders Street
Kent Town 5067, South Australia

If you liked this book, you'll love this series:

Little Giant Encyclopedia of Aromatherapy • Little Giant Encyclopedia of Baseball Quizzes • Little Giant Encyclopedia of Card & Magic Tricks • Little Giant Encyclopedia of Card Games • Little Giant Encyclopedia of Card Games Gift Set • Little Giant Encyclopedia of Checker Puzzles • Little Giant Encyclopedia of Dream Symbols •Little Giant Encyclopedia of Etiquette • Little Giant Encyclopedia of Fortune Telling • Little Giant Encyclopedia of Gambling Games • Little Giant Encyclopedia of Games for One or Two • Little Giant Encyclopedia of Handwriting Analysis • Little Giant Encyclopedia of Home Remedies • Little Giant Encyclopedia of IQ Tests • Little Giant Encyclopedia of Logic Puzzles • Little Giant Encyclopedia of Lucky Numbers • Little Giant Encyclopedia of Magic • Little Giant Encyclopedia of Mazes • Little Giant Encyclopedia of Meditations & Blessings • Little Giant Encyclopedia of Mensa Mind-Teasers • Little Giant Encyclopedia of Names • Little Giant Encyclopedia of Natural Healing • Little Giant Encyclopedia of One-Liners • Little Giant Encyclopedia of Palmistry • Little Giant Encyclopedia of Proverbs • Little Giant Encyclopedia of Puzzles • Little Giant Encyclopedia of Runes • Little Giant Encyclopedia of Spells & Magic • Little Giant Encyclopedia of Superstitions • Little Giant Encyclopedia of Toasts & Quotes • Little Giant Encyclopedia of Travel & Holiday Games • Little Giant Encyclopedia of UFOs • Little Giant Encyclopedia of Wedding Toasts • Little Giant Encyclopedia of Word Puzzles • Little Giant Encyclopedia of the Zodiac

Available at fine stores everywhere.